365 SLOW COOKER SUPPERS

Stephanie O'Dea

creator of crockpot365.blogspot.com

photography by Tara Donne

Houghton Mifflin Harcourt • Boston • New York •

Food styling by Vivian Lui

Prop styling by Martha Bernabe

Interior design by Waterbury Publications, Des Moines, IA

For information about permission to reproduce selections from this book, write to Permissions, Houghton Mifflin Harcourt Publishing Company, 215 Park Avenue South, New York, New York 10003.

www.hmhco.com

Library of Congress Cataloging-in-Publication Data

O'Dea, Stephanie.
  365 slow cooker suppers / Stephanie O'Dea ; Photography by Tara Donne.
    p. cm.
  Includes index.
  ISBN: 978-1-118-23081-7 (pbk); 978-0-544-18936-2 (ebk)

1. Electric cooking, Slow. 2. Suppers. I. Title. II. Title: Three hundred sixty-five slow cooker suppers.
  TX827.O315 2013
  641.5'884—dc23
                            2013026086

Printed in the United States of America

DOC 10 9 8 7 6 5 4

ACKNOWLEDGMENTS

This book is a group effort. I would not have been able to do it without my wonderfully supportive family and scores of readers from all over the world who write in with recipe suggestions and family favorites. Thank you. Thank you for holding my hand along the way. I've had an absolute ball with all of this, and am just so happy that I can be of some help in some way in your very busy lives.

Thank you especially to: Adam, Amanda, Molly, and Katie O'Dea, Perky, Bill, Andy, Karen, Anna and Bill Sr. Ramroth, Bunny and Ken Gillespie, John and Maureen O'Dea, Murielle Rose and Patrick Smiley, the Pellisier Family, the Peñas Family, the Bloom-Smith Family, the Evanchik Family, the Price Family, and the blogging community.

Thank you to the following websites for your inspiration and continuous friendship:
5dollardinners.com
adventuresofaglutenfreemom.com
BlogHer.com
cocktail365.blogspot.com
cookitallergyfree.com
dailybitesblog.com
elanaspantry.com
foodblogga.blogspot.com
glugleglutenfree.com
glutenfreeeasily.com
glutenfreegoddess.blogspot.com
godairyfree.org
kalynskitchen.com
lexieskitchen.com
lillianstestkitchen.com
moneysavingmom.com
onceamonthmom.com
perfectpantry.com
slowcookingfromscratch.com
soupchick.com
suddenlyfrugal.com
surefoodsliving.com
thewholegang.org
todayscreativeblog.net

Thank you to the following people who helped bring *365 Slow Cooker Suppers* to life:
Alison Picard
Justin Schwartz
Perky Ramroth
Bunny Gillespie
Adam O'Dea
Jennette Fulda
Lisa Irvine
Jenny Lauck
Thank you to Euro-Pro for providing The Ninja® Cooking System for the recipe development and photography.

CONTENTS

INTRODUCTION

I received my first slow cooker as a birthday present when I turned twenty-one. I asked for this gift, along with a food dehydrator and a pasta machine I saw advertised on late-night TV. I was newly engaged and determined to learn how to cook. I only used the food dehydrator twice and the pasta machine a handful of times before giving them away. I just wasn't thrilled with the amount of time and energy needed to achieve halfway decent results.

But the slow cooker? I still have it, and continue to use it quite often. I loved the ease of plugging it in, loading it up, and walking away. I became fascinated at how this simple appliance could bring a forgotten and frostbitten roast back to life or transform a ninety-nine-cent bag of lentils into an amazing meal with very little effort or kitchen know-how.

In 2008, I took my love of the slow cooker to the Internet. I decided to make a New Year's resolution to use my slow cooker every day for a year and document the results on a personal website. My first two cookbooks, *Make It Fast, Cook It Slow* and *More Make It Fast, Cook It Slow*, document the many different uses of this amazing machine— I've used it to make everything from a fabulous pumpkin spice latté to playdough and candles.

But at the end of the day? The most dreaded question will always be, "What's for dinner?" This book will help. It contains 365 new slow cooker dinners selected and tested in my own home kitchen by my family: my husband Adam, and my three children, who were ten, seven, and two years of age at the time. There are meals for all types of food—including meatless mains, pastas and casseroles, hot sandwiches, hearty soups and stews, and mouthwatering meat dishes.

One of my favorite things about cooking this way is that you don't need to cook nightly if you don't want to. Slow cooking lends itself to leftovers, which can be eaten the next night, repurposed into a new meal, or frozen for future meals. Although you can certainly use this book to cook a brand-new dinner each and every night for a whole year, you can also choose to cook three or four times a week and stretch the leftovers for subsequent meals—saving time and money.

REAL LIFE COOKING

I began using my slow cooker faithfully as a newlywed, but fell head over heels in love with it when I became a mother. I quickly learned that one of the best ways to ensure a healthy and hot dinner at six p.m. was to load the cooker up early in the morning while I was still wide awake and heavily caffeinated. It just wasn't safe to be chopping onions or standing over a stovetop in the late afternoon with tired and cranky kids hanging off my ankles. Now that my older two are school-aged, our afternoons are even more jam-packed with sports practice, music lessons, and homework. There's nothing better than coming home after a long day to a fully cooked meal. You'll love it.

I don't consider myself a very good traditional cook. I regularly walk away from the stove when things are cooking and come back to an overboiled pot or scorched food. I'm currently sporting a two-inch scar on my right wrist from baking cookies last week in the oven. I have little-to-no knife skills, and prefer to use my Pampered Chef handheld chopper to dice onions.

But I can slow cook. And so can you.

Cooking doesn't need to be scary. There's truly no easier way to cook than to dump in a bunch of ingredients, push a button, and walk away. I like that I can plug in the machine early in the morning while I'm packing school lunches and finishing breakfast instead of worrying about dinner in the late afternoon when my stomach is growling and the kids are getting cranky.

SAVE BOTH TIME AND MONEY

As I shared in my housekeeping shortcut book, *Totally Together: Shortcuts to an Organized Life*, I'm a meal planner. This doesn't mean that I'm an obsessive controller as much as it means that I am aware that our family runs better and sticks to our monthly budget when I take the time to plan our weekly meals in advance. It also keeps me from wasting valuable time and energy thinking up meal and snack ideas five to six times a day, every day.

The beauty of slow cooking is that it actually helps facilitate meal planning because it forces you to think ahead to your nightly dinners instead of waiting until the last minute when you're already famished. This is a good thing for both your wallet and your waistline because walking through the door at the end of a long day to a fully cooked meal keeps you out of the fast-food drive-through lane and away from the pizza delivery guy.

A WELL-STOCKED FREEZER AND PANTRY

Keeping a well-stocked freezer and pantry will also help save your family's valuable time and money. If you make a large batch of food, plan on serving half of it, and save the leftovers in the freezer. It was very comforting for me to come home from the hospital with my third baby, knowing I had about three weeks' worth of cooked food ready and waiting in the freezer.

One of my favorite ways to keep my freezer stocked is with what I call "slow cooker TV dinners." To do this, pick

out a slow cooker recipe, and instead of loading the meat, vegetables, sauce, and seasoning into the slow cooker, put it all into a plastic zippered bag (or other freezer-safe container). Write any extra directions on the outside of the bag with a permanent marker and place it into the freezer. The night before, take the bag out of the freezer to thaw overnight in the refrigerator. In the morning, plop all the ingredients into the insert and slow cook as directed in the recipe. Most recipes work quite well with this method, but I have found that freezing uncooked potato results in a rather mealy texture—I suggest adding room temperature potatoes to the cooker in the morning instead.

The recipes in this book have been prepared and photographed completely gluten-free, due to a family intolerance. If you are not gluten-free, feel free to ignore my notes, or file them away in case you ever need to cook for someone with a gluten sensitivity. Gluten is found in wheat, barley, and rye. Oats are off-limits, too, unless they come from a specified gluten-free source. Please read all manufacturer labels carefully; ingredients sometimes change with little to no warning.

I try to keep the following pantry and freezer staples on hand in our home kitchen:

All-purpose flour (I use Pamela's Baking & Pancake Mix as my gluten-free all-purpose flour)

Beans (dried and canned; if using canned, opt for low-sodium varieties)

Beef chuck roast and stew meat

Broth (chicken, beef, and vegetable as well as bouillon granules)

Brown and white rice (long-grain and instant)

Butter

Canned tomatoes

Cheese

Chicken thighs and breast pieces

Cornstarch

Cottage cheese

Cream (heavy whipping, half-and-half)

Cream cheese

Eggs

Fish (frozen tilapia, salmon, catfish fillets)

Fresh fruit: apples, bananas

Fresh vegetables (garlic, potatoes, onions, carrots, celery, bell peppers)

Frozen vegetables (peas, corn, bell pepper strips)

Ground beef and turkey

Ketchup (organic varieties do not contain high-fructose corn syrup)

Meatballs (frozen; Coleman Natural has a gluten-free variety)

Milk

Mustard (organic varieties do not contain high-fructose corn syrup)

Nut butter (peanut, almond, hazelnut)

Oatmeal (rolled and steel-cut; ours are certified gluten-free; we use Bob Red's Mill)

Orange juice

Pasta (all shapes and sizes; brown rice pasta for us!)

Pork (pork chops, tenderloin, shoulder roast)

Soy sauce (gluten-free; we use La Choy and wheat-free tamari)

Spices (a wide variety of dried spices; the more the better!)

Sugar (white and brown)

Vinegar (apple cider, red wine, balsamic, white wine)

Wine (white and red)

Worcestershire sauce (gluten-free, Lea & Perrins made in the USA is gluten free)

Yogurt

Please note that children under the age of four should not be given hot dogs, nuts, seeds, popcorn, large chunks of meat, whole grapes, carrots, or any other food that may cause choking.

CHOOSING A SLOW COOKER

Your basic slow cooker has a cooking element (the part with the cord) and an insert into which you load the food. Some of the older slow cooker models don't have this removable section, but all of the new ones on the market do.

Please refer to your owner's manual for proper use and care of your slow cooker. The cooking time when slow cooking is a range—if you know that your particular slow cooker seems to cook fast, stick to the low end of the cooking time. When preparing delicate dishes, and when baking, keep an eye on your slow cooker and don't venture too far away.

I highly recommend purchasing a programmable slow cooker. This type of slow cooker has either buttons or a knob that lets the home cook decide on the cooking temperature (high or low), and can be set to cook in 30-minute intervals ranging from 1 to 20 hours. When the set cooking time has elapsed, the machine automatically switches to a "warm" setting, keeping your food hot and ready to serve when you arrive home at the end of a busy day. When using this type of slow cooker, opt to set it for the lower end of the suggested cooking time. If you're out of the house for 10 hours, and the suggested cooking range is for between 6 and 8 hours, set it for 6 hours, and let the cooker stay on "warm" until you arrive home. If your meat and potatoes aren't quite bite tender, you can always flip it to "high" while you change clothes and set the table.

You can pick up a good programmable slow cooker for under a hundred dollars. I have an updated list of recommended slow cookers listed on stephanieodea.com.

I recommend keeping the cooker at least two-thirds full for optimum performance. Although there are many different sizes of slow cookers on the market, you do not need to go out and buy them all. If you are going to purchase one, and one only, opt for a 6-quart machine. You can still make all of the appetizers, dips, and fondues in this one machine by simply inserting an oven-safe dish (CorningWare, Pyrex) into the insert to create a smaller cooking vessel.

All the recipes in this book are for 4- or 6-quart machines. The 4-quart recipes will work just fine in the larger 6-quart machine, but will cook faster. I suggest reducing the cooking time by at least a third and then checking the food to ensure doneness, or you may opt to increase the ingredient amount by 50 percent to fill the pot properly, and use the stated cook times.

MODERN SLOW COOKING

In the past, slow cookers became synonymous with pot roasts, chili, and gloppy casseroles made with cream-of-something soup. While the slow cooker does make an awesome pot roast (try the Lazy Sunday Pot Roast on page 158 or the Sweet-and-Sour Pot Roast on page 178), it can do so much more. When I began using my slow cooker daily, I knew I would need to learn how to prepare much more than heavy comfort foods—it just wouldn't be healthy to eat that way on a daily basis. Through trial and error, I learned how to steam fish to perfection, and how to incorporate vegetarian and vegan food into our regular weekly menu. I learned to embrace the lentil and not shy away from kale or tofu. The slow cooker is a permanent fixture on our kitchen countertop (and tucked underneath the bed—we have 15 in the house!) and my hope is that you, too, will fall in love with this simple, yet remarkable appliance.

In the past, slow cookers became synonymous with pot roasts, chili, and gloppy casseroles made with cream-of-something soup. While the slow cooker does make an awesome pot roast (try the Lazy Sunday Pot Roast on page 158 or the Sweet-and-Sour Pot Roast on page 178), it can do so much more.

SOUPS & STEWS

BABY ONION AND SUMMER VEGETABLES STEW

Serves 8

1	(16-ounce) bag frozen red and white pearl onions
4	zucchini cut into ¼-inch-thick rounds
4	summer squash, washed and cut into ¼-inch-thick rounds
1	cup chopped baby carrots
½	cup sliced celery
⅓	cup dried chickpeas, rinsed or 1 (15-ounce) can, drained
4	cups chicken or vegetable broth
1	cup tomato-based pasta sauce
1	cup water
1	tablespoon dried Italian seasoning
½	cup pasta (I used gluten-free penne)
	Freshly grated Parmesan cheese, for serving (optional)

Use a 6-quart slow cooker. Add the onions, zucchini, squash, carrots, celery, and chickpeas to the insert. Add the broth, pasta sauce, and water. Stir in the Italian seasoning. Cover, and cook on low for 8 hours, or until the beans are bite-tender. About 20 minutes before serving, stir in the pasta and turn to high. Serve with cheese, if desired.

THE VERDICT

THE ONIONS BURST A BIT DURING THE SLOW COOKING PROCESS AND THE SQUASH BREAKS DOWN TO MELD WITH THE PASTA SAUCE, CREATING A THICKENED, LOVELY RED BASE TO THIS HEARTY SOUP. I LIKE TO SERVE THIS SOUP WITH HOMEMADE GLUTEN-FREE CORNBREAD MUFFINS, AND USE GLUTEN-FREE PASTA.

BAKED POTATO AND CAULIFLOWER SOUP

Serves 4

2   large baking potatoes, such as Russet or Yukon Gold, peeled and diced
1   small head cauliflower, stem removed, florets diced
1   cup chicken broth
1   cup milk
½   teaspoon kosher salt
¼   teaspoon ground black pepper
1   cup sour cream
    Optional toppings: shredded Cheddar cheese, crumbled cooked bacon, chopped fresh chives

Use a 6-quart slow cooker. Place the potatoes and cauliflower into the insert and top with the broth and milk. Stir in the salt and pepper. Cover, and cook on low for 6 to 7 hours, or on high for about 4 hours. Blend the soup fully with a handheld immersion blender, or let cool a bit and blend in small batches in a traditional blender. Stir in the sour cream, and ladle into bowls with desired toppings.

The Verdict

Adding cauliflower lowers the carb count for this soup, and adds lots of fiber and vitamins C and K. Opt for low-fat milk and sour cream if you'd like an even lighter version.

BEEF AND GREEN CHILE STEW

Serves 6

3   pounds beef stew meat
⅓   cup all-purpose flour
1   teaspoon kosher salt
1   teaspoon ground black pepper
1   teaspoon ground chipotle chile
1   teaspoon ground cumin
1   onion, diced
2   (4-ounce) cans whole chiles
1   (10-ounce) can tomatoes and chiles, undrained
1   cup beef broth
¼   cup barbecue sauce

Use a 6-quart slow cooker. Place the meat into the insert, and add the flour, salt, pepper, chipotle, and cumin. Toss the meat to evenly coat with the flour and seasoning. Add the onion, whole chiles, and tomatoes with chiles. Stir in the broth and barbecue sauce. Cover, and cook on low for 8 to 10 hours, or until the meat is tender and breaks apart easily with a fork.

The Verdict

My friend Lydia, who writes The Perfect Pantry website (theperfectpantry.com), came up with this slow cooker recipe. I've changed the chipotle chile in adobo sauce to ground chipotle chile to make it gluten-free, and I use a gluten-free baking mix as my all-purpose flour. I love how the sweet barbecue sauce interacts with the tangy heat from the chiles. Delicious!

BEEF AND HOMINY STEW

Serves 6

1	pound beef stew meat
4	cups beef broth
1	(15-ounce) can hominy, drained and rinsed
1	(4-ounce) can whole green chiles
2	Yukon Gold potatoes, peeled and diced
1	onion, sliced
2	garlic cloves, sliced
1	tablespoon chili powder
1	tablespoon ground cumin
1	teaspoon dried oregano
1	teaspoon kosher salt
½	teaspoon ground black pepper
¼	teaspoon cayenne pepper

Use a 4-quart slow cooker. Put the meat into the insert, and add all the remaining ingredients. Stir well to combine. Cover, and cook on low for 8 hours, or until the meat can shred easily with a fork. If you like, pulse the stew a few times with a handheld immersion blender (or puree a cup of stew in a traditional blender and mix back into the cooker) to naturally thicken the broth before serving.

 THE VERDICT

MY FRIEND LYDIA POSTED THIS STEW ON HER SOUP CHICK WEBSITE (SOUPCHICK.COM). I AGREE WITH HER—YOU CAN'T EVER HAVE TOO MANY SOUP OR STEW RECIPES. THIS IS A LOVELY STEW; THE HOMINY AND GREEN CHILES PROVIDE A WONDERFUL DEPTH OF TEXTURE AND FLAVOR.

BRANDY BEEF STEW WITH SQUASH AND CRANBERRIES

Serves 6

3	pounds beef short ribs
1	(2-pound) butternut squash, peeled and cubed
1	onion, sliced into thin rings
½	cup sweetened dried cranberries
2	tablespoons unsweetened cocoa powder
1	tablespoon garlic powder
1	teaspoon ground ginger
½	teaspoon kosher salt
1	orange, juiced
4	cups beef broth
¼	cup brandy or apple juice

Use a 6-quart slow cooker. Place the meat into the insert, and add the squash, onion, and cranberries. Add the cocoa powder, garlic powder, ginger, and salt. Add the orange juice, and pour in the broth and brandy. Stir well to distribute the ingredients. Cover, and cook on low for 8 to 10 hours, or until the meat has begun to lose its shape and can shred easily with a fork.

 **THE VERDICT**

I LIKE THIS STEW BECAUSE THE BROTH HAS A BITE TO IT—IT'S NOT SWEET, AND IT DOESN'T TASTE LIKE COOKED CARROTS OR CELERY THE WAY MOST BEEF STEWS DO. THE SQUASH AND CRANBERRIES WORK WELL TO BALANCE OUT THE BITTERNESS OF THE COCOA AND BRANDY. SERVE WITH CRUSTY BREAD (I USE A LOAF OF GLUTEN-FREE RICE BREAD) AND A GARDEN SALAD. MY WHOLE FAMILY ENJOYED THIS MEAL, AND I STRETCHED THE LEFTOVERS THE NEXT EVENING BY SERVING IT WITH POLENTA.

BEEF AND POTATOES AU CHOCOLAT

Serves 6

2	pounds rib eye steak, trimmed and cut into 2-inch pieces
1	onion, thinly sliced
4	red potatoes, washed and thinly sliced
1	cup baby carrots
2	stalks celery, thinly sliced
1	(4-ounce) can fire-roasted green chiles, undrained
5	garlic cloves, thinly sliced
2	tablespoons balsamic vinegar
1	tablespoon all-natural maple syrup
1	tablespoon ground chipotle chile
1	teaspoon ground cumin
1	teaspoon ground cinnamon
1	teaspoon kosher salt
½	teaspoon ground black pepper
½	cup golden raisins
2	tablespoons unsweetened cocoa powder
5	cups beef broth

Use a 6-quart slow cooker. Place the meat into the insert and add the onion, potatoes, carrots, celery, chiles, garlic, vinegar, and maple syrup. Stir to distribute the ingredients. Add the chipotle, cumin, cinnamon, salt, and pepper. Add the raisins, cocoa, and pour in the broth. Cover, and cook on low for 8 to 10 hours, or until vegetables are bite-tender, and meat has begun to shred.

THE VERDICT

THIS RECIPE COMES FROM KARINA, THE GLUTEN-FREE GODDESS (GLUTENFREEGODDESS. BLOGSPOT.COM), WHO WRITES THAT IF YOU'D PREFER TO USE CHICKEN OR TOFU, YOU SHOULD. SHE SUGGESTS (AND I AGREE) THAT IF YOU OPT FOR TOFU, USE A DRAINED EXTRA-FIRM VARIETY, AND ADD IT 2 HOURS BEFORE SERVING SO IT RETAINS ITS SHAPE AND TEXTURE. THIS IS A WONDERFUL, CHOCOLATY STEW—THE RAISINS PLUMP WHILE SLOW COOKING TO CREATE FUN BURSTS OF SWEETNESS IN EVERY BITE. SERVE WITH HOMEMADE DROP BISCUITS.

BEEF VEGETABLE SOUP

Serves 6

1   pound beef stew meat
1   (28-ounce) can stewed tomatoes, undrained
1   tablespoon Worcestershire sauce
1   tablespoon dried minced onion
1   teaspoon garlic powder
1   teaspoon kosher salt
2   teaspoons dried Italian seasoning
1   (16-ounce) package frozen mixed vegetables

Use a 6-quart slow cooker. Put the meat into the insert and add the tomatoes. Fill the empty tomato can with water and pour that into the pot. Add the Worcestershire sauce, dried onion, garlic powder, salt, and Italian seasoning. Stir in the bag of vegetables. Cover, and cook on low for 8 to 10 hours, or until the stew meat can shred easily with a fork.

🍲 The Verdict

This is so much better than the canned stuff—it is a great, simple, hearty, and inexpensive soup. I keep stew meat in the freezer and love how it comes "back to life" after slow cooking all day long. I have listed my gluten-free Worcestershire sauce recommendation in the Introduction.

BUFFALO CHICKEN STEW

Serves 6

1½ pounds boneless, skinless chicken breast, diced
1   white onion, diced
4   red potatoes, washed and cubed
1   cup chopped baby carrots
1   cup sliced celery
6   garlic cloves, minced
1   (1-ounce) packet ranch salad dressing mix (for homemade, see page 256)
6   cups chicken broth
⅔   cup prepared buffalo wing sauce
2   cups shredded mozzarella cheese
½   cup crumbled blue cheese

Use a 6-quart slow cooker. Place the chicken into the insert, and add the onion, potatoes, carrots, celery, and garlic. Sprinkle in the salad dressing mix, and stir in the broth and buffalo wing sauce. Cover, and cook on low for 8 to 10 hours, or on high for about 5 hours. Stir well and serve in wide-mouth bowls with a handful of mozzarella cheese and a spoonful of blue cheese crumbles.

🍲 The Verdict

I crave the tart tang of Buffalo wings, and go out of my way to hunt down new places to pick up wings when on vacation. This stew completely satisfies my wing craving without a drop of oil, and very little fat. If you'd prefer a low-carb version, swap out potatoes for a half head of diced cauliflower.

CARROT AND COCONUT CURRY BISQUE

Serves 4

2	pounds baby carrots
1	onion, diced
2	tablespoons grated fresh ginger
1	tablespoon curry powder
¼	teaspoon cayenne pepper
1	fully ripe banana, peeled
1	(13.5-ounce) can coconut milk
2	limes, juiced
1	teaspoon kosher salt
	Fresh flat-leaf parsley, for garnish (optional)

Use a 6-quart slow cooker. Add the carrots, onion, ginger, curry powder, and cayenne to the insert. Add the banana and coconut milk. Add the lime juice, and stir in the salt. Cover, and cook on low for 6 to 7 hours, or until onions are translucent and carrots are soft. Use a handheld immersion blender to blend until velvety smooth, or let cool partially and blend in batches in a traditional blender. Garnish with fresh parsley, if desired.

 **THE VERDICT**
WHAT A GORGEOUS SOUP—
IT'S VELVETY AND SMOOTH,
WITH THE PERFECT BLEND OF
CURRY AND A TOUCH OF SPICE.
I CAN'T WAIT TO MAKE IT
AGAIN. THANK YOU TO ALISA
FROM GODAIRYFREE.ORG FOR
INTRODUCING IT TO ME!

CHICKEN AND CHORIZO STEW

Serves 6

4 boneless, skinless chicken thighs
12 ounces fresh chorizo
1 medium onion, diced
4 garlic cloves, minced
2 red bell peppers, seeded and diced
1 (16-ounce) bag frozen white corn
1 (14.5-ounce) can diced tomatoes, undrained
1 cup diced baby carrots
½ cup chopped fresh flat-leaf parsley
1 teaspoon dried thyme
4 cups chicken broth
Sour cream, for serving (optional)

Use a 6-quart slow cooker. Place the chicken thighs into the insert. Remove the casings from the chorizo links, and crumble the meat into a large skillet over medium heat. Add the onion and garlic and cook, stirring, until the onion is translucent, about 5 minutes. Drain any accumulated grease, and pour the meat mixture into the insert. Add the bell peppers, corn, tomatoes, carrots, parsley, and thyme. Pour in the broth, and stir well to combine. Cover, and cook on low for 6 to 8 hours, or on high for 4 to 5 hours. Serve in a wide-mouth bowl with a dollop of sour cream, if desired.

 The Verdict

My baby, who was 11 months old at the time, ate three bowlfuls of this stew! There is a bit of spice, but it is not overpowering. My entire family ate happily, and the leftovers freeze marvelously.

CHICKEN ENCHILADA SOUP

Serves 6 to 8

1 pound boneless, skinless chicken, cut into thin strips
1 (1-ounce) packet taco seasoning (for homemade, see recipe below)
1 (32-ounce) can tomato juice
1 (16-ounce) jar salsa
½ cup chicken broth
1 (15-ounce) can black beans, drained and rinsed
1 (16-ounce) bag of frozen corn
Suggested toppings: sour cream, shredded Cheddar cheese, crumbled tortilla chips

Use a 6-quart slow cooker. Put the chicken into the insert, and sprinkle with the taco seasoning. Pour in the tomato juice, salsa, and broth. Add the beans and corn. Cover, and cook on low for 8 hours. Stir well and serve in bowls or mugs with sour cream, cheese, and tortilla chips, if desired.

The Verdict

I once bought six cans of tomato juice because they were heavily discounted and scrambled to find different ways to use them up. This soup was our absolute favorite—it's spicy enough to warm up your insides, but not enough to keep the baby from eating every last drop.

HOMEMADE TACO SEASONING

2 teaspoons dried onion flakes
1 teaspoon chili powder
½ teaspoon cornstarch
½ teaspoon crushed dried red pepper
½ teaspoon garlic powder
¼ teaspoon dried oregano
½ teaspoon ground cumin

Mix all ingredients together. This recipe equals one packet of purchased taco seasoning.

CHIPOTLE, LIME, AND CHICKEN SOUP

Serves 6

4	boneless, skinless chicken thighs, cut into 1-inch pieces
1	onion, diced
6	garlic cloves, sliced
1	tablespoon ground chipotle chile
6	cups chicken broth
3	limes, juiced
½	cup chopped fresh cilantro leaves
1	teaspoon kosher salt
	Suggested toppings: avocado slices, shredded mozzarella cheese, lime wedges

Use a 6-quart slow cooker. Place the chicken into the insert, and add the onion, garlic, and chipotle. Add the broth and the juice from 2 of the limes. Stir in the cilantro and salt. Cover, and cook on low for 6 to 7 hours. Ladle into wide-mouth bowls and add the avocado, a handful of cheese, and a lime wedge.

 **THE VERDICT**

THIS IS A SMOKY, SPICY VERSION OF TORTILLA SOUP. I LOVE THE CITRUS LIME FLAVOR, AND ADDED MORE TO MY BOWL. MY KIDS WEREN'T ALL THAT IMPRESSED AND STUCK TO QUESADILLAS, BUT ADAM AND I BOTH HAD TWO BOWLS. PAIRS WELL WITH MARGARITAS!

CHUNKY ARTICHOKE SOUP

Serves 4

1	pound lean ground beef or turkey
8	ounces fresh button mushrooms, sliced
1	onion, diced
3	garlic cloves, minced
2	(8.5-ounce) cans artichoke hearts, undrained
½	teaspoon kosher salt
½	teaspoon ground black pepper
¼	teaspoon dried oregano
¼	teaspoon ground sage
¼	teaspoon crushed red pepper flakes
1	cup chicken broth
1	cup heavy whipping cream

Use a 4-quart slow cooker. In a large skillet over medium heat, cook the meat, mushrooms, onion, and garlic, stirring, until the meat is browned. Drain any accumulated fat. Place the meat mixture into the insert. Strain the artichoke can liquid into the insert, and coarsely chop the artichoke hearts and then add to the pot. Add all the seasonings, and pour in the broth. Cover, and cook on low for 6 hours. In a mixing bowl, whip the cream until it's light and fluffy with a whisk, and fold that into the soup. Serve immediately.

THE VERDICT

OTT, OF ALATTEWITHOTTA.COM, POSTED THIS RECIPE IN A SOUP-A-PALOOZA ROUNDUP ONLINE, AND I'M SO GLAD SHE DID. IT IS PACKED WITH ARTICHOKE FLAVOR AND THE MEAT, CREAM, AND VEGETABLES REALLY MAKE IT A COMPLETE MEAL IN A BOWL.

CURRIED EGGPLANT SOUP

Serves 4

I   large (2-pound) eggplant, peeled and diced
I   (14.5-ounce) can diced tomatoes, undrained
I   onion, diced
I   Granny Smith or other tart green apple, peeled and diced
2   tablespoons curry powder
I   tablespoon soy sauce (I use gluten-free)
I   tablespoon honey
¼   teaspoon kosher salt
¼   teaspoon cayenne pepper
4   cups vegetable broth
     Suggested toppings: feta cheese, chopped fresh cilantro leaves

Use a 4-quart slow cooker. Add the eggplant, tomatoes, onion, and apple to the insert. Add the curry powder, soy sauce, honey, salt, and cayenne pepper. Stir in the broth. Cover, and cook on low for 7 to 8 hours. Before serving, blend with a handheld immersion blender until you have reached desired consistency or let cool a bit and blend in small batches in a traditional blender. I blended ours until it was velvety smooth. Add cheese and cilantro to each bowl, if desired.

The Verdict
I found this recipe on Susan Voisin's blog (blog.fatfreevegan. com) and adapted it to work in the slow cooker and to make it gluten-free. I had eggplant bisque at a restaurant that was delicious, but quite heavy since it was cream-based. I loved how light and flavorful this curry adaptation was without a drop of cream. Thank you, Susan!

FANCY PANTS LAMB STEW

Serves 6

4   pounds bone-in lamb shanks
2   onions, thinly sliced
2   (14-ounce) cans fire-roasted diced tomatoes
I   cup dried pitted plums (prunes)
½   cup golden raisins
½   cup whole almonds
I   tablespoon ground cumin
½   to I tablespoon crushed red pepper flakes
I   teaspoon kosher salt
I   (2-inch) piece fresh ginger, peeled

Use a 6-quart slow cooker. Put the lamb into the insert, and add the onions, tomatoes, dried plums, raisins, and almonds. Stir in the cumin, red pepper flakes (go slowly if you don't want it spicy), and salt. Toss in the ginger. Cover, and cook on low 8 to 10 hours. Remove the lamb bones and ginger; stir stew well to break up the dried plums.

The Verdict
This is a beautiful stew—fit for your favorite guests. I used the whole tablespoon of red pepper flakes and I liked how the stew slowly warmed up the back of my tongue. If you aren't a fan of pepper, start with the smaller amount; you can add more at the table if you'd like. Serve with a hearty red wine and a loaf of crusty bread.

FRENCH ONION SOUP WITH CAULIFLOWER

Serves 4

4	tablespoons butter
3	yellow onions, sliced into thin rings
6	cups beef broth
½	cup dry sherry
1	tablespoon sugar
½	teaspoon kosher salt
¼	teaspoon ground black pepper
1	small head cauliflower, florets separated
4	slices Gruyère or Swiss cheese

Use a 4-quart slow cooker. Melt 3 tablespoons of the butter and pour into the insert, and swish the onions around in it. Pour in the broth, and stir in the sherry, sugar, salt, and pepper. Cover and cook on low for 7 to 8 hours or high for 4 to 5 hours, until the onions are completely wilted and translucent.

In a covered microwave-safe dish, heat the cauliflower on high for 3 minutes, or until fork-tender. Drain any accumulated liquid. Use a potato masher or large fork to mash the cauliflower; lumps are okay. Separate the cooked cauliflower into 4 parts, and squish to form a patty. In a large skillet, fry the cauliflower patties in the remaining tablespoon of butter until golden brown. Ladle the soup into oven-safe bowls, and float the fried cauliflower on top. Add a piece of cheese, and broil in the oven for about a minute, or until cheese has melted and begun to brown.

 The Verdict

This completely gluten-free and low-carb soup is absolutely delicious—no bread is needed to re-create this restaurant classic at home.

GARDEN TOMATO AND SPINACH BISQUE

Serves 4 to 6

2	pounds ripe plum tomatoes, chopped, or 2 (14-ounce) cans crushed tomatoes
1	yellow onion, diced
1	(10-ounce) package frozen spinach, thawed and drained
1	cup beef broth
¼	cup packed dark brown sugar
¼	cup freshly grated Parmesan cheese
1	tablespoon Worcestershire sauce (I use gluten-free)
2	teaspoons dried basil
1	(14-ounce) can evaporated milk

Use a 4-quart slow cooker. In a blender or food processor, pulse the tomatoes, onion, and spinach. Pour this mixture into the insert. Stir in the broth, sugar, Parmesan cheese, Worcestershire sauce, and basil. Cover, and cook on low for 6 hours, or on high for about 4 hours. Stir in the evaporated milk and recover. Cook on high for 20 minutes, or until fully hot.

 The Verdict

Even tomato-phobes will be wowed by this soup. Packed with vegetables, this filling soup makes a fantastic lunch or light dinner. If you'd like to use fat-free evaporated milk, you may do so without sacrificing flavor.

GREEK STEW

Serves 6

2	pounds boneless, skinless chicken thighs (frozen is fine)
1	small head cauliflower, stem removed and florets separated
1	red onion, diced
6	garlic cloves, minced
1	(28-ounce) can diced tomatoes, undrained
1	cup chicken broth
1	tablespoon red wine vinegar
½	teaspoon ground cinnamon
½	teaspoon dried thyme
¼	teaspoon ground black pepper
⅓	cup pitted kalamata olives
¼	cup crumbled feta cheese (optional)

Use a 6-quart slow cooker. Place the chicken into the insert. Add the cauliflower, onion, and garlic. Pour in the tomatoes and broth. Stir in the vinegar, cinnamon, thyme, and pepper. Drop in the olives, and cover. Cook on low for 8 hours, or until the chicken breaks apart easily with a fork. Serve in large bowls with the cheese, if desired.

 THE VERDICT

HOLLEE SCHWARTZ TEMPLE, AUTHOR OF *GOOD ENOUGH IS THE NEW PERFECT*, RECOMMENDED THIS STEW TO ME. SHE ADAPTED IT TO WORK IN THE SLOW COOKER, AND IT HAS A TREMENDOUS MIXTURE OF FLAVORS. I LOVED HOW THE CINNAMON WORKS—IT'S DELICIOUS!

HONEY AND DIJON BEEF STEW

Serves 6

2	pounds beef stew meat
1	(16-ounce) bag frozen pearl onions
4	red potatoes, washed and sliced into ½-inch rounds
1	cup chopped baby carrots
½	cup chopped celery
8	garlic cloves, peeled
2	tablespoons honey
2	tablespoons tomato paste
1	tablespoon Dijon mustard
1	tablespoon herbes de Provence
1	teaspoon kosher salt
½	teaspoon ground black pepper
1	(750-ml) bottle of dry red wine

Use a 6-quart slow cooker. Place the meat into the insert. Add the onions and the potatoes. Add the carrots, celery, and garlic. Add the honey, tomato paste, mustard, and seasonings. Stir in the entire bottle of red wine. Cover, and cook on low for 8 to 10 hours, or until the garlic cloves smash easily with the back of a spoon and the meat has reached desired tenderness.

 THE VERDICT
EVERY TIME I MAKE A NEW STEW RECIPE I DECLARE THAT "THIS IS IT! THIS ONE IS MY FAVORITE!" TRY THIS STEW. IT'LL BE YOUR NEW FAVORITE, TOO!

ITALIAN MINESTRONE

Serves 6

- 1   pound ground beef
- 1   onion, diced
- 4   ounces fresh button mushrooms, thinly sliced
- 4   garlic cloves, chopped
- 4   cups beef broth
- 1   (14.5-ounce) can diced tomatoes, undrained
- 2   stalks celery, thinly sliced
- 1   cup chopped baby carrots
- 1   tablespoon dried oregano
- 1   teaspoon kosher salt
- ⅔   cup uncooked macaroni pasta (I use brown rice pasta), to add at the very end

Use a 6-quart slow cooker. In a large skillet over medium heat, add the beef, onion, mushrooms, and garlic and cook, stirring, until the meat is browned. Drain any accumulated fat. Transfer the meat and mushroom mixture to the slow cooker. Add the broth, tomatoes, celery, and carrots. Stir in the oregano and salt. Cover, and cook on low for 7 to 8 hours, or on high for about 4 hours. Stir in the pasta, recover, and cook on high for 20 to 30 minutes, or until the pasta is bite-tender.

 The Verdict

My kids ate bowl after bowl—this is a wonderful traditional minestrone. If you'd like to stretch it farther, try adding a can of beans, or sneaking in a handful of spinach or kale.

ITALIAN WEDDING SOUP

Serves 4

- 1   pound Italian-style meatballs (check for gluten; we like Coleman Natural)
- 1   onion, diced
- 1   cup chopped baby carrots
- ½   cup sliced celery
- 4   garlic cloves, minced
- 6   cups chicken broth
- 1   tablespoon dried Italian seasoning
- ½   cup elbow pasta (I use gluten-free)
- 2   cups fresh spinach
       Freshly grated Parmesan cheese (optional)

Use a 6-quart slow cooker. Place the meatballs into the insert (frozen is fine). Add the onion, carrots, celery, and garlic. Stir in the broth and Italian seasoning. Cover, and cook on low for 7 to 8 hours. Stir in the uncooked pasta and spinach. Recover, and cook on high for 30 minutes, or until the pasta has reached desired tenderness. Serve with Parmesan cheese, if desired.

The Verdict

I love meatballs in soup, and now that there are gluten-free varieties readily available, I'm having a lot of fun trying recipes that used to be off-limits to us (or labor-intensive). This is a delightfully comforting soup—we all really liked it.

LASAGNA SOUP

Serves 6

I   **pound lean ground turkey or beef**

I   **red onion, diced**

I   **(26-ounce) jar prepared pasta sauce**

I   **pound fresh button mushrooms, thinly sliced**

4   **cups beef broth**

I   **red bell pepper, seeded and thinly sliced**

I   **tablespoon dried Italian seasoning**

6   **lasagna noodles, broken in half (I use brown rice noodles)**

2   **cups shredded mozzarella cheese**

Use a 6-quart slow cooker. Add the meat and onion to a large skillet over medium heat and cook, stirring, until the meat is browned. Drain any accumulated fat and pour the pan contents into the insert. Add the pasta sauce and mushrooms. Next add the broth, bell pepper, and Italian seasoning, and stir in the broken lasagna noodles. Cover, and cook on low for 7 to 8 hours, or until fully hot and pasta has reached desired consistency. Serve in large bowls with a small bowl of cheese per person to stir in at the table.

 The Verdict

Liquid lasagna—could anything possibly taste any better? If you don't have lasagna noodles in the house, go ahead and use a half cup or so of whatever pasta you have on hand. The pasta will swell quite a bit—less is better than more.

LEFTOVER LAMB AND WHITE BEAN SOUP

Serves 6

3   **cups diced cooked lamb**

I   **onion, diced**

2   **cups dried small white beans, soaked overnight and drained (for quick-soak method, see page 82)**

I   **cup diced baby carrots**

I   **cup cherry tomatoes, halved**

I   **teaspoon ground thyme**

I   **teaspoon kosher salt**

½   **teaspoon ground black pepper**

4   **cups beef or chicken broth**

Use a 6-quart slow cooker. Place the lamb into the insert with the onion. Add the beans. Add the carrots, tomatoes, thyme, salt, and pepper. Stir in the broth. Cover, and cook on low for 7 to 8 hours, or on high for 4 to 5 hours. The soup is finished when the beans are soft and the onion is translucent.

The Verdict

I hate wasting food, and this is a great use for leftover meat that's been hanging out in the freezer after your last holiday dinner. The beans, tomato, and carrots work well to stretch the odds and ends of the meat into a complete meal. Serve with a garden salad and sliced bread.

LEFTOVER TURKEY (WITH A KICK) SOUP

Serves 6

FOR THE BROTH

1   turkey carcass
1   cup diced cooked turkey meat
8   cups water

FOR THE SOUP

1   (14.5-ounce) can diced tomatoes, undrained
1   cup water
1   onion, diced
8   garlic cloves, peeled
2   chicken bouillon cubes
1   tablespoon ground cumin
½   to 1 tablespoon Tabasco sauce

Use a 6-quart slow cooker. This is a two-day process. On the first day (or overnight), put the turkey carcass and meat into the insert, and add the water. Cover, and cook on low 8 to 12 hours. Unplug the cooker and let it cool to room temperature before refrigerating the turkey carcass and meat and broth in the insert overnight. In the morning, skim off any accumulated fat, and remove all turkey bones and skin. Add the soup ingredients. Cover, and cook on low for 6 to 8 hours, or until the onion is translucent and the garlic cloves smash easily when pressed with a spoon. Stir well before serving.

 THE VERDICT

NOW THAT I KNOW HOW EASY IT IS TO MAKE HOMEMADE BROTH AND SOUP, I'LL NEVER AGAIN THROW AWAY ANOTHER TURKEY OR CHICKEN CARCASS. THIS IS A WONDERFUL SOUP. THE GARLIC AND CUMIN PROVIDE A SLIGHTLY SMOKY, NUTTY FLAVOR TO THE BROTH, AND YOU CAN CUSTOMIZE THE HEAT TO YOUR LIKING WITH THE TABASCO SAUCE. I COULD EAT THIS DAILY.

MATZO BALL SOUP

Serves 8

3   pounds bone-in chicken parts
2   onions, cut into quarters
6   garlic cloves, peeled
1   cup baby carrots
3   stalks celery, cut in large chunks, leaves reserved
    for garnish
1   tablespoon kosher salt
1   teaspoon whole black peppercorns
12 cups water
1   package matzo ball mix or make your own gluten-
    free variety (recipe follows)

Use a 6-quart slow cooker. This is a 2-day process. On the first day (or overnight), make the chicken broth. Place the chicken parts into the insert. (I use chicken quarters and try to take as much of the skin off as I can.) Add the vegetables, salt, and peppercorns. Pour in the water— the cooker will be quite full. Cover, and cook on low for 8 to 10 hours. Unplug the slow cooker, and let it sit for 3 hours, or until the meat is cool enough to handle.

Remove the meat from pot, and discard the bones. Scoop out the vegetables and set aside. Some people prefer their matzo soup to be simply broth, some like chunks of meat and vegetables—it's up to you. Strain the broth through a cheesecloth or fine-mesh sieve to remove the peppercorns and extra bits. Return the broth to the cooker.

Plug the cooker back in and cook on high for 2 hours. While the broth is reheating, make the matzo ball dough (if using packaged mix, prepare according to the package instructions).

Once the soup is hot, drop rounded spoonfuls of matzo mix into the insert. Cover, and cook on high for about 30 minutes, or until the dough is cooked through and "bounces" in the broth when poked with a spoon. Garnish with celery leaves, if desired.

GLUTEN-FREE MATZO BALLS

Makes 8

½   cup finely ground almond meal
½   cup potato starch
2   large eggs
2   tablespoons vegetable shortening
2   tablespoons ground flax seed
1   tablespoon fresh dill or 1½ teaspoons dried dill
½   teaspoon kosher salt
¼   teaspoon ground black pepper

In a bowl, use a handheld mixer or stand mixer to blend the matzo ball ingredients together to form a dough. Refrigerate for 1 to 2 hours before using in the soup.

 **THE VERDICT**
MATZO BALL SOUP IS KNOWN FOR BEING THE CURE FOR WHATEVER AILS YOU: THE SNIFFLES, THE FLU, LONELINESS, OR EVEN HEARTACHE. THE MATZO COOKS PERFECTLY IN THE SLOW COOKER—MOIST, FLUFFY BALLS OF GOODNESS.

MOROCCAN TAGINE

Serves 8

4   pounds beef or lamb stew meat
2   onions, thinly sliced
4   garlic cloves, minced
1   tablespoon paprika
1   tablespoon ground cumin
1   teaspoon ground turmeric
1   teaspoon ground cinnamon
1   teaspoon ground ginger
1   teaspoon kosher salt
½   teaspoon cayenne pepper
3   cardamom pods
1   (14.5-ounce) can diced tomatoes, undrained
½   cup pitted kalamata olives
2   tablespoons tomato paste
2   cups beef broth

Use a 6-quart slow cooker. Put the meat into the insert, and add the onion, garlic, and all the seasonings, including the cardamom pods. Add diced tomatoes, olives, and tomato paste. Stir in the broth. Cover and cook on low for 8 to 10 hours, or until the meat shreds easily with a fork. Fish out the cardamom pods and discard. Stir well and serve with a nice crusty bread.

 The Verdict

Yum—this is a great meal to serve to company. My friend Diane got this recipe from her mother-in-law who serves this stew every Christmas Eve. It's rich, hearty, and presents well with very little effort from the chef!

MUSHROOM AND WILD RICE SOUP

Serves 4

1   cup boiling water
½   cup dried shiitake mushrooms
1   onion, diced
1   cup diced baby carrots
1   cup wild rice, rinsed
6   cups chicken or vegetable broth

Use a 4-quart slow cooker. In a saucepan, combine the water and mushrooms. Cover, and let the mushrooms sit for 15 minutes, before draining and placing the mushrooms into the insert. Add the onion, carrots, and rice. Pour in the broth. Cover, and cook on low for 6 to 7 hours, or on high for about 3½ hours.

 The Verdict

Shiitake mushrooms provide lots of flavor to this classic soup. The wild rice bursts a bit while slow cooking, resembling barley—this makes a wonderful light meal.

OLD-FASHIONED CHICKEN AND DUMPLINGS SOUP

Serves 4

2	pounds boneless, skinless chicken thighs
1	onion, diced
½	cup chopped baby carrots
½	cup sliced celery
½	teaspoon kosher salt
½	teaspoon ground black pepper
½	teaspoon ground thyme
4	cups chicken broth
½	cup heavy whipping cream
1	(10-ounce) can refrigerated biscuits (see below for gluten-free variation)

Use a 4-quart slow cooker. Place the chicken into the insert, and add the onion, carrots, and celery. Add all the spices, and stir in the chicken broth and heavy cream. Cover, and cook on low for 7 to 8 hours, or until the onion is translucent and the chicken shreds easily. Shred the chicken completely, and drop in the biscuit dough. Cover, and cook on high for an hour, or until a knife inserted into the dough comes out clean. The dumplings will be brown on top and a bit spongy when they are fully cooked. Serve in bowls with a dumpling or two per person.

 The Verdict

Tina, a longtime reader, sent me this recipe and promises that it tastes "just like the soup at Cracker Barrel." We don't have that restaurant close by, so I can't testify to the comparison, but I can attest that my entire family loved this soup. Thank you, Tina!

GLUTEN-FREE DROP BISCUITS

1	cup gluten-free baking mix
¼	cup melted butter
⅓	cup milk

Stir together with a large fork until dry ingredients are fully incorporated.

ROASTED BUTTERNUT SQUASH SOUP

Serves 4 to 6

1	(2-pound) butternut squash
2	large onions
1	head garlic
2	tablespoons olive oil
4	cups vegetable broth
¼	cup chopped fresh flat-leaf parsley
1	tablespoon chopped fresh sage
¾	teaspoon chopped fresh thyme or ¼ teaspoon dried thyme
	Kosher salt and ground black pepper, to taste

Use a 4-quart slow cooker. There are two steps here—we need to roast the vegetables before placing them into the slow cooker. This will create a delicious nutty flavor; you'll thank me for the bit of extra work! Preheat the oven to 375°F. Cut the butternut squash in half, and scoop out the seeds. Cut the onions and the head of garlic in half (no need to peel). Rub the exposed squash, onion, and garlic flesh with the oil, and place the halves facedown on a baking sheet. Bake for about 45 minutes. When the vegetables are soft, and have begun to brown and wrinkle, scoop the cooked flesh out of the butternut squash skin and place it into the insert. Add the roasted onion and garlic (discard the skins).

Add the broth and herbs. Cover and cook on low for 5 hours, or until the flavors have melded and the soup is fully hot. Use a handheld immersion blender and blend until the soup has reached desired consistency or let cool a bit and blend in small batches in a traditional blender (I like a few chunks here and there). Add the salt and pepper at the table.

 The Verdict

My mom has been making this soup for years—she still has the photocopied recipe out of a 1997 *Sunset* magazine. I love how buttery and rich this soup is although there isn't a drop of cream or butter; it's absolutely delicious. The soup freezes and reheats well, although you may need to add a bit of broth or water to thin it a bit.

ROASTED GARLIC POTATO CHOWDER

Serves 6

8	baking potatoes, such as Yukon Gold or Russet, peeled and cubed
2	onions, diced
1	cup chopped baby carrots
3	stalks celery, sliced
1	head garlic, peeled (approximately 10 cloves)
1	teaspoon kosher salt
½	teaspoon ground black pepper
5	cups chicken broth
1	cup heavy whipping cream

Use a 6-quart slow cooker. Place the vegetables into the insert, and add the salt and pepper. Stir in the broth. Cover, and cook on low for 7 to 8 hours, or until the garlic smooshes easily with the back of a spoon. Use a potato masher (or handheld immersion blender) to squish a few of the potatoes to thicken the broth. Stir in the cream. Cover, and cook on high for 20 minutes, or until the soup is hot.

 The Verdict

The whole cloves of garlic really give a wonderful smoky, nutty flavor to this chowder. If you'd prefer to keep it vegetarian, swap out the chicken broth for a veggie broth.

SHIITAKE MUSHROOM AND TOFU SOUP

Serves 4

6	cups beef broth
12	ounces extra-firm tofu, cut into tiny cubes
1	(1-inch) piece fresh ginger, peeled and grated
1	tablespoon soy sauce (I use gluten-free)
3	green onions, thinly sliced
½	cup dried shiitake mushrooms, coarsely chopped

Use a 4-quart slow cooker. Pour the broth into the insert, and add the tofu, ginger, and soy sauce. Stir in the green onions and mushrooms. Cover, and cook on low for 6 to 7 hours. The mushrooms will reconstitute and swell while cooking.

 The Verdict

This is a great soup to sip on for a light lunch, or to soothe a sore throat on a rainy day. If serving for dinner, pair it with a large salad and a bowl of rice or pasta. I enjoy sipping it from a large mug for lunch at my desk.

SOUTHWESTERN TURKEY SOUP

Serves 4

2½ pounds turkey drumsticks, skin removed
1 onion, diced
1 (15-ounce) can corn, undrained
1 (14.5-ounce) can stewed tomatoes, undrained
1 (4-ounce) can diced jalapeño peppers, undrained
1 tablespoon ground cumin
1 teaspoon chili powder
½ teaspoon kosher salt
4 cups chicken broth
   Sour cream, for serving (optional)

Use a 6-quart slow cooker. Place the turkey into the insert. Add the onion, corn, tomatoes, and the jalapeños. Add the spices and salt, and pour in the broth. Cover, and cook on low for 7 to 8 hours, or on high for about 4 hours. Carefully remove the turkey meat from the bones with kitchen tongs and return to the soup. Serve in a large bowl with a dollop of sour cream, if desired.

The Verdict

While you can certainly use chicken instead of turkey in this soup, I like the richer flavor turkey provides. I tend to forget about turkey in the middle of the year, and need to cook it more often. My kids all ate this soup—the jalapeños do have heat, but not enough to deter my kids (they crumbled Fritos into their helpings).

SNOWY DAY SQUASH AND CHICKEN STEW

Serves 8

1 (2-pound) butternut squash, peeled, seeded, and cut into 1-inch pieces
1 pound chicken breast, pounded thin and cut into ½-inch pieces
1 onion, diced
1 red bell pepper, seeded and chopped
4 garlic cloves, minced
2 tablespoons chili powder
1 tablespoon dried oregano
2 teaspoons ground cumin
1 teaspoon kosher salt
½ teaspoon ground black pepper
1 (15-ounce) can white beans, drained and rinsed
1 (15-ounce) can pinto beans, drained and rinsed
1 (15-ounce) can corn, drained
2 (10-ounce) cans tomatoes and chiles, undrained
1 cup chicken broth
   Freshly grated Parmesan cheese (optional)

Use a 6-quart or larger slow cooker. Place the squash into the insert, and add the chicken. Add the onion, bell pepper, and garlic. Sprinkle in all the dried seasonings, salt, and black pepper, and then stir well to distribute the spices. Add the beans, corn, and tomatoes and chiles. Stir in the broth (the cooker will be quite full—stir the best you can). Cover, and cook on low for 10 hours, or on high for about 6 hours. Stir well before serving, and add a bit of grated Parmesan cheese, if you'd like.

The Verdict

This is a great stew to come home to after a day out in the cold—it'll warm you up without weighing you down—allowing plenty of room for seconds and thirds. This makes a lot, but freezes and reheats beautifully.

SPANISH CHICKEN STEW

Serves 6

3	pounds bone-in chicken thighs, skin removed
1	onion, sliced into rings
8	garlic cloves, peeled
1	cup frozen peas
1	cup pitted green olives
1	(14.5-ounce) can diced tomatoes, undrained
1	teaspoon paprika
1	teaspoon chili powder
½	teaspoon ground white pepper
1	cup dry white wine
	Hot cooked quinoa, for serving

Use a 4-quart slow cooker. Place the chicken into the insert, and add the onion and garlic. Add the peas, olives, tomatoes, and spices, and pour in the wine. Cover, and cook on low for 8 hours. Serve with the quinoa in a large bowl with a ladleful of broth over the top.

THE VERDICT

THIS DELICIOUS STEW HAS A NICE AMOUNT OF HEAT THAT SNEAKS UP ON YOUR TONGUE; IF YOU DON'T CARE FOR SPICY FOOD, CUT THE WHITE PEPPER AMOUNT IN HALF. THE PEAS, OLIVES, AND TOMATOES COOK DOWN TO A BEAUTIFUL GRAVY.

SPICED CHICKEN AND VEGETABLE STEW

Serves 6

2	pounds boneless, skinless chicken thighs
I	onion, thinly sliced
6	garlic cloves, peeled
I	head cauliflower, florets separated
2	medium zucchini, thickly sliced
I	(14.5-ounce) can diced tomatoes, undrained
I	teaspoon ground cumin
I	teaspoon ground coriander
½	teaspoon ground turmeric
½	teaspoon kosher salt
½	teaspoon cayenne pepper
2	cups chicken broth

Use a 6-quart slow cooker. Put the chicken into the insert, and add the onion and garlic. Toss the cauliflower and zucchini on top, and pour in the tomatoes. Add all the spices, and stir in the broth, taking care not to crumble the cauliflower. Cover, and cook on low for 6 to 8 hours, or on high for about 5 hours.

 THE VERDICT

THIS IS A GREAT WAY TO GET EXTRA VITAMINS INTO YOUR DIET IF YOU AREN'T NORMALLY A FAN OF ZUCCHINI AND CAULIFLOWER, WHICH COMBINED GIVE YOU A FANTASTIC DOSE OF VITAMINS A, B, AND C. MY CHILDREN HAPPILY ATE THEIR SERVINGS, AND I SHARED THE LEFTOVERS WITH MY GRANDMOTHER WHO REPORTED THAT THE FLAVORS WERE EVEN MORE PRONOUNCED THE NEXT DAY.

SPINACH AND TOMATO SOUP (SWAMP SOUP)

Serves 4 to 6

2	tablespoons olive oil
1	onion, diced
3	stalks celery, thinly sliced
4	garlic cloves, diced
1	(26-ounce) jar prepared pasta sauce
1	(14.5-ounce) can fire-roasted tomatoes, undrained
2	cups chicken or vegetable broth
1	(10-ounce) package frozen spinach
1	tablespoon dried Italian seasoning
½	teaspoon kosher salt
½	teaspoon ground black pepper
2	cups shredded Swiss cheese

Use a 6-quart slow cooker. In a large skillet over medium heat, heat the oil, then add the onion, celery, and garlic and cook, stirring, until the onion is translucent. Scrape the skillet contents into the insert. Add the pasta sauce and tomatoes. Add the broth and spinach. Stir in the Italian seasoning, salt, and pepper. Cover, and cook on low for 7 to 8 hours. Stir well to break up the spinach. Place a handful of cheese into each bowl, and ladle the soup on top.

 The Verdict

The inspiration from this soup comes from budgetbytes. com. It serves up to six people and the entire pot cost right around seven dollars. While the vegetables will cook just fine in the slow cooker without browning beforehand, I recommend doing so—the bit of oil and caramelized onions really add a great depth of flavor.

SPLIT PEA SOUP WITH HAM

Serves 6

1	ham bone
1	cup diced ham
1	onion, diced
1	pound dried split peas, rinsed
4	cups chicken broth
4	cups water
½	teaspoon celery seed
½	cup chopped baby carrots
¼	teaspoon kosher salt
¼	teaspoon ground black pepper

Use a 6-quart slow cooker. Put the ham bone and diced ham into the insert. Add the onion, split peas, broth, and water. Drop in the celery seed, carrots, salt, and pepper. Cover, and cook on low for 8 to 10 hours, or until onion is translucent and peas are soft. Carefully remove the ham bone. Pulse the soup with a handheld immersion blender (or let cool and blend in small batches in a traditional blender) until you've reached the desired consistency.

 The Verdict

This is a fantastic pea soup, smoky and perfectly seasoned. Everyone I've served it to loves it—unless they don't like peas. Then I can't be of help.

STEAK SOUP WITH SALSA AND WHITE BEANS

Serves 6

2   cups diced cooked steak
1   cup salsa
2   cups dried small white beans, soaked overnight and drained (for quick-soak method, see page 82)
1   cup frozen corn
4   cups beef or chicken broth
    Kosher salt, to taste

Use a 6-quart slow cooker. Put the meat into the insert, and add the salsa and beans. Add the corn, and stir in the broth. Cover and cook on low for 7 hours, high for 4 hours, or until the beans are soft. Add salt to taste at the table, if needed.

 The Verdict

This is my favorite summertime and early fall lunch. My husband likes to grill steak, but usually overestimates how much meat our family will actually eat. I like how this is low in calories but packed with flavor and (relatively) mild heat, thanks to the salsa.

SUPER SIMPLE TORTILLA SOUP

Serves 6

4   boneless, skinless chicken thighs or breast halves (frozen is fine)
1   (14.5-ounce) can pinto beans, undrained
1   (14.5-ounce) can diced tomatoes, undrained
1   (4-ounce) can diced green chiles, undrained
1   tablespoon ground cumin
4   cups chicken broth
    Suggested toppings: corn chips, shredded Cheddar cheese

Use a 6-quart slow cooker. Place the chicken into the insert, and add the beans, tomatoes, and chiles. Add the cumin, and stir in the broth. Cover, and cook on low for 8 to 10 hours. Shred the chicken before serving. To thicken the broth a bit, pulse a few times with a handheld immersion blender, or scoop out a ½ cup of pinto beans to blend in a traditional blender before stirring back into the soup. Serve with a handful of corn chips and cheese, if desired.

 The Verdict

I love how uncomplicated this soup is—I had pinto beans on hand the day I made it, but feel free to use whatever happens to be in your pantry. My kids like to spoon their soup with Tostitos Scoops chips.

SWEET CORN CHOWDER

Serves 6

1	(16-ounce) package frozen white corn
4	cups chicken broth
2	Yukon Gold potatoes, peeled and diced
4	garlic cloves, minced
1	teaspoon kosher salt
½	teaspoon ground black pepper
1	cup heavy whipping cream

Use a 4-quart slow cooker. Put the corn into the insert, and add the broth, potatoes, garlic, salt, and pepper. Cover, and cook on low for 7 hours, or until the potatoes are bite-tender. Use a handheld immersion blender to blend until you've reached desired consistency (or blend in small batches in a traditional blender)—super chunky or smooth; your choice. Stir in the cream. Cover, and cook on high for 30 minutes, or until the soup is hot.

 THE VERDICT
WHITE CORN MAKES THIS CHOWDER NICE AND SWEET, A DEFINITE KID PLEASER. IF YOU ONLY HAVE YELLOW CORN IN THE HOUSE, GO AHEAD AND USE IT, BUT STIR IN ABOUT 1 TABLESPOON SUGAR, OR TO TASTE, AT THE VERY END.

TANGY BLACK BEAN SOUP

Serves 8

1	pound dried black beans, soaked overnight and drained (for a quick-soak method, see page 82)
1	(14.5-ounce) can diced tomatoes, drained
1	red bell pepper, seeded and diced
2	garlic cloves, chopped
1	teaspoon ground cinnamon
1	teaspoon ground allspice
1	tablespoon ground cumin
1	teaspoon ground chipotle chile
1	orange, juiced
1	lime, juiced
4	cups chicken broth
1	lemon, sliced into 8 wedges, for serving

Use a 6-quart slow cooker. Put the beans into the insert. Add the tomatoes, bell pepper, garlic, and all the dried spices. Add the orange and lime juices, and stir in the broth until the spices and broth are completely distributed. Cover and cook on low for 8 to 10 hours, or until the beans are soft. Blend with a handheld immersion blender or carefully scoop the soup into a traditional blender and pulse until the soup is fully blended. Serve each bowl with a lemon wedge at the table for an even more pronounced burst of citrus.

 **THE VERDICT**
THIS SOUP FEELS LIKE A VACATION IN A BOWL. THE BIT OF HEAT FROM THE CHIPOTLE CHILE POWDER IS WASHED AWAY BY THE FRESH CITRUSY TANG. MY WHOLE FAMILY LOVED THIS SOUP, AS DID OUR NEIGHBORS UP THE STREET.

TEX-MEX CHICKEN SOUP

Serves 4

2   frozen chicken breast halves
1   onion, diced
1   (10-ounce) can tomatoes and chiles, undrained
1   (15-ounce) can black beans, drained and rinsed
1   (15-ounce) can corn, undrained
1   (1-ounce) packet ranch salad dressing mix (for homemade, see page 256)
1   tablespoon ground cumin
1   teaspoon chili powder
1   cup chicken broth
1   (8-ounce) package cream cheese

Use a 4-quart slow cooker. Place the chicken into the insert, and add the onion, tomatoes and chiles, black beans, and corn. Stir in the salad dressing mix, cumin, chili powder, and broth. Cover, and cook on low for 8 hours. Shred the chicken with a fork, and stir in the cream cheese. Cover, and cook on high for 30 minutes, or until the cream cheese is completely dissolved.

The Verdict

This warm, comforting, creamy chicken soup pairs well with cornbread and a green salad. It freezes and reheats well.

THAI CHICKEN AND COCONUT SOUP

Serves 4

1   pound boneless, skinless chicken thighs, cut into thin strips
1   cup fresh green beans, trimmed and chopped
2   garlic cloves, chopped
1   tablespoon sugar
1   to 2 teaspoons chili-garlic sauce
1   teaspoon grated fresh ginger
4   cups chicken broth
1   (14.5-ounce) can diced tomatoes, drained
1   (15-ounce) can coconut milk
3   tablespoons fish sauce
3   limes, juiced

Use a 4-quart slow cooker. Place the chicken into the insert, and add the green beans and garlic. Add the sugar, 1 teaspoon of the chili-garlic sauce (if desired, stir in more after the cooking time for additional heat), and the ginger. Pour in the broth, tomatoes, coconut milk (don't forget the cream on top), and fish sauce. Stir well and add the lime juice. Cover and cook on low for 6 hours, or on high for 4 hours. Stir well before serving.

The Verdict

Coconut soup is one of my comfort foods. I love the creamy texture with the bite of lime. When I make it for the family I add very little heat, but if I have the house to myself, I make it spicy enough for my nose to run. You can omit the chicken and add cubed tofu, if you'd prefer.

THAI PEANUT CHICKEN NOODLE SOUP

Serves 4

1	pound boneless, skinless chicken, cut into ½-inch pieces
1	(14.5-ounce) can diced tomatoes, undrained
1	red bell pepper, seeded and thinly sliced
1	cup bean sprouts
3	green onions, thinly sliced
1	(2-inch) piece fresh ginger, peeled and grated
4	garlic cloves, minced
6	cups chicken broth
½	cup smooth, all natural peanut butter
1	tablespoon fish sauce
1	tablespoon soy sauce (I use gluten-free)
1	teaspoon sesame oil
1	(6-ounce) package rice noodles, rinsed
	Suggested toppings: chopped peanuts, chopped fresh cilantro leaves, lime wedges

Use a 6-quart slow cooker. Place the chicken into the insert and add the tomatoes. Add the bell pepper, bean sprouts, green onions, ginger, and garlic. Stir in the broth, peanut butter, fish sauce, soy sauce, and oil; the peanut butter will be clumpy, but don't worry about it. Cover, and cook on low for 7 to 8 hours. Stir well, and drop in the rice noodles. Cover, and cook on high for 20 to 30 minutes, or until the noodles are bite-tender. Serve in large bowls with chopped peanuts, a bit of cilantro, and a squeeze of lime, if desired.

 The Verdict

Thai food at home just couldn't be easier. Everything about this soup works—the bean sprouts, the salty peanut taste, and the tiny bit of fresh tartness at the end with the lime wedge. Score!

TOMATO BASIL SOUP

Serves 6

1	onion, diced
2	stalks celery including leaves, sliced
1	(46-ounce) container tomato juice
1	(8-ounce) can tomato sauce
½	cup chicken or vegetable broth
1	teaspoon dried basil
1	bay leaf
½	cup heavy whipping cream (optional)

Use a 4-quart slow cooker. Place the onion and celery into the insert, and add the tomato juice, tomato sauce, and broth. Add the basil and bay leaf. Cover, and cook on low for 6 hours, or until onion is translucent and flavors have melded. Discard the bay leaf, and use a handheld immersion blender to completely blend the soup, or blend in batches in a traditional blender. If desired, stir in the cream, and turn to high for 20 minutes, or until soup is fully hot.

 The Verdict

Tomato soup and grilled cheese sandwiches are one of my husband's favorite meals. My kids like it when I serve the cream separately and they each stir a tablespoon or so into their own bowls at the table.

TOMATO BEEF SOUP

Serves 8

2	pounds fajita meat (thinly sliced beef)
1	onion, diced
2	stalks celery, thinly sliced
1	(16-ounce) bag frozen mixed vegetables
1	tablespoon dark brown sugar
1	teaspoon paprika
1	tablespoon garlic powder
1	teaspoon seasoned salt
½	teaspoon ground black pepper
2	teaspoons chili powder
2	(28-ounce) cans tomato sauce
2	cups beef broth

Use a 6-quart slow cooker. Place the beef into the insert, and add the onion, celery, and the vegetables. Add the sugar, all the spices, and stir in the tomato sauce and broth. Cover, and cook on low for 8 to 10 hours—the longer the better for this one!

 THE VERDICT

DO ME A FAVOR AND EAT THIS SOUP CUDDLED UP ON THE COUCH WITH A HANDMADE AFGHAN OVER YOUR SHOULDERS—IT'S PURE COMFORT IN A BOWL. MY KIDS ADDED PARMESAN CHEESE ON TOP, AND REFUSED TO EAT ANY OF THE LIMA BEANS FROM THE FROZEN VEGETABLE MIX, BUT ALL IN ALL THIS WAS A VERY SUCCESSFUL MEAL IN OUR HOUSEHOLD. IT FREEZES AND REHEATS BEAUTIFULLY, ALTHOUGH YOU MAY HAVE TO THIN IT A BIT WHEN REHEATING.

TRADITIONAL BEEF STEW

Serves 8

2	pounds lean beef stew meat
4	cups beef broth
2	cups tomato juice
8	garlic cloves, peeled
2	onions, thinly sliced
2	pounds red potatoes, washed and cubed
I	cup frozen peas
I	cup diced celery
I	cup diced baby carrots
I	tablespoon dried Italian seasoning
I	tablespoon Worcestershire sauce (I use gluten-free)
I	teaspoon kosher salt
½	teaspoon ground black pepper
2	bay leaves

Use a 6-quart slow cooker. Put the meat into the insert, and add the broth, tomato juice, and garlic. Then add all the vegetables and seasonings. Drop in the bay leaves. Cover, and cook on low for 8 to 10 hours, or until beef has reached desired tenderness and garlic smooshes easily with a spoon. Remove the bay leaves before serving.

THE VERDICT

I ONCE JOKED THAT THERE ARE AS MANY VERSIONS OF BEEF STEW AS THERE ARE MISSING BARBIE SHOES, AND I CONTINUE TO STAND BY THAT ASSERTION. I DO LOVE THIS VERSION, THOUGH, BECAUSE THE BROTH IS RICH AND FLAVORFUL THANKS TO THE GARLIC AND TOMATO JUICE. WE SHARED THIS STEW WITH FAMILY AND FRIENDS, AND EVERYBODY LOVED IT.

TURKEY DRUMSTICK AND ONION GOULASH

Serves 6 to 8

4	turkey drumsticks (frozen is fine)
3	onions, thinly sliced
8	garlic cloves, peeled
1	tablespoon ground cumin
1	tablespoon paprika
1	tablespoon chicken bouillon granules
1	teaspoon ground black pepper
½	cup pitted green olives
4	tablespoons (½ stick) butter
	Hot cooked brown rice or quinoa, for serving (optional)

Use a 6-quart slow cooker. Place the drumsticks into the insert. Add the onion and garlic. Sprinkle in the spices, and add the olives and butter. Cover, and cook on low for 8 hours. Carefully remove the turkey bones and skin and serve the soup over a bowl of steamed brown rice or quinoa—or eat as is, like a stew, to keep the carb count low.

🍲 The Verdict

I had a quarter jar of olives left in the fridge and decided to toss them into this turkey dish, and I'm so glad I did. The olives plump and then break down during slow cooking, which creates a marvelous broth when mixed with the seasoned turkey and butter. You can eat this as is, or serve it over a starch to stretch the meal to serve up to 8 people.

WHITE BEAN AND KALE SOUP

Serves 8

1	cup dried white beans, soaked overnight and drained or 1 (15-ounce) can, drained and rinsed
1	pound kale, stems removed and leaves torn
1	onion, diced
6	garlic cloves, sliced
1	tablespoon olive oil
1	(14.5-ounce) can fire-roasted tomatoes, undrained
1	teaspoon kosher salt
½	teaspoon crushed red pepper flakes
3	cups chicken or vegetable broth
	Freshly grated Parmesan cheese, for serving (optional)

Use a 6-quart slow cooker. Put the beans into the insert, and add the kale, onion, and garlic. Add the oil, and swirl the beans and vegetables around until they are fully coated with the oil. Add the tomatoes, salt, and red pepper flakes, and stir in the broth. Cover, and cook on low for 8 hours, or on high for about 4 hours. Serve with cheese, if desired.

🍲 The Verdict

Kale is packed with vitamins and fiber and is becoming the new "it" vegetable. This soup is a great way to introduce this nourishing green to your family. Serve with homemade sourdough or cornbread.

WILD MUSHROOM BEEF STEW

Serves 6

2	pounds beef chuck, cut in 1-inch pieces
3	tablespoons all-purpose flour (I used rice flour)
1	tablespoon dried Italian seasoning
1	teaspoon ground black pepper
1	pound fresh wild mushrooms, thinly sliced
1	onion, diced
4	garlic cloves, minced
1	cup beef broth
1	(6-ounce) can tomato paste
½	cup dry red wine
1	tablespoon Worcestershire sauce (I use gluten-free)

Use a 6-quart slow cooker. Place the meat into the insert, and add the flour, Italian seasoning, and pepper. Toss the meat to coat each piece with flour and seasoning. Add the mushrooms, onion, and garlic. In a mixing bowl, whisk together the broth, tomato paste, wine, and Worcestershire sauce. Pour the liquid evenly over the slow cooker contents. Cover, and cook on low for 8 hours or on high for about 4 hours. The stew is finished when the meat has reached the desired tenderness.

 The Verdict

I found this recipe from chickinthekitchen.com via slowcookerfromscratch.com, and I'm so glad I did! I tend to shy away from wild mushrooms, but loved how they provided a hearty "meaty" texture to the broth—this is an excellent stew, and a nice change from our regular carrots, celery, and potato beef stew standby.

YEMENI CHICKEN SOUP

Serves 6

3	pounds chicken quarters
1	onion, thinly sliced
4	garlic cloves, chopped
6	carrots, cut into 2-inch pieces
6	small yellow potatoes, washed and cubed
6	small zucchini, cut into 1-inch coins
5	teaspoons ground cumin
2	teaspoons ground turmeric
1	teaspoon kosher salt
½	teaspoon ground black pepper
8	cups water

Use a 6-quart or larger slow cooker. Place the chicken into the insert, and add the onion, garlic, carrots, potatoes, and zucchini. Add all the spices and seasonings, and pour in the water. Cover, and cook on low for 8 hours. Remove the lid, and carefully pick out and discard all the chicken skin and bones. Stir well. Season with additional salt and pepper, if desired, at the table.

The Verdict

Kate from New York wrote to me and shared that she loves to adapt this Yemeni staple according to whatever fresh vegetables she has on hand. This is a traditional midday meal in the Yemeni culture, and Kate pairs it with pita bread and zhug, a hot sauce made from chiles, cilantro, and lemon.

ZERO POINTS VEGETABLE SOUP

Serves 8

6	**cups chicken or vegetable broth**
1	**onion, diced**
2	**carrots, diced**
½	**head cabbage, chopped**
½	**pound frozen green beans**
4	**garlic cloves, minced**
2	**tablespoons tomato paste**
1	**teaspoon dried basil**
1	**teaspoon dried oregano**
1	**teaspoon kosher salt**
½	**teaspoon ground black pepper**
1	**large zucchini, diced**
	Freshly grated Parmesan cheese, for serving (optional)

Use a 6-quart slow cooker. Put the broth into the insert, and add the onion, carrots, cabbage, green beans, and garlic. Stir in the tomato paste, basil, oregano, salt, and pepper. Cover, and cook on low for 8 to 10 hours, or until the onion is translucent and the flavors have melded. Add the zucchini 1 hour before serving. Top with cheese, if desired.

 **THE VERDICT**

THIS SOUP COMES FROM ALANNA KELLOGG, OF A VEGGIE VENTURE (KITCHEN-PARADE-VEGGIEVENTURE.BLOGSPOT.COM). IT'S A ZERO-POINTS WEIGHT WATCHER SOUP (WITH NO CHEESE) AND IS A GREAT SOUP TO EAT DAILY FOR LUNCH. IT'S PACKED WITH VEGETABLES AND FIBER, AND IT FREEZES AND REHEATS WELL.

BEANS

21-INGREDIENT CHILI

Serves 8

2	pounds boneless, skinless chicken thighs, cut into 1-inch chunks (frozen is fine)
1	onion, diced
1	(15-ounce) can kidney beans, drained and rinsed
1	(15-ounce) can white cannellini beans, drained and rinsed
1	(15-ounce) can corn, drained and rinsed
1	(14.5-ounce) can fire-roasted tomatoes, undrained
1	medium sweet potato, peeled and grated
1	(4-ounce) can diced green chiles, undrained
½	cup spicy brown mustard
2	tablespoons soy sauce (I use gluten-free)
2	tablespoons honey
3	tablespoons chili powder
1	tablespoon ground chipotle chile, or to taste (if you are sensitive to heat, start with 1 teaspoon)
1	tablespoon onion powder
1	tablespoon garlic powder
1	teaspoon ground white pepper, or to taste (if you are sensitive to heat, add less or omit)
1	teaspoon dried oregano
1	teaspoon ground cumin
¼	teaspoon ground cinnamon
¼	teaspoon ground cloves
2	cups chicken broth
	Suggested toppings: shredded Cheddar cheese, sour cream

Use a 6-quart or larger slow cooker. Put the chicken into the insert. Add the onion, beans, corn, tomatoes, sweet potato, and chiles. Now add the mustard, soy sauce, honey, and all the seasonings. Carefully stir well to distribute the spices the best you can. Pour in the broth. Cover and cook on low for 8 to 10 hours, or until the chicken easily shreds with a fork. Stir very well and serve in a large bowl with your favorite chili toppings. We like cheese and sour cream.

THE VERDICT

SUCH. GOOD. CHILI. THIS IS A WHOLE MEAL IN A BOWL. MY TONGUE WAS FIRST HIT WITH SWEETNESS, THEN A SLOW HEAT CAME OUT. THE CHILDREN ATE THEIR SERVINGS—IT WAS NOT OVERLY SPICY (THE BABY HAD THREE HELPINGS!). THE HEAT IS FROM THE WHITE PEPPER MORE THAN THE CHILI POWDER. IF YOU'VE GOT SENSITIVE PALATES, CUT BACK ON THE WHITE PEPPER (YOU CAN ALWAYS ADD MORE AT THE TABLE).

3-BEAN CHILI

Serves 10

- 1   **pound lean ground beef**
- 1   **pound Italian sausage, casings removed**
- 1   **onion, diced**
- 6   **garlic cloves, chopped**
- 2   **(10-ounce) cans tomatoes and chiles, undrained**
- 2   **(8-ounce) cans tomato sauce**
- 1   **(16-ounce) can black beans, drained and rinsed**
- 1   **(16-ounce) can chickpeas, drained and rinsed**
- 1   **(16-ounce) can kidney beans, drained and rinsed**
- 2   **tablespoons ground cumin**
- 2   **tablespoons chili powder**
- 1   **teaspoon paprika**
- 1   **teaspoon liquid smoke**
- ½   **teaspoon kosher salt**
-       **Suggested toppings: shredded Cheddar cheese, sour cream**

Use a 6-quart slow cooker. In a large skillet over medium heat, cook the beef, sausage, onion, and garlic, stirring, until the meat is browned. Drain off any accumulated fat. Transfer the meat mixture to the insert. Add the tomatoes and tomato sauce. Add all the beans and all the seasonings. Stir well to combine the ingredients. Cover, and cook on low for 8 to 10 hours. Serve with cheese and sour cream, if desired.

 The Verdict

I made this on Super Bowl Sunday and everyone loved it—it's got a bit of heat that sneaks up the back of your tongue—absolutely the right amount. This is award-winning chili—two of my readers have won cook-offs with this recipe!

BAKED BEANS WITH ROOT BEER

Serves 8

- 6   **slices applewood-smoked bacon, diced**
- 1   **onion, diced**
- 4   **garlic cloves, minced**
- 4   **(15-ounce) cans white beans, drained and rinsed**
- 1   **cup root beer**
- 1   **tablespoon apple cider vinegar**
- 2   **tablespoons molasses**
- 2   **tablespoons tomato paste**
- 2   **tablespoons Dijon mustard**
- 1   **teaspoon chili powder**
- 1   **teaspoon kosher salt**
- ½   **teaspoon ground black pepper**

Use a 4-quart slow cooker. In a large skillet over medium heat, cook the bacon, onion, and garlic, stirring, until the bacon is cooked. Drain off any accumulated fat, and transfer the bacon mixture into the insert. Add the beans and root beer. In a small bowl, combine the vinegar, molasses, tomato paste, mustard, chili powder, salt, and pepper. Stir this sauce into the beans. Cover, and cook on low for 8 hours.

 The Verdict

Ah, American comfort cuisine at its finest. Donna, from Madison, Wisconsin, adapted this recipe from one she found in *Bon Appétit* magazine. We all loved the sweet and smoky root beer flavor. We saved the rest of the root beer and had floats for dessert! Try serving this with cornbread and a large salad.

BBQ BEAN CHILI

Serves 8

1	**pound dried small red beans**
1	**pound lean ground beef**
2	**onions, diced**
6	**garlic cloves, chopped**
4	**ripe tomatoes, chopped**
1	**cup frozen white corn**
1	**cup barbecue sauce**
¼	**cup minced fresh cilantro leaves**
2	**tablespoons chili powder**
1	**tablespoon ground cumin**
1	**cup chicken broth**

Use a 6-quart slow cooker. Add the beans to a pot with water to cover and cook for 10 minutes at a rapid boil. Let the beans sit in the hot water for 1 hour before draining and placing into the insert. (Red beans must be boiled before putting into the slow cooker to remove a naturally occurring potential toxin.)

In a large skillet over medium heat, cook the beef, onions, and garlic, stirring, until the meat has browned. Drain off any accumulated fat. Transfer the mixture to the insert. Add the tomatoes, corn, barbecue sauce, cilantro, chili powder, and cumin. Stir in the broth. Cover, and cook on low for 8 to 10 hours, or until the beans have reached desired tenderness and have begun to split.

 **THE VERDICT**

I WAS INTRIGUED BY THIS INGREDIENT LIST—I HADN'T PREVIOUSLY MADE A CHILI WITH A BARBECUE BASE. MY CHILDREN WERE THRILLED, AND EACH ATE A BUNCH. THE LEFTOVERS MAKE A FANTASTIC NACHO TOPPING, AND I'M ALREADY LOOKING FORWARD TO COOKING IT AGAIN. THIS FREEZES AND REHEATS WELL.

BLACK BEAN AND CHORIZO CHILI

Serves 8

1   **pound dried black beans, soaked overnight and drained (for quick-soak method, see page 82)**
12 **ounces fresh chorizo**
1   **onion, diced**
4   **garlic cloves, minced**
1   **cup diced baby carrots**
1   **red bell pepper, seeded and diced**
¼   **cup chopped fresh flat-leaf parsley**
2   **teaspoons ground cumin**
4   **cups beef broth**
     Suggested toppings: shredded Cheddar cheese, sour cream

Use a 6-quart slow cooker. Place the beans into the insert. Remove the casings from the chorizo, and crumble it into a large skillet over medium heat. Add the onion and garlic, and cook, stirring, until the mixture is browned. Drain off any accumulated fat, and pour the meat mixture into the insert. Add the carrots, bell pepper, parsley, and cumin. Stir in the broth. Cover, and cook on low for 8 hours, or on high for 4 to 5 hours. Your chili is complete when the beans are fully cooked and soft. Serve with Cheddar cheese and a dollop of sour cream, if desired.

THE VERDICT

I LOVE THIS CHILI—I LIKE THAT IT'S NOT TOMATO-BASED, AND I LOVE THE FLAVOR, TEXTURE, AND HEAT THE CHORIZO PROVIDES. THE CARROTS, BELL PEPPER, AND PARSLEY ARE NICE SURPRISES MINGLED THROUGHOUT THE BEANS AND MEAT. WE SHARED THIS CHILI WITH OUR NEIGHBORS, JENNY AND STEVE, WHO ALSO LIKED IT A LOT. MY GIRLS FOUND IT A BIT SPICY FOR THEIR LIKING.

BLACK BEAN CHILI SOUP

Serves 6

2 **(15-ounce) cans black beans, undrained**
1 **(28-ounce) can crushed tomatoes, undrained**
1 **(15-ounce) can white corn, undrained**
¼ **cup dried minced onion**
2 **tablespoons chili powder**
1 **tablespoon tomato paste**
1 **tablespoon unsweetened cocoa powder**
1 **teaspoon garlic powder**
1 **teaspoon ground cumin**
 **Suggested toppings: shredded Cheddar cheese,
 sour cream**

Use a 6-quart slow cooker. Pour the beans, tomatoes, and corn into the insert. Add the dried onion, chili powder, tomato paste, cocoa powder, garlic powder, and cumin. Stir well to distribute ingredients. Cover, and cook on low for 6 to 8 hours. Thicken the broth by using a handheld immersion blender to blend 1 cup or so of the ingredients or blend in a traditional blender. Top with cheese and sour cream, if desired.

 The Verdict

Deborah sent me this recipe via e-mail, and it was a hit in our house. It's thicker than a soup, but not quite as thick as a chili, and it's absolutely delicious. Soak up the juice with a big hunk of cornbread. Thank you, Deborah!

CARIBBEAN BLACK BEANS

Serves 8

1 **pound dried black beans, soaked overnight and
 drained (for quick-soak method, see page 82)**
2 **mangoes, peeled, pitted, and diced**
4 **garlic cloves, minced**
1 **teaspoon curry powder**
1 **teaspoon ground allspice**
1 **teaspoon paprika**
1 **teaspoon ground ginger**
1 **teaspoon Tabasco sauce, plus more for serving**
4 **cups chicken broth**

Use a 6-quart slow cooker. Place the beans into the insert. Add all but ½ cup of the diced mango, the garlic, and all the spices. Add the Tabasco sauce, and stir in the broth. Cover and cook on low for 7 to 8 hours, or until the beans are fully softened. The mango will have disappeared while cooking—gingerly fold in the remaining ½ cup mango just before serving. If you'd like more of a spicy tang, add Tabasco at the table.

The Verdict

Just when I thought I couldn't like black beans any more than I already do, I opened my e-mail and got this wonderful new recipe from Meg. These beans are dual purpose—you can eat them hot for dinner or lunch, or the next day cold, as a salad.

CHEESY LENTIL BAKE

Serves 6 to 8

2	cups dried brown or green lentils, rinsed
1	(14.5-ounce) can diced tomatoes, undrained
1	red onion, diced
½	cup chopped baby carrots
½	cup sliced celery
1	teaspoon herbes de Provence
½	teaspoon kosher salt
¼	teaspoon ground black pepper
2½	cups chicken or vegetable broth
2	cups shredded Cheddar cheese
1	cup shredded mozzarella cheese

Use a 4-quart slow cooker. Dump the lentils into the insert and add the tomatoes, onion, carrots, celery, and all the seasonings. Stir in the broth. Add the cheeses to the top and cover. Cook on low for 5 to 6 hours, or until the lentils are bite-tender and the cheeses are fully melted and have begun to brown on top and pull away from the sides.

 **THE VERDICT**
WHO NEEDS MAC AND CHEESE WHEN YOU CAN HAVE LENTILS AND CHEESE? I KEEP THIS DISH VEGETARIAN, BUT YOU CAN CERTAINLY ADD SLICED SMOKED SAUSAGE TO "BEEF" IT UP A BIT. MY KIDS LOVE THE STRINGY CHEESE ON TOP.

CHILEAN BLACK BEAN STEW

Serves 6

2	(15-ounce) cans black beans, drained and rinsed
1	(16-ounce) bag frozen corn
1	medium butternut squash, peeled, seeded, and cubed
1	large onion, diced
¼	cup tightly packed fresh basil leaves, chopped
¼	teaspoon cayenne pepper
½	teaspoon kosher salt
4	cups vegetable broth

Use a 6-quart slow cooker. Put the beans into the insert, and add the corn. Add the squash, onion, basil, cayenne pepper, and salt. Stir in the broth. Cover, and cook on low for 6 hours, or until the onion is translucent.

 The Verdict

The teensy bit of cayenne is noticeable, but not spicy—just flavorful and yummy. The squash breaks down quite a bit in the cooker, coating the beans with buttery sweetness. My youngest will eat these beans all day long. Serve this with a dinner salad if you'd like.

CHOCOLATE CHILI

Serves 6

1	pound dried small red beans
1	yellow onion, diced
1	cup diced baby carrots
4	garlic cloves, chopped
3	tablespoons chili powder
1	tablespoon sugar
½	to 1 tablespoon ground chipotle chile
1	teaspoon paprika
1	teaspoon ground cumin
1	teaspoon dried oregano
1	teaspoon kosher salt
1	(28-ounce) can crushed tomatoes
½	cup brewed coffee
½	cup water
1	ounce unsweetened baking chocolate

Use a 6-quart slow cooker. Add the beans to a pot with water to cover and cook on the stovetop for 10 minutes at a rapid boil and then let the beans sit in the hot water, covered, for 1 hour. Drain and place the beans into the insert. (Red beans must be boiled before slow cooking to remove a naturally occurring potential toxin.) Add the onion, carrots, garlic, and all the seasonings. Slowly stir in the tomatoes, coffee, water, and chocolate. Cover and cook on low for 8 to 10 hours, or until the beans are soft. Stir well before serving.

 **The Verdict**

This is a rich, velvety chili with a nice punch of heat that sneaks up on you. The boldness created by the chipotle, chocolate, and coffee is startling—it's a combination that makes your tongue want more.

INDIAN-SPICED CHILI

Serves 6

I	**(15-ounce) can kidney beans, drained and rinsed**
I	**(15-ounce) can chickpeas, drained and rinsed**
I	**(14.5-ounce) can diced tomatoes, undrained**
I	**onion, diced**
4	**stalks celery, diced**
2	**pounds red potatoes, washed and cubed**
3	**tablespoons curry powder**
I	**tablespoon chili powder**
I	**teaspoon ground turmeric**
½	**teaspoon garam masala (for homemade, see page 264)**
I	**teaspoon kosher salt**
4	**cups chicken or vegetable broth**
I	**to 2 jalapeño peppers or to taste**
	Corn tortillas or naan, for serving

Use a 6-quart slow cooker. Put all the beans into the insert, and add the tomatoes. Add the onion, celery, potatoes, and all the seasonings. Pour the broth evenly over the top. Drop in 1 or 2 jalapeños. Cover, and cook on low for 8 hours, or until the onions are translucent, the potatoes are soft, and the flavors have melded. Discard the jalapeños. If you'd like to thicken the chili, pulse a few times with a handheld immersion blender to puree some of the potatoes and beans or puree a cup in a traditional blender and return to the cooker. Serve with tortilla wedges or naan.

THE VERDICT

THIS RECIPE WAS ADAPTED FROM A RECIPE ON DAILYGARNISH.COM AND IT COOKS BEAUTIFULLY IN THE SLOW COOKER. THERE ISN'T A DROP OF OIL IN HERE, AND IF YOU USE VEGETABLE BROTH IT'S COMPLETELY VEGAN. I LIKE USING WHOLE JALAPEÑO PEPPERS IN THE COOKER— THE FLAVOR STEAMS OUT WITHOUT NEEDING TO DICE THEM. THIS CHILI FREEZES AND REHEATS WELL; FREEZE IN LITTLE CONTAINERS AND BRING TO WORK FOR LUNCH.

CHICKEN CURRY CHILI

Serves 6

1	pound boneless, skinless chicken breast, cut into strips
1	red onion, diced
1	small butternut squash, peeled, seeded, and cubed
1	medium zucchini, peeled if desired, and diced
1	red bell pepper, seeded and diced
6	garlic cloves, minced
2	(15-ounce) cans white beans, drained and rinsed
2	(14.5-ounce) cans diced tomatoes, undrained
1	tablespoon chili powder
1	tablespoon curry powder
1	teaspoon ground cumin
1	teaspoon smoked paprika
1	teaspoon kosher salt
½	teaspoon ground black pepper
½	cup chicken broth
1	to 2 dried red chile peppers (optional)

Use a 6-quart slow cooker. Put the chicken into the insert, and add the onion, squash, zucchini, bell pepper, and garlic. Add the beans, tomatoes, and the spices. Stir in the broth. If desired, drop 1 or 2 of the chiles on top. Cover, and cook on low for 8 hours, or until the onions are translucent, and the flavors have melded. Discard the chiles, and stir very well before serving; the squash will break up quite a bit.

THE VERDICT

THE FLAVORS PLAY SO NICELY TOGETHER IN THIS POT OF CHILI. I LIKE THE MILD CURRY FLAVOR MIXED WITH THE SWEET BUTTERNUT SQUASH. THIS IS A GREAT WAY TO GET EXTRA VEGETABLES INTO YOUR DIET (OR YOUR CHILDREN'S) IN A ONE-POT EASY MEAL.

LEFTOVER PULLED PORK POTLUCK BEANS

Serves 8

1	pound shredded cooked pork
2	(15-ounce) cans kidney or pinto beans, drained and rinsed
1	(15-ounce) can pork and beans
1	cup barbecue sauce
1	onion, diced
6	garlic cloves, chopped
¼	cup packed dark brown sugar
¼	cup spicy brown mustard
3	tablespoons soy sauce (I use gluten-free)
1	(20-ounce) can pineapple chunks, drained

Use a 6-quart slow cooker. Put the pork into the insert, and add the beans and the pork and beans. Add the barbecue sauce, onion, garlic, sugar, mustard, and soy sauce. Stir in the pineapple chunks. Cover, and cook on low for 8 to 10 hours, or until flavors have melded and the onions are translucent.

The Verdict

I came up with this recipe after finding a plastic bag full of pulled pork in the back of the freezer. The sauce and pineapple complement the meat beautifully—you can serve it in hamburger buns or spooned into a bowl.

LENTIL AND CORN CHILI

Serves 8

1	(16-ounce) bag dried green or brown lentils, rinsed
1	(28-ounce) can diced tomatoes, undrained
1	onion, diced
1	cup chopped baby carrots
1	cup chopped celery
4	garlic cloves, minced
¼	cup chopped fresh cilantro leaves
1	(16-ounce) bag frozen white corn, thawed
2	tablespoons chili powder
2	tablespoons ground cumin
1	teaspoon kosher salt
½	teaspoon cayenne pepper
2	cups vegetable broth

Use a 6-quart slow cooker. Place the lentils into the insert. Add the tomatoes, onion, carrots, celery, and garlic. Then add the cilantro, the corn, and all the seasonings. Stir in the broth. Cover, and cook on low for 8 to 10 hours. Stir well before serving, and add a bit more chopped cilantro, if desired.

The Verdict

I saw Mario Batali making a lentil chili with corn on *The Chew* and wondered if I could make it in the slow cooker. So I did! This is a great chili—super light, with a slight crunch from the white corn, even after slow cooking all day long. I purposely kept the spice quotient quite low. If you'd like a spicier result, add more cayenne pepper.

MAIN DISH BBQ BEANS

Serves 6 to 8

1	pound lean ground beef
1	onion, diced
4	garlic cloves, minced
1	(28-ounce) can baked beans
2	(15-ounce) cans navy beans, drained and rinsed
1	cup barbecue sauce
¼	cup yellow mustard
2	tablespoons Worcestershire sauce (I use gluten-free)
½	teaspoon kosher salt
½	teaspoon ground black pepper
4	slices bacon
	Cornbread or buttermilk biscuits, for serving

Use a 6-quart slow cooker. In a large skillet over medium heat, cook the beef, onion, and garlic, stirring, until the meat is browned. Drain off any accumulated fat. Transfer the meat mixture to the insert. Add the baked beans and the navy beans. Stir in the barbecue sauce, mustard, Worcestershire sauce, salt, and pepper. Lay the bacon over the top. Cover, and cook on low for 7 to 8 hours, or on high for about 5 hours. Discard the bacon and serve with cornbread or buttermilk biscuits (I make ours gluten-free).

 The Verdict

This is perfect camping food—although it sounds odd to bring a slow cooker camping, if your site or pop-up trailer has an outlet, it's wonderful to come back "home" after a long day of swimming and hiking to a fully cooked meal. I brown the meat at home, and bring everything ready to go in zippered plastic bags.

MISCELLANEOUS BEAN STEW

Serves 8

2	cups assorted dried beans
1	onion, finely diced
¼	cup wild rice, rinsed
1	tablespoon dried Italian seasoning
1	tablespoon garlic powder
½	teaspoon ground black pepper
6	cups beef or broth of your choice
	Salt, to taste

Use a 6-quart slow cooker. Soak the beans overnight. If you are using any type of red bean, cook the beans in water to cover for 10 minutes at a rapid boil, then let the beans soak in the hot water for 1 hour. Drain and place the beans into the insert. (Red beans must be boiled before slow cooking to remove a naturally occurring potential toxin.) Add the onion, rice, and spices. Stir in the broth. Cover, and cook on low for 10 hours, or until all the beans are bite-tender and have begun to split. Salt to taste, if necessary, and serve.

The Verdict

I make this simple bean soup about once a month to use up the odds and ends of the bagged dried beans I have in the pantry. I love how it's full of fiber, no fat, and crazy filling. It freezes and reheats well, and my friend Barb takes a small container to work every day to have for lunch.

NEW YEAR'S DAY HOPPIN' JOHN

Serves 6

1	pound dried black-eyed peas, soaked overnight and drained (for quick-soak method, see page 82)
4	cups beef broth
1	pound Cajun-spiced smoked sausage, sliced
1	bunch collard greens or kale, stems removed and leaves torn
1	(10.5-ounce) can tomatoes and chiles, undrained
½	teaspoon kosher salt
¼	teaspoon ground black pepper
1	cup hot cooked brown rice

Use a 6-quart slow cooker. Put the beans into the insert, and add the broth and sausage. Add the greens to the pot with the tomatoes and chiles, salt, and pepper. Stir to combine. Cover, and cook on low for 8 to 10 hours, or until beans are bite-tender and flavors have melded. Stir in the rice and serve.

 **THE VERDICT**

HOPPIN' JOHN IS TRADITIONALLY SERVED ON NEW YEAR'S DAY TO BRING PROSPERITY AND GOOD LUCK— BOTH WONDERFUL THINGS TO ATTRACT TO A BRAND-NEW YEAR. THIS WAS THE FIRST TIME I HAD COOKED WITH COLLARD GREENS AND WAS HAPPY HOW THEY HELD BOTH SHAPE AND COLOR IN THE SLOW COOKER. WE SHARED THIS HOPPIN' JOHN WITH OUR NEW NEIGHBORS, WHO REPORTED BACK THAT THEY LIKED EVERYTHING ABOUT IT.

ROASTED POTATO AND WHITE BEAN SOUP

Serves 8

8   small red potatoes, washed and cut into
    1-inch pieces
1   head garlic, peeled (about 10 cloves)
1   onion, diced
1   cup chopped broccoli
1   (14.5-ounce) can fire-roasted tomatoes, undrained
1   tablespoon dried Italian seasoning
2   (15-ounce) cans white cannellini beans, drained
    and rinsed
6   cups chicken or vegetable broth
    Salt, to taste
    Crusty bread, for serving (optional)

Use a 6-quart slow cooker. Place the potatoes and garlic
into the insert, and add the onion and broccoli. Pour in
the tomatoes and add the Italian seasoning. Pour in the
beans and broth and stir. Cover, and cook on low for 8 to
10 hours or until garlic squishes easily with the back of
a spoon and the onions are translucent. Salt to taste and
serve with a hunk of crusty bread, if desired.

 The Verdict

I adapted this soup from a recipe found on
cleaneatingchelsey.com and loved everything about it. The
garlic cloves flavor the broth with a rich, nutty flavor and a
hint of spice.

SAUSAGE AND LENTIL STEW

Serves 4

1   cup dried green or brown lentils, rinsed
2   cups beef broth
1   (12-ounce) package smoked turkey or chicken
    sausage, sliced
1   (14.5-ounce) can diced tomatoes, undrained
1   cup chopped baby carrots
1   (12-ounce) bag fresh spinach, to add later

Use a 6-quart slow cooker. Place the lentils into the insert,
and add the broth, sausage, tomatoes, and carrots. Stir
well. Cover, and cook on low for 5 hours. Remove the lid,
and add the spinach. You may need to push it down with
a spoon to get it all to fit. Cover, and cook on high for
20 to 30 minutes, or until spinach has completely wilted.
Stir again and serve.

The Verdict

This entire meal cost me eight dollars, and that was
without coupons. I have fallen in love with lentils, and
am trying to incorporate them more often into our nightly
meals. I served this dish with homemade cornbread, and
we were all happy and full. I like how the sausage provides
all of the flavor—no additional seasoning is required.

SAUSAGE AND RED BEANS FOR A CROWD

Serves 10

1	pound dried small red beans, soaked overnight
1	pound spicy smoked sausage, thickly sliced
2	onions, diced
8	garlic cloves, peeled
1	tablespoon dried Italian seasoning
6	cups chicken broth
	Hot cooked white rice, for serving

Use a 6-quart slow cooker. Drain the beans and add to a pot of fresh water and cook at a rapid boil for 10 minutes, then let the beans sit in the hot water, covered, for one hour. (Red beans must be boiled before slow cooking to remove a naturally occurring potential toxin.) Put the boiled beans into the insert, and add the sausage, onion, garlic, and Italian seasoning. Stir in the broth. Cover, and cook on low for 8 to 10 hours, or until the beans are bite-tender. Serve over a scoop of hot white rice.

🍲 The Verdict

This New Orleans classic is a slow cooker staple. I like cooking my dried beans in broth instead of water to infuse more flavor into the beans. I keep granulated bouillon on hand to keep this cost-effective.

SMOKY BEAN SOUP

Serves 8

2	cups dried pinto beans, soaked overnight and drained (for quick-soak method, see page 82)
1	(14.5-ounce) can diced tomatoes, undrained
1	onion, diced
4	garlic cloves, minced
1	teaspoon ground cumin
1	teaspoon paprika
1	teaspoon kosher salt
½	teaspoon ground black pepper
5	cups water
4	cups chicken or vegetable broth
	Suggested toppings: sour cream, shredded Cheddar cheese, tortilla chips, jalapeño slices

Use a 6-quart slow cooker. Add the beans to the insert. Add the tomatoes, onion, and garlic. Sprinkle in all the seasonings, and stir in the water and broth. Cover and cook on low for 8 to 10 hours. (NOTE: If you live in a high elevation and have a hard time with beans softening in the cooker in this time frame, don't add the salt until the beans are fully soft.) Use a handheld immersion blender and pulse a few times to get the desired consistency (or carefully remove a cup of beans, puree in a traditional blender, and mix back into the soup). Serve with your favorite toppings!

🍲 The Verdict

This recipe came from one of my Twitter friends, @tiamimi, who writes the blog Cookin' Mimi (cookingmimi.wordpress.com). Adam and I loved the smoky flavor, and the kids liked to scoop up their soup with tortilla chips. Fun!

SMOKY BLACK-EYED PEA SOUP

Serves 8

1	**pound dried black-eyed peas, soaked overnight and drained (for quick-soak method, see page 82)**
6	**cups beef broth**
1	**bunch kale, stems removed and leaves torn**
1	**pound smoked sausage, sliced**
1	**(15-ounce) can corn, drained**
1	**(10.5-ounce) can tomatoes and chiles, undrained**
¼	**teaspoon liquid smoke (optional)**
1	**teaspoon kosher salt**
½	**teaspoon ground black pepper**

Use a 6-quart slow cooker. Put the beans into the insert. Add the broth, kale, sausage, corn, and tomatoes and chiles. Stir in the liquid smoke if desired, and the salt and pepper. Cover, and cook on low for 8 to 10 hours, or until beans are soft and have begun to split. Pulse a few times with a handheld immersion blender to smash up the beans and thicken the broth (or carefully remove a cup of beans, puree in a traditional blender, and mix back into the soup).

THE VERDICT

MMM. WHAT A WONDERFUL, SOOTHING, COMFORTING SOUP. JUST LIKE THE SONG: IT KIND OF MAKES YOU WANT TO JUMP OFF THE SOFA AND GO OUT AND SMASH THINGS!

TEXAS TACO SOUP

Serves 6

1½   pounds beef or pork stew meat (frozen is fine)
1   onion, diced
2   (15-ounce) cans ranch-style beans, undrained
2   (15-ounce) cans corn, undrained
2   (14.5-ounce) cans diced tomatoes, undrained
1   (1-ounce) packet taco seasoning (for homemade,
     see page 28)
     Suggested toppings: shredded Cheddar cheese,
     sour cream

Use a 6-quart slow cooker. Put the meat into the insert.
Add the onion, beans, corn, and tomatoes. Stir in the
taco seasoning. Cover, and cook on low for 8 to 10 hours,
or until the meat shreds easily with a fork. Serve with a
handful of cheese and a dollop of sour cream, if desired.

 The Verdict

I made a batch of this soup on a rainy day when I had
three extra kids for the afternoon, and all the children sat
around the table and ate happily. They seemed to really
enjoy dipping Tostitos Scoops chips into their bowls and
eating the soup that way.

TOMATO CURRIED LENTILS

Serves 4

1   cup dried green or brown lentils, rinsed
2   cups chicken or vegetable broth
1   (14.5-ounce) can diced tomatoes, undrained
1   onion, diced
4   garlic cloves, diced
2   teaspoons curry powder
½   teaspoon ground black pepper
     Hot cooked white rice, pita bread, naan, or corn
     tortilla wedges, for serving

Use a 4-quart slow cooker. Place the lentils into the
insert, and add the broth and tomatoes. Stir in the onion,
garlic, curry powder, and pepper. Cover and cook on low
for 6 hours. Serve over rice or with pita bread, naan, or
gluten-free corn tortilla wedges.

The Verdict

Lentils are crazy good for you, along with being low in
fat, inexpensive, and packed with fiber. If you'd like to add
meat, you can place chicken breasts or thighs right on top
and increase cooking time 1 to 2 hours.

TURKEY CHILI

Serves 6

1	pound dried kidney beans, soaked overnight
1	pound ground turkey
1	onion, diced
4	garlic cloves, diced
2	red bell peppers, seeded and diced
1	tablespoon chili powder
2	teaspoons ground cumin
1	teaspoon dried Italian seasoning
½	teaspoon kosher salt
½	teaspoon ground black pepper
1	(15-ounce) can refried beans
2	cups chicken broth
	Suggested toppings: shredded Cheddar cheese, sour cream

Use a 6-quart slow cooker. Drain the beans and cook them in fresh water to cover for 10 minutes at a rapid boil, then let the beans sit in the hot water, covered, for 1 hour. (Red beans must be boiled before slow cooking to remove a naturally occurring potential toxin.) Drain the beans and place into the insert. In a skillet over medium heat, add the turkey, onion, and garlic and cook until browned. Pour the mixture into the insert. Add the bell peppers and all the seasonings. Add the refried beans, and stir in the broth. Cover, and cook on low for 8 to 10 hours, or until the kidney beans are soft. Serve with cheese and a dollop of sour cream, if desired.

The Verdict

What a beautifully mild chili—my children will each eat seconds. The canned refried beans thickens the broth while providing a slight smoky flavor. This is a fantastic high-fiber, low-fat chili that freezes exceptionally well.

TUSCAN WHITE BEAN AND TOMATO SOUP

Serves 8

2	(15-ounce) cans white cannellini beans, drained and rinsed
1	pound potatoes, peeled and diced
1	fennel bulb, diced
1	leek, diced
1	onion, diced
1	cup diced baby carrots
1	cup diced celery
1	(28-ounce) can plum tomatoes, undrained
1	tablespoon dark brown sugar
1	tablespoon dried Italian seasoning
1½	teaspoons kosher salt
½	teaspoon ground black pepper
6	cups chicken or vegetable broth

Use a 6-quart slow cooker. Put the beans into the insert, and add all the vegetables and tomatoes. Add the sugar, Italian seasoning, salt, and pepper. Stir in the broth. Cover, and cook on low for 8 to 10 hours. Before serving, pulse a few times with a handheld immersion blender to thicken the broth (or carefully remove a cup of beans and potatoes, blend in a traditional blender, and mix back into the soup).

The Verdict

This recipe was modified for the slow cooker from the *Los Angeles Times'* adaptation of Bewley's Grafton Street Café in Dublin, Ireland's, Tuscan bean and tomato soup. This is a hearty, filling, one-pot meal. You'll love the tiny bit of sweetness from the brown sugar.

VEGETARIAN BARBECUED BAKED BEANS

Serves 8

1	pound dried small white beans, soaked overnight and drained (for quick-soak method, see page 82)
1	onion, diced
4	garlic cloves, chopped
1	cup barbecue sauce
¼	cup packed dark brown sugar
1	tablespoon spicy brown mustard
1	tablespoon soy sauce (I use gluten-free)
1	tablespoon molasses
½	to 1 teaspoon Tabasco sauce
3	cups water
1	cup freshly brewed coffee

Use a 6-quart slow cooker. Put the beans into the insert. Add the onion, garlic, barbecue sauce, sugar, mustard, soy sauce, molasses, and Tabasco sauce. Stir in the water and coffee until fully combined. Cover, and cook on low for 8 to 10 hours. If you'd like a thicker consistency, you can leave the lid off of the cooker for the last hour to allow condensation to dissipate, or pulse a few times with a handheld immersion blender.

 THE VERDICT

YOU CAN NEVER HAVE TOO MANY BARBECUE BEAN RECIPES, AND THIS CAME FROM KATHY, A READER OF MINE, WHO LOVES THAT SHE CAN PLEASE HER VEGAN IN-LAWS AND HER MEAT-LOVING BROTHER WITH THE SAME DISH—IT HAS SUCH A HEARTY TEXTURE AND AMAZING FLAVOR. I LOVE THE WAY THE BITTER COFFEE AND MUSTARD COMPLEMENT THE SWEET MOLASSES AND BROWN SUGAR. DELICIOUS!

VEGETARIAN 16-BEAN SOUP

Serves 8

1 **(16-ounce) package 16-bean soup mix**
1 **(14.5-ounce) can Italian-style stewed tomatoes, undrained**
1 **onion, diced**
6 **garlic cloves, chopped**
1 **tablespoon ground cumin**
2 **teaspoons kosher salt**
1 **teaspoon ground black pepper**
2 **bay leaves**
8 **cups vegetable broth**

Use a 6-quart slow cooker. Discard the included flavor packet in the package of beans. Soak the beans overnight in water to cover, and then drain the beans. (For a quick-soak method, see the Tip below.) Place the drained beans into the insert. Add the tomatoes, onion, garlic, cumin, salt, pepper, and bay leaves. Stir in the broth. Cover, and cook on low for 8 to 10 hours, or until the beans have reached desired thickness. Remove the bay leaves. If you'd like, you can smash a few beans with a potato masher to thicken the broth.

Tip: To quick-soak dried beans, bring the beans to a boil in a large pot of fresh water to cover. Remove from the heat, cover the pot, and let sit for an hour. Drain.

THE VERDICT
THIS SMOKY, DELICIOUS BEAN SOUP IS LIGHT IN CALORIES AND QUITE FILLING. I LIKE TO EAT IT FOR LUNCH—THIS SOUP FREEZES AND REHEATS WELL (YOU MAY NEED TO THIN IT WITH A BIT OF WATER BECAUSE THE BEANS SWELL).

POULTRY

2-PACKET CHICKEN

Serves 4

2   pounds boneless, skinless chicken breast
    (frozen is fine)
1   (1-ounce) packet taco seasoning (for homemade,
    see page 28)
1   (1-ounce) packet ranch salad dressing mix
    (for homemade, see page 256)
1   (14.5-ounce) can diced tomatoes, undrained
    Taco shells, corn tortillas, or hot cooked rice or
    quinoa, for serving

Use a 6-quart slow cooker. Put the chicken into the insert,
and sprinkle with the seasoning mixes. Top with the
tomatoes. And that's it—no need to add any additional
liquid. Cover, and cook on low for 8 hours. Serve shredded
in taco shells or corn tortillas, or on top of rice or quinoa.

 The Verdict

This is lazy cooking at its finest—this flavorful dinner
comes together in roughly 2½ minutes, and utilizes pantry
and freezer staples. I toss my chicken halves in frozen
solid, and they cook beautifully. If you're feeding more
people, you can add a can of rinsed beans and/or a can of
corn niblets.

ARTICHOKE CHICKEN LASAGNA

Serves 6

⅓   cup butter
⅓   cup all-purpose flour (I use rice flour)
3   cups milk
1   teaspoon kosher salt
1   teaspoon ground nutmeg
1   teaspoon dried thyme
½   teaspoon ground black pepper
10 lasagna noodles (I use gluten-free)
2   cups diced cooked chicken
2   (14-ounce) cans artichoke hearts packed in water,
    drained and chopped
4   cups shredded Italian cheese blend

Use a 6-quart slow cooker. In a large pot over medium
heat, melt the butter and stir in the flour to make a roux.
Whisk in the milk, salt, nutmeg, thyme, and pepper. Bring
this sauce to a boil, then reduce heat to a simmer (DON'T
walk away from the stove, this happens VERY quickly!)
and cook until sauce thickens slightly, about 2 minutes.
Remove the pot from the heat. Spoon out about ⅓ cup
of the white sauce and spread into the bottom of the
insert. Add a layer of lasagna noodles (you may need to
break them to get a good fit). Put a handful of chicken
and artichoke hearts on top, and add a healthy topping of
cheese. Top with another ⅓ cup or so of the white sauce,
and repeat the layers. Pour the remaining white sauce
evenly over the top, and add the rest of the cheese. Cover,
and cook on low for 6 hours, then uncover and cook on
high for about 20 minutes to release condensation (if
necessary, push the lasagna noodles on top back into the
sauce with the handle of a wooden spoon).

The Verdict

I'm usually a red-sauce lasagna girl, but the nutmeg and
thyme really takes this white sauce to a whole new level—
this is a fabulously decadent lasagna, and the artichoke
hearts mixed with chicken is a fantastic combination. Yum.

BAKED CHICKEN WITH PESTO

Serves 4

I	cup packed fresh basil leaves
⅓	cup freshly grated Parmesan cheese
2	garlic cloves
2	tablespoons olive oil
2	tablespoons pine nuts
I	lemon, juiced
½	teaspoon kosher salt
¼	teaspoon ground black pepper
4	boneless, skinless chicken breast halves, pounded thin
I	cup shredded mozzarella cheese
	Hot cooked pasta, for serving

Use a 4-quart slow cooker. In a food processor, add the basil, Parmesan, garlic, oil, pine nuts, lemon juice, salt, and pepper. Pulse until the ingredients are blended and have reached the desired consistency—I like a chunky pesto. Smear a bit of the pesto into the insert, and add 2 of the chicken breasts. Top with half of the mozzarella and a heaping spoonful of pesto. Add the rest of the chicken and mozzarella cheese. Pour the remaining pesto on top. Cover, and cook on low for 6 hours, or on high for about 4 hours. Serve over pasta.

 THE VERDICT

THIS IS A TAKE ON MY FRIEND KALYN DENNY'S (KALYNSKITCHEN.COM) BAKED CHICKEN WITH PESTO. I LOVE HOW SHE ADDS LEMON TO HER PESTO; IT GIVES IT A GREAT FRESH FLAVOR. IF YOU'D PREFER TO MAKE A BIG BATCH OF PESTO, IT FREEZES BEAUTIFULLY.

BARBECUE CHICKEN THIGHS

Serves 4

4	skinless chicken thighs (frozen is fine)
1	onion, thinly sliced
1	cup ketchup
2	tablespoons soy sauce (I use gluten-free)
2	tablespoons dark brown sugar
2	tablespoons Worcestershire sauce (I use gluten-free)
½	teaspoon ground black pepper
1	cup baby carrots
2	red bell peppers, seeded and thinly sliced
	Hot cooked brown rice or quinoa, for serving

Use a 4-quart slow cooker. Place the chicken into the insert, and add the onion on top. In a small bowl, combine the ketchup, soy sauce, sugar, Worcestershire sauce, and black pepper. Pour this mixture evenly over the top of the chicken and onion. Add the carrots and bell peppers. Cover, and cook on low for 6 to 7 hours. Serve over rice or quinoa.

THE VERDICT

THIS IS A SIMPLE, EASY BARBECUE CHICKEN THAT ISN'T OVERLY SWEET. I LOOK FOR ORGANIC KETCHUP THAT DOESN'T CONTAIN HIGH-FRUCTOSE CORN SYRUP. I LIKE THAT THE CARROTS AND PEPPER ARE ON TOP AND DON'T GET DROWNED IN SAUCE.

BASIL CHICKEN WITH FETA

Serves 4

4   skinless chicken thighs
I   (14.5-ounce) can fire-roasted tomatoes, undrained
I   (14.5-ounce) can chickpeas, drained and rinsed
½   cup pitted green olives
¼   cup tightly packed fresh basil leaves
8   ounces crumbled feta cheese
     Hot cooked brown rice or couscous, for serving

Use a 4-quart slow cooker. Place the chicken into the insert, and add the tomatoes and chickpeas. Add olives and basil, and sprinkle in the cheese. Cover, and cook on low for 6 to 7 hours. Serve over brown rice or couscous (there is a gluten-free variety found in a box in the rice aisle).

 The Verdict

This is a dump-and-go recipe that rivals fancy restaurant food. My kids love feta in any form, and practically lick their plates when I make this chicken.

BEER-BRAISED TURKEY WITH POTATOES

Serves 4 to 6

2   pounds potatoes, washed and quartered (such as Yukon Gold or Russet; no need to peel)
I   onion, thinly sliced
3   pounds turkey drumsticks, skin removed if desired
4   tablespoons (½ stick) butter, melted
I   lemon, juiced
I   tablespoon dried basil
½   teaspoon kosher salt
I   (12-ounce) bottle beer (Redbridge by Anheuser-Busch is gluten-free)

Use a 6-quart slow cooker. Place the potatoes and onion into the insert, and place the turkey on top. Drip in the butter and lemon juice, and sprinkle with the basil and salt. Pour in the beer. Cover, and cook on low for 6 to 8 hours, or on high for 4 to 5 hours. Your dinner is complete when the turkey is no longer pink, and has reached desired tenderness.

 The Verdict

Don't save turkey for only once or twice a year—this is a simple, family-pleasing meal that can be enjoyed at any time. Serve with steamed broccoli or brussels sprouts.

BUTTERMILK BRINED CHICKEN

Serves 4 to 6

1	**4-pound roaster chicken, cleaned (I remove the skin; it's up to you)**
2	**cups buttermilk**
¼	**cup packed dark brown sugar**
1	**tablespoon plus 1 teaspoon paprika**
1	**tablespoon garlic powder**
1½	**teaspoons kosher salt**
1½	**teaspoons ground black pepper**
	Hot cooked wild rice pilaf, for serving

Use a 6-quart slow cooker. In a large zippered plastic bag or covered bowl, combine the chicken with the buttermilk, sugar, 1 tablespoon of the paprika, the garlic powder, 1 teaspoon of the salt, and 1 teaspoon of the pepper. Seal well, and refrigerate for 24 to 48 hours. Remove the chicken from the bag and discard the marinade. Place the chicken into the insert, breast-side down. Sprinkle the remaining paprika, salt, and pepper on top of the chicken. Cover, and cook on low for 7 hours, or on high for about 4 hours. Check the temperature with a meat thermometer to ensure the meat has reached an internal temperature of at least 165°F before serving.

THE VERDICT

THE RECIPE TRAIL FOR THIS CHICKEN IS LONG: IT CAME FROM A RECIPE ON PINTEREST FOR OVEN-FRIED BUTTERMILK CHICKEN FROM THE PICKYIN. BLOGSPOT.COM WEBSITE, WHICH HAD ADAPTED A RECIPE FROM DEB AT SMITTENKITCHEN.COM, WHO PERSONALIZED A RECIPE FROM NIGELLA LAWSON. IT'S RECIPE GENEALOGY! SERVE WITH A GREEN VEGETABLE ON THE SIDE, IF YOU'D LIKE.

B.L.T. CHICKEN

Serves 4

4   **boneless, skinless chicken breast halves (frozen is fine)**

1   **(1-ounce) packet ranch salad dressing mix (for homemade, see page 256)**

1   **(14.5-ounce) can stewed tomatoes, undrained**

⅓   **cup crumbled cooked bacon or bacon bits**

4   **ounces cream cheese, softened**

    Hot cooked penne pasta, for serving

Use a 4-quart slow cooker. Place the chicken into the insert, and sprinkle in the ranch dressing mix. Add the tomatoes and bacon. Dot on pieces of cream cheese. Cover, and cook on low for 6 hours, or on high for about 3 hours. Stir the topping before serving the creamy chicken over a bed of penne pasta (I use brown rice pasta).

🍲 The Verdict

I made this on a night that Adam was working late, and he didn't have a chance to eat any. My kids ate so much of this, I thought they'd explode. This is definitely a kid-pleasing meal. I sliced the chicken into long strips and stirred the sauce into the penne pasta.

BUFFALO CHICKEN AND POTATO CASSEROLE

Serves 6

3   **pounds red potatoes, washed and cubed**

2   **pounds boneless, skinless chicken breast, cubed**

½   **pound bacon (about 6 thick slices), cooked until crisp and diced**

4   **green onions, thinly sliced**

6   **garlic cloves, minced**

1   **tablespoon paprika**

¼   **teaspoon ground black pepper**

⅓   **cup prepared buffalo wing sauce (I use Frank's)**

2   **cups shredded mozzarella cheese**

Use a 6-quart slow cooker. Place the potatoes into the insert, and add the chicken. Add the bacon, green onions, garlic, paprika, and pepper. Stir in the buffalo wing sauce, and top with the cheese. Cover, and cook on low for 7 hours, or until the potatoes have reached the desired tenderness.

🍲 The Verdict

This casserole has all the good parts of loaded potatoes and buffalo wings—in a bowl! This is a fun dish to serve to company; it's packed with flavor and memorable.

CARDAMOM CHICKEN

Serves 4

1	**4- to 5-pound roaster chicken, cleaned (I remove the skin; it's up to you)**
½	**cup sour cream**
1½	**teaspoons ground cardamom**
1	**teaspoon kosher salt**
½	**teaspoon ground allspice**
½	**teaspoon ground black pepper**
1	**lemon, juiced**

Use a 6-quart slow cooker. Place the chicken into the insert, breast-side down. In a small bowl, combine the sour cream and all the seasonings. Rub this sauce on all sides of the chicken, inside and out. Add the lemon juice. Cover, and cook on low for 6 to 7 hours, or on high for 4 to 5 hours. Check the temperature with a meat thermometer to ensure the meat has reached an internal temperature of at least 165°F.

 **THE VERDICT**
CARDAMOM IS WHAT GIVES CHAI TEA ITS UNIQUE FLAVOR. THIS CHICKEN TASTES JUST LIKE CHAI TEA—A GOOD THING IF YOU LIKE CHAI, A NOT-SO-GOOD THING IF YOU DON'T. THE MEAT IS QUITE MOIST, AND THE CROCK DRIPPINGS CREATE A FABULOUS GRAVY, OR YOU CAN USE THE JUICE TO COOK RICE AS A SIDE DISH.

CARIBBEAN JERK CHICKEN

Serves 6

1   **4- to 5-pound roaster chicken, cleaned (I remove the skin; it's up to you)**
1   **tablespoon dark brown sugar**
1   **tablespoon ground allspice**
1   **teaspoon ground cinnamon**
2   **teaspoons kosher salt**
½   **teaspoon cayenne pepper**
3   **limes, juiced, plus lime wedges, for serving (optional)**

Use a 6-quart slow cooker. Place the chicken into the insert breast-side down. (I prefer to cook my chickens upside down, to keep the breast meat as juicy as possible.) In a small bowl, combine the sugar and all the seasonings. Rub this spice and sugar mixture all over the bird, inside and out. Pour on the lime juice. Cover, and cook on low for 6 to 7 hours, or on high for 4 hours. Check the temperature with a meat thermometer to ensure the meat has reached an internal temperature of at least 165°F. Usually the bird falls completely apart, which is great. You can serve with lime wedges for a bit of extra citrus flavor, if you'd like.

THE VERDICT

MY FAMILY AND MY FRIEND SHARYL'S FAMILY ATE THIS CHICKEN AND WE ALL LOVED IT. EVEN MY NOW-TURNED-SUPER-PICKY TEN-YEAR-OLD ATE HER SERVING AND SAID IT WAS GOOD.

THE BIT OF HEAT FROM THE CAYENNE IS THERE—BUT NOT ENOUGH TO CAUSE ANY OF THE KIDS (SIX IN ALL) TO COMPLAIN. MAKE RICE USING THE PAN DRIPPINGS FOR A GREAT SIDE DISH.

CHAMPION CHICKEN

Serves 4 to 6

3   pounds chicken drumsticks, skin removed if desired
1   medium onion, thinly sliced
1   red bell pepper, seeded and thinly sliced
1   (6-ounce) can tomato paste
4   garlic cloves, chopped
2   tablespoons apple cider vinegar
1   teaspoon smoked paprika
1   teaspoon sugar
1   teaspoon ground cumin
¼   cup fresh cilantro leaves

Use a 4-quart slow cooker. Place the chicken into the insert. Add the onion and bell pepper. In a small bowl, mix together the tomato paste, garlic, vinegar, paprika, sugar, cumin, and cilantro. Spread this mixture evenly over the top of the vegetables and chicken. Cover, and cook on low for 6 to 7 hours, or on high for about 4 hours.

The Verdict

With a name like Champion Chicken, it has to be good! This dish was adapted from a recipe on Alanna Kellogg's kitchenparade.com, and it works beautifully in the slow cooker. I paired it with baked sweet potato fries, and then forced the kids to sing the Queen song with me.

CHICKEN AND CREAMED CORN

Serves 4

1   (16-ounce) package frozen white corn
1   (15-ounce) can corn, undrained
1   tablespoon butter
1   tablespoon cream cheese
2   tablespoons all-purpose flour (I use rice flour)
¼   cup milk
¼   teaspoon ground black pepper
4   boneless, skinless chicken thighs

Use a 4-quart slow cooker. Place the frozen corn and canned corn (reserve the juice from the canned corn) into the insert. In a small saucepan over medium heat, melt the butter and cream cheese and whisk in the flour to create a roux. Once combined, whisk in the milk, reserved juice from the canned corn, and the pepper. Stir well, and pour this mixture evenly over the corn in the insert. Stir to combine. Place the chicken thighs on top. Cover, and cook on low for 6 to 8 hours. The chicken will shred easily when finished cooking; serve over rice, or eat as a thick chowder out of bread bowls.

The Verdict

Guess what? There is hardly any cream or butter in this dish, yet it tastes like each serving should have 100 million calories. Eat up and enjoy without the guilt!

CHICKEN AND QUINOA WITH GREEN OLIVES

Serves 6

6   boneless, skinless chicken thighs
1   teaspoon ground cumin
1   teaspoon ground coriander
1   teaspoon dried oregano
1   (14.5-ounce) can fire-roasted tomatoes, undrained
1   (15-ounce) can chickpeas, drained and rinsed
½   cup pitted green olives
3   cups chicken broth
2   cups quinoa, rinsed

Use a 4-quart slow cooker. Place the chicken into the insert and add all the spices. Top with the tomatoes and chickpeas. Add the olives, and stir in the broth. Cover, and cook on low for 6 hours, or on high for about 3 hours. When the cooking time has elapsed, carefully remove the chicken from the pot, and set aside. Pour in the quinoa, and stir well. Cover, and cook on high for 20 to 30 minutes, or until the quinoa is bite-tender. Let sit with the lid off to release condensation for a few minutes before serving with the chicken.

 The Verdict

Everything cooks in the same pot —I love it! This is a reader recipe from Ann, whose husband will only eat "flavored" quinoa. I don't blame him! Adam, the three girls, and I all enjoyed our dinner. Thank you, Ann!

CHICKEN AND WILD RICE

Serves 8

2   cups cubed cooked chicken
2   cups wild rice, rinsed
1   onion, diced
8   ounces fresh button mushrooms, thinly sliced
1   tablespoon dried parsley
1   teaspoon garlic powder
½   teaspoon kosher salt
½   teaspoon ground black pepper
6   cups chicken broth
1   cup shredded mozzarella cheese

Use a 6-quart slow cooker. Put chicken into the bottom of the insert, and add the rice, onion, mushrooms, parsley, garlic powder, salt, and pepper. Stir in the broth. Cover, and cook on low for 4 to 5 hours, or until rice is bite-tender. Remove the lid to release the steam, and add the cheese. Cook for an additional 20 minutes with the lid off.

 The Verdict

Wild rice has a rather thick hull and holds up nicely in the slow cooker. This is a creamy, delicious chicken and rice dish that doesn't use canned condensed soup. Score! Serve with steamed vegetables or a dinner salad.

CHICKEN COCONUT CURRY

Serves 4

4   **boneless, skinless chicken thighs**
I   **onion, diced**
2   **tablespoons curry powder**
½   **teaspoon kosher salt**
¼   **teaspoon ground black pepper**
I   **(14-ounce) can coconut milk**
I   **cup chicken broth**
I   **cup instant brown rice, rinsed**
     Steamed broccoli, for serving (optional)

Use a 4-quart slow cooker. Put the chicken into the insert and add the onion. Sprinkle the curry powder, salt, and pepper evenly over the top. Pour in the coconut milk and add the broth. Stir well to combine. Cover, and cook on low for 5 to 6 hours. Carefully remove the chicken from the pot and set aside in a covered dish. Stir in the rice. Cover, and cook on high for 10 to 15 minutes, or until the rice is bite-tender. Serve with the chicken and broccoli, if desired.

 THE VERDICT

THIS IS A BEAUTIFUL YELLOW CURRY THAT MY KIDS ABSOLUTELY ADORE. IF YOU LIKE HEAT IN YOUR CURRY, ADD I TEASPOON OF RED PEPPER FLAKES, OR SPRINKLE SOME ON INDIVIDUAL SERVINGS AT THE TABLE.

CHICKEN IN ROMESCO SAUCE

Serves 6

6   boneless, skinless chicken thighs
1   (16-ounce) jar roasted bell peppers, drained
3   ripe tomatoes, halved
½   cup almonds
½   cup hazelnuts
¼   cup fresh cilantro leaves
3   garlic cloves, peeled
1   teaspoon paprika
     Hot cooked rice or rigatoni pasta, for serving (I use gluten-free pasta)

Use a 4-quart slow cooker. Place the chicken into the insert. In a food processor, combine the peppers, tomatoes, nuts, cilantro, garlic, and paprika, and pulse until everything is fully combined into a sauce. Pour this sauce evenly over the top of the chicken. Cover, and cook on low for 6 to 7 hours, or on high for about 4 hours. Serve over rice or rigatoni.

THE VERDICT

I ADAPTED THIS RECIPE FROM ONE FEATURED ON JEANETTESHEALTHYEATING. COM AND LOVED HOW IT WORKED IN THE SLOW COOKER. I WAS UNFAMILIAR WITH ROMESCO SAUCE, BUT LEARNED THAT IT ORIGINATES FROM TARRAGONA, IN CATALONIA, SPAIN. ALL THESE INGREDIENTS WORK WELL BLENDED TOGETHER TO CREATE A VERY RICH, PACKED-WITH-FLAVOR SAUCE WITH NO ADDED OIL OR DAIRY.

CHICKEN MOLÉ SOFT TACOS

Serves 4 to 6

- 2 pounds boneless, skinless chicken thighs
- 1 onion, diced
- 1 (15-ounce) can kidney beans, drained and rinsed
- 1 (14.5-ounce) can diced tomatoes, undrained
- 2 tablespoons unsweetened cocoa powder
- 1 teaspoon ground cumin
- ½ teaspoon ground chipotle chile
- ½ teaspoon ground cinnamon
- 1 cup chicken broth
    Warmed corn tortillas and sour cream, for serving

Use a 4-quart slow cooker. Put the chicken into the insert and add the onion. Add the beans and tomatoes. Add the cocoa powder, cumin, chipotle, and cinnamon. Stir in the broth. Cover, and cook on low for 7 to 8 hours. Shred the chicken completely and spoon into warmed corn tortillas and garnish with a dollop of sour cream.

🍲 The Verdict

I love this easy, shortcut molé. This is completely nut-free, and can be stretched to feed up to six grown-ups. The ground chipotle chile mixes with the cocoa powder to create a dark chocolaty sauce—it's delicious.

CHICKEN PAPRIKASH

Serves 6

- 2 pounds boneless, skinless chicken breast, cut into 1-inch pieces
- 3 tablespoons all-purpose flour (I use rice flour)
- 2 tablespoons Hungarian sweet paprika
- 1 teaspoon kosher salt
- ½ teaspoon ground black pepper
- 1 onion, sliced into thin rings
- 1 red bell pepper, seeded and thinly sliced
- ½ cup shredded carrots
- 8 ounces fresh button mushrooms, thinly sliced
- 4 garlic cloves, chopped
- 1 cup chicken broth
- 1 cup sour cream, at room temperature (to add later)
    Hot cooked wide flat noodles

Use a 6-quart slow cooker. Put the chicken into a large zippered plastic bag and add the flour, paprika, salt, and black pepper. Seal the bag and shake to coat the chicken pieces evenly. Pour the contents of the bag into the insert, and add the onion, bell pepper, carrots, mushrooms, and garlic. Pour the broth evenly over the top. Cover, and cook on low for 6 to 7 hours. Add the sour cream and stir well before serving over wide, flat noodles (I use gluten-free noodles).

🍲 The Verdict

I've wanted to try paprikash since I first saw the *When Harry Met Sally* movie and Billy Crystal says "paprikash" in a funny voice. This is good chicken—the paprika gives it a sweet and smoky flavor that we all really enjoyed.

CHICKEN PARMIGIANA MEATLOAF

Serves 6

1	pound lean ground chicken or turkey
1	onion, finely diced
2	large eggs
½	cup breadcrumbs (I use gluten-free)
1	tablespoon dried Italian seasoning
1	tablespoon garlic powder
1	cup prepared pasta sauce (divided)
2	cups shredded mozzarella cheese (divided)

Use a 6-quart slow cooker with an inserted 9 x 5 x 3-inch loaf pan. In a mixing bowl, combine the chicken, onion, eggs, breadcrumbs, Italian seasoning, garlic powder, ½ cup of the pasta sauce, and ½ cup of the cheese. Mix well (I use my hands) and press the meat into the loaf pan. Smear the remaining pasta sauce on top, and top with the remaining cheese. Lower the pan into the cooker insert (do not add water) and cover. Cook on low for 7 to 8 hours, or on high for 4 hours.

 THE VERDICT
THIS IS EXACTLY HOW YOU'D EXPECT IT TO TASTE: CHEESY, GOOEY, ITALIAN-Y GOODNESS. IF YOU'D LIKE, YOU MAY NESTLE WASHED BAKING POTATOES AROUND THE PAN IN THE COOKER TO MAKE A COMPLETE MEAL.

CHICKEN PICCATA

Serves 4

2	pounds boneless, skinless chicken thighs, cut into thin strips
2	tablespoons all-purpose flour (I use rice flour)
½	teaspoon kosher salt
½	teaspoon ground black pepper
I	onion, sliced into thin rings
8	ounces fresh button mushrooms, thinly sliced
⅓	cup capers, drained
¼	cup dry white wine or chicken broth
2	lemons, juiced
2	tablespoons sugar
2	tablespoons butter, melted
I	tablespoon olive oil
	Hot buttered cooked pasta, for serving (I use gluten-free)

Use a 4-quart slow cooker. Put the chicken into a large zippered plastic bag and add the flour, salt, and pepper. Seal the bag, and shake the chicken until it's evenly coated. Dump the chicken into the insert, and add the onion, mushrooms, and capers. In a mixing bowl, whisk together the wine, lemon juice, sugar, butter, and oil. Pour this mixture evenly over the top of the crock contents. Cover, and cook on low for 6 hours, or on high for about 3 hours. Serve over hot pasta.

 The Verdict

My kids really like capers—the baby calls them "tiny pickles," and they all enjoy this dish. Adam isn't a caper fan, but eats them to be a good sport. We put a bit of Parmesan cheese on top at the table.

CHICKEN PUTTANESCA

Serves 4

4	boneless, skinless chicken thighs
I	pint cherry tomatoes, halved
3	garlic cloves, chopped
I	tablespoon dried oregano
½	teaspoon crushed red pepper flakes
½	teaspoon ground black pepper
¼	teaspoon kosher salt
I	cup kalamata olives, pitted
4	ounces fresh mozzarella cheese, sliced
	Hot cooked pasta, for serving (I use gluten-free)

Use a 4-quart slow cooker. Place the chicken into the insert. Add the tomatoes, garlic, oregano, red pepper flakes, black pepper, and salt. Toss all the ingredients with a spoon. Pour the olives on top. Cover and cook on low for 5 to 6 hours, or on high for about 4 hours. Remove the lid and place slices of cheese on top. Recover, and cook on high for about 15 minutes, or until the cheese has fully melted. Serve with pasta.

The Verdict

This delicious chicken dinner is super easy to throw together, yet looks and tastes like restaurant fare. I prefer thighs in the slow cooker, but any chicken parts will work.

CHICKEN TIKKA MASALA

Serves 6

OVERNIGHT MARINADE

3   pounds boneless, skinless chicken thighs, cut into
      thin strips
2   cups plain yogurt
1   tablespoon ground coriander
1   tablespoon ground cumin
1   teaspoon salt

IN THE MORNING, ADD

2   (14.5-ounce) cans diced tomatoes, undrained
1   onion, diced
4   garlic cloves, diced
4   tablespoons (½ stick) butter
3   tablespoons garam masala (for homemade,
      see page 264)
1   tablespoon kosher salt
1   tablespoon ground ginger
2   red chile peppers
      Hot cooked white or brown basmati rice, for serving

Use a 6-quart slow cooker. Place the chicken into a large zippered plastic bag or sealable bowl, and add 1 cup of the yogurt, the coriander, cumin, and salt. Toss to fully coat the chicken, and refrigerate overnight (6 to 8 hours). In the morning, squeeze out the bag contents into the insert, and add the tomatoes, onion, garlic, butter, garam masala, salt, ginger, and chiles (simply toss them in whole). Cover, and cook on low for 8 hours. Stir in the remaining cup of yogurt and discard the chile peppers. Serve over white or brown basmati rice.

 THE VERDICT

THIS IS FANTASTIC. I ADAPTED A RECIPE FOUND ON REE DRUMMOND'S TASTY KITCHEN WEBSITE (TASTYKITCHEN. COM), AND LOVED EVERY SECOND OF MY DINNER. ADAM DID, TOO. WE FOUND THIS TO BE MEDIUM-SPICED; YOU CAN ADJUST THE HEAT LEVEL BY USING MORE (OR NONE AT ALL!) OF THE WHOLE CHILES. THE CAPSAICINOIDS STEAM OUT OF THE PEPPERS' SKIN WITHOUT YOU NEEDING TO CUT THEM.

CHICKEN SATAY

Serves 4

FOR THE CHICKEN

2	pounds boneless, skinless chicken thighs
1	tablespoon soy sauce (I use gluten-free)
1	tablespoon creamy peanut butter
1	tablespoon dark brown sugar
1	teaspoon grated fresh ginger
1	teaspoon seasoned rice wine vinegar
½	teaspoon sesame oil
¼	cup chopped roasted peanuts
1	green onion, sliced
	Hot cooked basmati rice

FOR THE PEANUT DIPPING SAUCE

1	(14-ounce) can coconut milk
½	cup creamy peanut butter
1	tablespoon dark brown sugar
1	tablespoon red curry paste
1	tablespoon fish sauce
1	teaspoon grated fresh ginger

Use a 6-quart slow cooker. Slice the chicken into long, thin strips and fold a few times, before inserting a bamboo skewer into each one. Layer the skewers into an insert that has been sprayed with cooking spray. In a small bowl, combine the soy sauce, peanut butter, sugar, ginger, vinegar, and oil. Pour this mixture evenly over the top of the skewered chicken. Cover, and cook on low for 4 to 5 hours, or on high for about 3 hours. The chicken will be fully cooked and browned when it's finished.

While the meat is cooking, in a medium bowl, combine the dipping sauce ingredients. (The sauce can be stored in an air-tight container in the refrigerator for 3 to 4 days or frozen for up to 3 months.) Sprinkle the chicken with the peanuts and green onions before serving. Serve the chicken on the skewers on a bed of white basmati rice with the dipping sauce on the side.

THE VERDICT

DON'T BE INTIMIDATED BY THIS DISH. WHILE IT IS RATHER LABOR INTENSIVE FOR A SLOW COOKER MEAL, THE END RESULT AND PRESENTATION IS WELL WORTH IT. THE FLAVORS ARE SPOT ON, AND THE RECIPE CAN EASILY BE DOUBLED FOR SERVING AT AN APPETIZER PARTY. JUST THROW IN MORE SKEWERS—YOU CAN FIT UP TO 24 SKEWERS IN A STANDARD 6-QUART SLOW COOKER.

CITRUS CHICKEN

Serves 6

2	oranges, peeled and separated into segments
6	boneless, skinless chicken thighs
1	onion, sliced into thin rings
1	cup orange juice
½	cup chili sauce (in the ketchup aisle)
4	garlic cloves, minced
1	tablespoon soy sauce (I use gluten-free)
1	tablespoon molasses
1	teaspoon ground mustard
1	teaspoon ground ginger
¼	teaspoon ground black pepper
	Hot cooked rice, for serving

Use a 4-quart slow cooker. Put the orange segments into the insert, place the chicken directly on top, and add the onion. In a mixing bowl, combine the orange juice, chili sauce, garlic, soy sauce, molasses, mustard, ginger, and pepper. Whisk everything together and pour evenly on top of the chicken. Cover, and cook on low for 5 to 6 hours, or on high for about 4 hours. Serve on a bed of rice with a spoonful of the juices.

 **THE VERDICT**

THIS DELIGHTFUL CHICKEN RECIPE IS SURE TO PLEASE EVERYONE AT YOUR KITCHEN TABLE. MY CHILDREN ARE BIG FANS, AND I'VE SERVED IT TO THEIR FRIENDS AT SLEEPOVERS (WITH TATER TOTS) WITH GREAT SUCCESS.

CLASSIC CHICKEN (CROCK) POT PIE

Serves 6

2	pounds boneless, skinless chicken breast, diced
2	cups frozen mixed vegetables
1	teaspoon onion powder
½	teaspoon dried marjoram
½	teaspoon dried thyme
½	teaspoon celery seed
1	tablespoon cream cheese
3	tablespoons all-purpose flour (I use rice flour)
½	cup milk
½	cup chicken broth
¼	teaspoon kosher salt
¼	teaspoon ground black pepper

FOR THE BISCUIT TOPPING

2	cups biscuit mix (I use a gluten-free variety)
8	tablespoons (1 stick) butter, melted
¾	cup milk
½	tablespoon sugar

Use a 4-quart slow cooker. I know it looks like there are a lot of ingredients listed, but this will come together pretty quickly. Read through all the directions before getting started. First off, coat the insert well with cooking spray. Place the chicken and vegetables into the insert. Add the onion powder, marjoram, thyme, and celery seed. In a small saucepan over medium heat, melt the cream cheese, and stir in the flour to make a roux. Whisk in the milk, broth, salt, and pepper until fully incorporated—do not bring to a boil. Pour this sauce over the contents in the slow cooker and stir. In a medium bowl, make the biscuit topping by combining the biscuit mix, butter, milk, and sugar. The dough will be quite thick and have the texture of sticky playdough. Spread this topping on top of the ingredients in the slow cooker—I use my hands. Cover, and cook on low for 6 to 7 hours, or on high for 3 to 4 hours. The pot pie is finished when the biscuit topping is golden brown and is hard to the touch in the middle. Uncover, and let the condensation evaporate before cutting.

The Verdict

This is such a fun dish to make in the slow cooker, and I love how everything cooks so well together. My kids are huge fans of the biscuit topping, and end up stealing it from one another's plates. The filling is creamy, delicious, and thanks to the thyme, tastes a bit like stuffing.

COCONUT CHICKEN

Serves 6

6	boneless, skinless chicken thighs, cut into chunks
1	(14-ounce) can coconut milk, divided
1	tablespoon ground ginger
1	teaspoon crushed red pepper flakes
¼	cup seasoned rice wine vinegar
¼	cup soy sauce (I use 1 gluten-free)
¼	cup sugar
3	green onions, thinly sliced
	Hot cooked sticky white or brown rice, for serving

Use a 4-quart slow cooker. The night before you're going to make the chicken, place the chicken into a large zippered plastic bag, and add ¾ cup of the coconut milk (save the rest of the can for the next day!), the ginger, and crushed red pepper. Seal the bag well and shake. Marinate overnight in the refrigerator (6 to 10 hours). In the morning, dump the bag contents into the insert and add the rest of the coconut milk, the vinegar, soy sauce, sugar, and green onions. Stir well and cover. Cook on low for 7 to 8 hours, or on high for about 4 hours. Serve over sticky white or brown rice.

The Verdict

I adapted this recipe from a camping/grilling suggestion on the website merrywithchildren.com that had been adapted from *Sunset* magazine. It cooked beautifully in the slow cooker, and my kids loved every single bite. The leftovers are delicious—even cold, right out of the fridge!

COFFEE BRINED CHICKEN

Serves 4

FOR THE BRINE

3   **cups cold brewed coffee**

2   **oranges, juiced**

I   **tablespoon peppercorns**

I   **tablespoon whole cloves**

3   **whole star anise**

I   **4- to 5-pound roaster chicken, cleaned (I remove the skin; it's up to you)**

FOR COOKING

⅓   **cup packed dark brown sugar**

I   **tablespoon kosher salt**

Use a 6-quart slow cooker. In a large covered bowl or zippered plastic bag, combine the coffee, orange juice, peppercorns, cloves, and star anise. Soak the chicken in the brine overnight (6 to 8 hours) in the refrigerator. In the morning, remove the chicken from the brine, and place breast-side down into the insert. Rub the sugar and salt all over the bird, inside and out. Cover, and cook on low for 7 to 8 hours, or on high for 4 to 5 hours. Check the temperature with a meat thermometer to ensure the meat has reached an internal temperature of at least 165°F before serving.

 The Verdict

I really liked this chicken. It's quite dark in color and very moist, with a rather exotic flavor—I think this is from the cloves. The first time I tried it I was stingy with the brown sugar, but this seems to be the right amount to cut the coffee's acidity. My kids dipped their chicken into barbecue sauce, but they always do.

CRANBERRY GLAZED CHICKEN THIGHS

Serves 6

6   **boneless, skinless chicken thighs (frozen is fine)**

I   **large onion, diced**

6   **garlic cloves, minced**

I   **(16-ounce) can whole-berry cranberry sauce**

½   **cup cranberry juice**

2   **tablespoons soy sauce (I use gluten-free)**

I   **lime, juiced**

2   **tablespoons cold water**

I   **tablespoon cornstarch**

   Hot mashed potatoes or polenta, for serving

Use a 6-quart slow cooker. Place the chicken into the insert. Add the onion and garlic. In a medium bowl whisk together the cranberry sauce, cranberry juice, soy sauce, and lime juice. Pour this mixture evenly over the top of the chicken. Cover, and cook on low for 6 to 7 hours, or until the chicken is fully cooked (if you cook it longer, it'll shred—it's up to you!). Carefully remove the chicken and place on a serving platter. In a small bowl, whisk together the water and cornstarch to create a slurry. Stir this into the insert to thicken the accumulated juices. Drizzle this sauce over the chicken, and serve with mashed potatoes or polenta.

The Verdict

My ten-year-old ate three chicken thighs the night I made this—the sauce is tangy and delicious. If you'd like an easy prep/cleanup in the morning, this is a great candidate for a slow cooker TV dinner meal (see page 10).

CRANBERRY TURKEY LEGS

Serves 4

3   **to 4 pounds turkey drumsticks, skin removed if desired**

1   **(1-ounce) packet onion soup mix (for homemade, see recipe below)**

1   **(14-ounce) can whole-berry cranberry sauce**

½   **cup orange juice**

Use a 6-quart slow cooker. Place the drumsticks side by side into the insert. Sprinkle on the onion soup mix, and spread the cranberry sauce on top. Pour on the orange juice. Cover, and cook on low for 6 to 7 hours, or on high for about 3 hours, or until turkey is no longer pink and has reached desired tenderness.

ONION SOUP MIX

¼   **cup dried minced onion**

2   **tablespoons chicken bouillon granules**

¼   **teaspoon paprika**

¼   **teaspoon ground black pepper**

Combine all ingredients in a small bowl and mix well. Recipe equals one packet of store-bought soup mix.

 **THE VERDICT**

MY CHILDREN COULDN'T GET ENOUGH OF THIS TURKEY. MY SEVEN-YEAR-OLD SPENT A LOT OF TIME DIPPING HER TURKEY LEG INTO THE SAUCE SO SHE COULD HAVE MORE. THE TURKEY IS SWEET AND PINK IN COLOR—A PERFECT PRINCESS DINNER. IT PAIRS BEAUTIFULLY WITH MASHED POTATOES.

CREAM OF MUSHROOM CHICKEN (WITHOUT CONDENSED SOUP)

Serves 4

4	skinless chicken breasts (frozen is fine)
2	teaspoons garlic powder
1	teaspoon paprika
½	teaspoon kosher salt
½	teaspoon ground black pepper
1	pound fresh button mushrooms
1	cup chicken broth
1	(8-ounce) package cream cheese, softened (to add at the end)
	Hot cooked rice or buttered noodles, for serving (I use gluten-free fusilli pasta)

Use a 4-quart slow cooker. Place the chicken breasts into the insert, and add all the seasonings. Flip the breast halves over a few times to get the spices (somewhat) evenly dispersed. Add the mushrooms, and pour in the broth. Cover, and cook on low for 6 hours, or on high for about 4 hours. When the chicken is fully cooked, remove carefully from the pot, and scoop out the mushrooms with a slotted spoon. Put the cream cheese into the insert, and cook on high for 15 minutes, or until fully melted. Stir well, and add the chicken and mushrooms back into the pot to get coated in the sauce. Serve over rice or buttered noodles.

 **THE VERDICT**
THIS IS CREAMY AND DELICIOUS—EVERYONE IN MY FAMILY LOVES THIS DISH. I CAUGHT MY TEN-YEAR-OLD LICKING HER PLATE BEFORE LOADING IT INTO THE DISHWASHER.

CURRIED CHICKEN WITH CAULIFLOWER

Serves 4

2　pounds boneless, skinless chicken thighs, cut into 1-inch chunks
1　head cauliflower, stem removed and florets cut into 1-inch pieces
2　cups fresh green beans, cut into 1-inch pieces
1　red bell pepper, seeded and cut into 1-inch pieces
1　onion, thickly sliced
1　(15-ounce) can coconut milk
3　tablespoons fish sauce
2　tablespoons sugar
1½　tablespoons red curry paste
1　tablespoon dried basil

Use a 6-quart slow cooker. Place the chicken into the insert, and add the cauliflower, green beans, bell pepper, and onion. Toss to distribute the vegetables. In a small bowl, combine the coconut milk, fish sauce, sugar, curry paste, and basil. Pour this mixture evenly over the top of the chicken and vegetables in the insert. Cover, and cook on low for 6 hours, or until the chicken is cooked and vegetables have reached desired tenderness.

The Verdict

Curry paste and fish sauce can both be found in the Asian foods aisle in your grocery store (the coconut milk might be there, too). This is delicious—the coconut pairs well with the curry and fish sauce and creates a beautiful mild curry that coats the vegetables. I'm not a big cauliflower fan, but love it in curry dishes. If you'd prefer to keep this vegetarian, simply omit the chicken and add a can of drained chickpeas.

DIJON CHICKEN WITH LEMON CREAM SAUCE

Serves 6

4　pounds chicken parts, skin removed
⅓　cup chicken broth
¼　cup Dijon mustard
2　lemons, juiced
1　tablespoon dried tarragon
1　(8-ounce) package cream cheese, softened (to add at the very end)
　Hot mashed potatoes or cooked rice, for serving

Use a 6-quart slow cooker. Place the chicken into the insert. In a small bowl, whisk together the broth, Dijon mustard, lemon juice, and tarragon. Pour this sauce evenly over the chicken. Cover, and cook on low for 6 to 8 hours, or on high for 4 to 5 hours. Check the temperature with a meat thermometer to ensure the chicken has reached an internal temperature of at least 165°F. Carefully remove the chicken from the pot—it'll be super tender and fall easily from the bone. Stir the cream cheese into the pot drippings to make a creamy gravy. Serve the chicken with mashed potatoes or rice, with a spoonful of the sauce over the top.

The Verdict

Luscious. The sour bite from the lemon and mustard harmonizes beautifully with the cream cheese. This is a great company meal—adults and kids alike are impressed. I like to pair our chicken with rice pilaf and steamed asparagus.

DUMP IT IN CHICKEN

Serves 4

2	pounds boneless, skinless chicken thighs or breasts
1	cup frozen roasted corn
1	(14.5-ounce) can fire-roasted tomatoes, drained
1	(15-ounce) can pinto beans, drained and rinsed
4	ounces cream cheese
	Hot cooked rice, tortilla chips, or taco shells, for serving

Use a 4-quart slow cooker. Put the chicken into the insert. Add the corn, tomatoes, and beans. Cover, and cook on low for 6 to 7 hours. Stir well, and drop in the cream cheese. Recover, and cook on high for 30 minutes, or until the cream cheese has fully melted. Stir again, and serve over rice, or with tortilla chips, or scooped into taco shells.

 The Verdict

I have my ten-year-old throw this in the pot. No knife-wielding is required, and she likes to open cans with the handheld can opener. Although my kids have been on a pinto bean kick lately, you can use whatever beans happen to be in your pantry. Easy and delicious.

FOIL PACKET HOBO DINNER

Serves 6

8	smoked chicken or turkey sausage links, such as chicken and apple, thickly sliced
6	red potatoes, washed and cut into 1-inch chunks
6	garlic cloves, minced
2	tablespoons olive oil
1	tablespoon rosemary
½	teaspoon kosher salt
¼	teaspoon ground black pepper
6	2-foot-length pieces of aluminum foil

Use a 6-quart slow cooker. In a large bowl, toss together the sausage, potatoes, garlic, oil, rosemary, salt, and pepper. Spoon equal amounts of the sausage mixture onto each of the six pieces of foil. Fold the foil over and crimp the edges to create a fully enclosed packet. Stack the packets in the insert. Cover, and cook on low for 6 to 7 hours, or on high for about 4 hours. Remove the packets with tongs, and carefully open—the steam will be quite hot, be aware!

 The Verdict

This classic campfire dish works beautifully in the slow cooker. My kids love eating directly out of the foil packets, and I appreciate the super-easy prep and cleanup.

GINGER CHICKEN

Serves 4

1	**pound baby carrots**
1	**pound potatoes, peeled and cut into 1-inch chunks**
2	**stalks celery, thinly sliced**
2	**pounds boneless, skinless chicken thighs, cut into 1-inch chunks**
1	**tablespoon ground ginger**
1	**teaspoon ground thyme**
½	**teaspoon kosher salt**
¼	**teaspoon ground black pepper**
1	**cup white wine or lemon-lime soda**
	Hot cooked quinoa or brown rice, for serving (optional)

Use a 4-quart slow cooker. Put the carrots, potatoes, and celery into the insert. In a zippered plastic bag, toss the chicken and seasonings together. Pour the chicken in on top of the vegetables. Add the wine. Cover, and cook on low for 6 to 7 hours, or on high for about 4 hours. Serve as is, or on top of a bed of quinoa or brown rice.

 **THE VERDICT**
A QUICK, EASY, ONE-POT MEAL THAT MAKES EVERYBODY HAPPY. WHO COULD ASK FOR MORE? THE LEFTOVERS FREEZE AND REHEAT QUITE WELL.

HONEY-LIME CHICKEN SOFT TACOS

Serves 8

3	**pounds boneless, skinless chicken breast, cut into 1-inch strips**
⅓	**cup honey**
2	**limes, juiced**
3	**garlic cloves, minced**
2	**teaspoons chili powder**
1	**(14-ounce) can green enchilada sauce**
½	**cup heavy whipping cream**
	Corn tortillas, for serving
	Suggested toppings: shredded Cheddar cheese, sour cream, sliced olives

Use a 6-quart slow cooker. Place the chicken into the insert. Add the honey, lime juice, garlic, and chili powder. Stir in the enchilada sauce. Cover, and cook on low for 6 to 7 hours. Shred the chicken meat completely and stir in the cream. Scoop with a slotted spoon into warmed corn tortillas. Garnish with cheese, sour cream, and sliced olives.

 **THE VERDICT**
I ADAPTED THIS FROM A RECIPE SENT BY A READER FROM OHSWEETBASIL.COM AND AM THRILLED WITH THE RESULTS. WE SERVED THIS CHICKEN TO SIX KIDS, AND THEY ALL LOVED IT. I LOVED HOW THE HONEY AND LIME MIXED WITH THE ENCHILADA SAUCE TO CREATE A SWEET NOTE. THE HEAVY CREAM LIGHTENS THE COLOR AND CREATES A VELVETY SMOOTHNESS.

HONEY MUSTARD CHICKEN WITH BACON

Serves 4

4	boneless, skinless chicken breast halves, pounded thin
⅓	cup honey
¼	cup yellow mustard
2	tablespoons mayonnaise
1	tablespoon dried minced onion
1	teaspoon seasoned salt
1	cup shredded Colby cheese
1	cup shredded Monterey Jack cheese
1	cup sliced fresh button mushrooms
8	slices bacon, cooked until quite crisp

Use a 6-quart slow cooker. Put the chicken into a large zippered plastic bag and add the honey, mustard, mayonnaise, dried onion, and salt. Seal the bag and toss the chicken in the sauce to fully coat. Squeeze the bag contents into the slow cooker. Add both the cheeses and the mushrooms on top. Cover, and cook on low for 6 to 7 hours, or until the chicken is cooked through and tender. Add 2 pieces of the bacon to the top of each chicken breast and serve.

THE VERDICT
JAN, A READER FROM TALLAHASSEE, SENT ME THIS RECIPE. SHE WROTE THAT WHENEVER SHE EATS AT AN OUTBACK STEAKHOUSE RESTAURANT, SHE ORDERS THE ALICE SPRINGS CHICKEN, AND THAT THIS DISH TASTES EXACTLY LIKE IT. I CAN SOLEMNLY SWEAR THAT MY KIDS AND HUSBAND LOVED EVERYTHING ABOUT THIS CHICKEN. THANK YOU, JAN! SERVE THIS WITH A LARGE SPINACH SALAD.

HONEY MUSTARD CHICKEN WITH CURRY

Serves 4

4   to 6 boneless, skinless chicken thighs
¼   cup honey
2   tablespoons Dijon mustard
1   tablespoon yellow curry powder
½   teaspoon kosher salt
½   teaspoon ground black pepper
    Hot cooked brown basmati rice, for serving

Place the chicken into the insert. In a small bowl, combine the honey, mustard, curry powder, salt, and pepper. Pour this sauce evenly over the top of the chicken. Cover, and cook on low for 6 hours, or on high for about 4 hours. Serve over rice, with a scoop of sauce spooned on top.

The Verdict

My kids loved how bright yellow their chicken was, and licked the sauce up, using their fingers. This is a super-easy dinner that tastes wonderful. This is a great slow cooker TV dinner candidate: Freeze all the ingredients together in a zippered plastic bag, then thaw overnight in the fridge. Dump the ingredients out of the bag and slow cook in the morning.

HUNGARIAN CHICKEN

Serves 6

6   chicken quarters, skin removed if desired
1   tablespoon Hungarian sweet paprika
1   (16-ounce) bag frozen pearl onions
1   (14.5-ounce) can diced tomatoes, undrained
1   tablespoon Dijon mustard
1   tablespoon tomato paste
1   lemon, juiced
    Hot cooked polenta or mashed potatoes, for serving

Use a 6-quart slow cooker. Place the chicken into the insert and sprinkle with the paprika. Add the onions. In a medium bowl, whisk together the tomatoes, mustard, tomato paste, and lemon juice. Pour this sauce evenly over the top of the onions and chicken. Cover, and cook on low for 7 to 8 hours, or on high for 4 to 5 hours. Serve with polenta or mashed potatoes.

The Verdict

I came across a variation of this recipe in an old *Bon Appétit* magazine I found at the dentist's office. The Hungarian sweet paprika sounds like it'd be hard to find, but I was able to locate it easily at my grocery store, although you can certainly use regular paprika as a substitute. The tomatoes, Dijon, and lemon create a fantastic tangy sauce for the chicken.

ITALIAN LEMON CHICKEN

Serves 6

- 1   4-pound roaster chicken, cleaned and skin removed
- ⅓   cup grated Parmesan cheese
- 1   tablespoon dried Italian seasoning
- 1   tablespoon garlic powder
- 1   tablespoon onion powder
- 1   tablespoon paprika
- 1   tablespoon sesame seeds
- 1   teaspoon celery seed, crushed
- 1   teaspoon kosher salt
- ¼   teaspoon ground black pepper
- 2   lemons, juiced
- 4   tablespoons (½ stick) butter, melted

Use a 6-quart slow cooker. Place the chicken into the insert breast-side down. Combine the cheese and all the seasonings in a small bowl. Rub the seasoning mixture into the meat, inside and out. Pour on the lemon juice and butter. Cover, and cook on low for 7 to 8 hours, or on high for 4 to 5 hours. Check the temperature with a meat thermometer to ensure the chicken has reached an internal temperature of at least 165°F. Remove the chicken and place in a serving dish to keep warm.

 The Verdict

Having company for Sunday dinner? Make this chicken— it's moist, flavorful, and will make everyone happy. I use the drippings to cook rice, but you can quarter red or white potatoes and nestle them around the chicken in the cooker for a complete meal-in-a-pot.

ITALIAN SAUSAGE SPAGHETTI

Serves 8

- 1   pound smoked turkey Italian sausage links, thickly sliced
- 1   (28-ounce) can crushed tomatoes
- 1   (15-ounce) can tomato sauce
- 2   large yellow onions, diced
- 1   (6-ounce) can tomato paste
- 6   to 8 garlic cloves, diced
- 2   tablespoons sugar
- 1   tablespoon dried oregano
- 1   tablespoon dried basil
- 1   teaspoon kosher salt
- ½   cup dry red wine (optional)
-    Hot cooked spaghetti, for serving

Use a 6-quart slow cooker. Place the sausage into the insert. Add the crushed tomatoes, tomato sauce, onions, tomato paste, garlic, sugar, oregano, basil, and salt. If desired, stir in the wine; otherwise just stir well to combine. Cover, and cook on low for 8 hours, or until onions are translucent and flavors have fully melded. Serve over hot spaghetti.

 The Verdict

Please make this on the next stormy day when you're stuck in the house, shivering by the fire. The aroma is out of this world—and the taste is rich and satisfying. I serve our spaghetti dinners with salad and garlic bread (I use the Against The Grain gluten-free baguettes for our bread).

JALAPEÑO CHICKEN

Serves 6

6   boneless, skinless chicken thighs
12 slices of pepperoni, diced
½   cup sliced pickled jalapeño peppers
4   ounces cream cheese, softened
1   cup shredded mozzarella cheese

Use a 4-quart slow cooker. Place the chicken into the insert. Top with the pepperoni and jalapeños. Dot cubes of cream cheese on the top, and add the mozzarella. Cover, and cook on low for 6 hours.

 The Verdict

Creamy and delicious. We had this for dinner on a very stormy night and shared it with our neighbors. It pairs well with beer and tortilla chips, or serve this with pasta and a green vegetable.

KFC-INSPIRED CHICKEN

Serves 4

1   4-pound roaster chicken, cleaned (I remove the skin; it's up to you)
1   teaspoon paprika
1   teaspoon garlic salt
1   teaspoon onion powder
1   teaspoon sugar
½   teaspoon ground thyme
½   teaspoon dried oregano
½   teaspoon ground sage
½   teaspoon ground black pepper
¼   teaspoon ground ginger
¼   teaspoon dried marjoram
¼   teaspoon celery salt
¼   teaspoon ground cardamom

Use a 6-quart slow cooker. Place the chicken into the insert, breast-side down (to ensure moist meat). In a small bowl, combine the remaining ingredients. Rub this spice blend evenly all over the bird, inside and out. Do not add liquid. Cover, and cook on high for 4 hours, or on low for 6 to 7 hours. Retain the pan drippings to make rice or mashed potatoes, if you'd like. Check the temperature with a meat thermometer to ensure the chicken has reached an internal temperature of at least 165°F before serving.

The Verdict

My little one with Celiac disease has never had Kentucky Fried Chicken and was disappointed when we watched a *Top Secret Recipe* episode featuring the famous food. The very next day we made this after some extensive spice research, and our entire family scarfed it down. If you'd like to make the spice mix in bulk, use about ¼ cup for the rub.

LEMON ROASTED CHICKEN

Serves 4 to 6

2 onions, cut into wedges
1 head garlic, peeled (about 10 cloves)
1 4-pound roaster chicken, cleaned (I remove the skin; it's up to you)
2 lemons, juiced
1 tablespoon olive oil
1 tablespoon butter, melted
1 tablespoon dried oregano
1 tablespoon dried parsley

Use a 6-quart slow cooker. Put the onions and garlic into the insert, and place the chicken on top. In a small bowl, combine the lemon juice, oil, butter, oregano, and parsley. Spread this mixture evenly over the entire chicken, inside and out. Cover, and cook on low for 7 to 8 hours, or on high for about 5 hours. Check the temperature of the chicken with a meat thermometer to ensure the chicken has reached an internal temperature of at least 165°F before serving.

 The Verdict

The meat falls right off the bones after slow cooking—it's juicy and flavorful and completely awesome. The drippings create a great gravy if you thicken with a cornstarch slurry, or you can use the accumulated liquid to make quinoa or brown rice as a side.

MAKES EVERYBODY HAPPY CHICKEN

Serves 4 to 6

3 to 4 pounds boneless, skinless chicken thighs
½ cup Dijon mustard
¼ cup all-natural maple syrup
1 tablespoon seasoned rice wine vinegar
1 tablespoon chopped fresh rosemary

Use a 4-quart slow cooker. Place the chicken into the insert. In a medium bowl, whisk together the mustard, maple syrup, and vinegar. Pour this sauce evenly over the top of the chicken. Cover, and cook on low for 6 to 7 hours. Before serving, sprinkle the rosemary on top.

 **The Verdict**

This fun recipe comes from the website wittyinthecity.com where it is called "Man Pleasing Chicken," but since I mostly feed girls, I've decided this chicken is guaranteed to make everyone happy. I know the ingredient list is a funky combination, but you're going to have to trust me on this one—you'll be glad you did!

MANGO CHICKEN BAKE

Serves 4

2	pounds boneless, skinless chicken thighs, cut into thin strips
1	red onion, thinly sliced
1	large mango, peeled, pitted, and thinly sliced
1	yellow bell pepper, seeded and thinly sliced
1	orange bell pepper, seeded and thinly sliced
1	red bell pepper, seeded and thinly sliced
4	garlic cloves, thinly sliced
1	teaspoon chili powder
1	teaspoon kosher salt
½	teaspoon ground black pepper
	Hot cooked quinoa or couscous, for serving (optional)

Use a 6-quart slow cooker. Place the chicken into the insert, and add the onion on top. Add the mango, bell peppers, and garlic. Sprinkle the seasonings on top. Toss all the ingredients in the pot until the seasonings are evenly dispersed. Cover, and cook on low for 6 to 7 hours, or on high for about 4 hours. Serve as is, or with a side of quinoa or couscous.

 **THE VERDICT**

THIS LIGHT, HEALTHY, DINNER REALLY LETS THE MANGO AND PEPPER BECOME THE STARS OF THE DISH—THE CHICKEN TAKES SECOND BILLING. I LIKED THIS DISH EVEN BETTER THE NEXT DAY, WHEN I ATE THE LEFTOVERS COLD FOR LUNCH. MY KIDS LOVE MANGO ANYTHING.

MYSTERY CHICKEN

Serves 4

2   pounds chicken parts (drumsticks, thighs, your
     choice)
¼   cup buffalo wing sauce
¼   cup ranch salad dressing
¼   cup barbecue sauce

Use a 4-quart slow cooker. Place the chicken into the
insert, and add the sauces. Using tongs, flip the chicken
over a few times to evenly distribute the sauce and coat
the chicken. Cover, and cook on low for 6 to 7 hours, or
on high for 4 hours.

 The Verdict

It's probably best to keep this sauce a mystery from your
guests—it sounds super bizarre, but it is SO. VERY.
TASTY. Some things are better being left to mystery! Serve
with baked potatoes and a green vegetable.

NO-BOURBON CHICKEN

Serves 6

2½   pounds boneless, skinless chicken breast, cut into
     1-inch pieces
½   cup water
⅓   cup packed dark brown sugar
⅓   cup soy sauce (I use gluten-free)
¼   cup apple or pineapple juice
6   garlic cloves, chopped
2   tablespoons ketchup
1   tablespoon apple cider vinegar
¼   teaspoon crushed red pepper flakes
     Hot steamed vegetables and cooked rice, for serving

Use a 4-quart slow cooker. Place the chicken into the insert
along with all the other ingredients. Stir well and cover.
Cook on low for 6 to 7 hours, or on high for 4 hours.
Uncover, and cook on high for an additional 20 minutes
to release steam. Serve with steamed vegetables over rice
with a scoop of the sauce.

 The Verdict

This is a fantastic chicken from Jamie at jamiecooksitup.
net. The chicken is moist and enveloped in a sweet and
(slightly) spicy sauce. If you'd like, you can substitute the
same amount of bourbon for the juice.

ORANGE GLAZED CHICKEN

Serves 4 to 6

4	to 6 boneless, skinless chicken thighs
1	orange, juiced
½	cup ketchup
½	cup soy sauce (I use gluten-free)
⅓	cup orange marmalade
3	garlic cloves, chopped
1	teaspoon dried basil
	Hot cooked white or brown basmati rice, for serving

Use a 4-quart slow cooker. Place the chicken into the insert. In a small bowl, combine the orange juice, ketchup, soy sauce, marmalade, garlic, and basil. Pour this sauce evenly over the top of the chicken. Cover, and cook on high for 3 to 4 hours, or on low for 6 hours. Serve over rice.

 The Verdict

Just like Chinese takeout, but without the oil, fat, or gluten. If you'd like steamed vegetables as a side dish, put a foil packet of freshly washed broccoli on top for the last hour. The broccoli will steam perfectly in the pouch.

OVERNIGHT VINEGAR CHICKEN

Serves 6

4	pounds chicken parts (I remove the skin; it's your choice)
⅓	cup soy sauce (I use gluten-free)
⅓	cup apple cider vinegar
6	garlic cloves, thinly sliced
2	green onions, thinly sliced
	Hot cooked rice, for serving (optional)

Use a 6-quart slow cooker. Place the chicken into the insert, and add the rest of the ingredients. Cover, and cook on low for 12 to 18 hours. Uncover, and carefully remove the bones. If you'd like, stir hot, cooked rice directly into the pot or you can spoon the chicken and broth over rice in a bowl.

 The Verdict

I prefer to use boneless, skinless thighs for this dish because I don't like messing around with the bones, but the bones can be saved to make broth or a soup—it's completely up to you. This chicken melts in your mouth—it's beautiful. I prepare everything in the evening and plug the pot in around 10 p.m., then we eat our chicken for dinner the next day.

PARMESAN-CRUSTED CHICKEN

Serves 4

4   boneless, skinless chicken breast halves, pounded thin
½   cup mayonnaise
⅓   cup freshly grated Parmesan cheese
⅓   cup panko-style breadcrumbs (I use gluten-free)
1   tablespoon dried Italian seasoning
    Hot cooked pasta and green salad, for serving

Use a 4-quart slow cooker. Place the chicken into the insert. In a small bowl, combine the rest of the ingredients. Spread this sauce evenly over the top of the chicken. Cover, and cook on low for 5 to 6 hours, or on high for about 3 hours. Serve with pasta and a green salad.

🍲 The Verdict

This recipe was adapted from one found on the side of the Best Foods/Hellmann's mayonnaise jar. My kids love this chicken—it's juicy, tangy, and the Parmesan and panko make a great cheesy crust. Panko-style breadcrumbs retain their shape and texture in the slow cooker much better than traditional breadcrumbs, although those would work in a pinch.

POTATO CASSEROLE

Serves 6

3   baked potatoes, peeled
4   green onions, thinly sliced
1   (16-ounce) container sour cream
2   teaspoons kosher salt
1   teaspoon ground black pepper
3   cups shredded Cheddar cheese
4   smoked chicken and apple sausages, thinly sliced

Use a 6-quart slow cooker. Coat the insert well with cooking spray, and set aside. In a large bowl, crumble the pulp of the baked potatoes, and add the green onion, sour cream, salt, pepper, and half of the cheese. Mix well to combine—I use my hands. Press this gloppy potato mixture into your greased insert, and place slices of sausage on top. Add the rest of the cheese. Cover, and cook on low for 6 to 7 hours, then uncover and cook on high for 20 minutes to release condensation. Serve hot or at room temperature.

🍲 The Verdict

I may or may not have eaten about a third of this straight out of the crock while waiting for Adam to bring the kids home from gymnastics. This is perfect potluck (or mommy's home alone) fare. Delicious.

PIZZA-STUFFED PEPPERS

Serves 6

1   pound lean ground turkey
20 slices turkey pepperoni, diced
1   cup prepared pizza sauce
2   teaspoons dried basil
1   teaspoon dried oregano
6   bell peppers, any color, cored, seeded, and
    left whole (retain tops)
1   cup shredded mozzarella cheese
½   cup warm water

Use a 6-quart slow cooker. In a large mixing bowl, combine the turkey, pepperoni, pizza sauce, basil, and oregano. Divide the mixture into 6 parts, and put a portion of the mixture into each bell pepper. Put the peppers into the insert, and top each one with some of the cheese. Put the tops back onto the peppers. Carefully pour the water around the base of the peppers. Cover, and cook on low for 7 hours, or until the meat is fully cooked, and the peppers have begun to wilt. Let stand for 10 minutes in the cooling slow cooker before serving.

The Verdict

These pizza peppers are a great low-carb and naturally gluten-free alternative to traditional pizza. The pepperoni provides a nice amount of spice; if you'd prefer a spicier pepper, you can put a half teaspoon or so of dried red pepper flakes into the meat mixture.

RIO RANCH CHICKEN

Serves 6

2   pounds boneless, skinless chicken parts
    (frozen is fine)
1   (1-ounce) packet ranch dressing mix
    (for homemade, see page 256)
½   tablespoon ground cumin
½   tablespoon chili powder
1   (15-ounce) can black beans, drained and rinsed
1   (15-ounce) can corn, drained
½   cup Italian salad dressing
    Hot cooked rice or corn tortillas, for serving

Use a 4-quart slow cooker. Place the chicken into the insert, and sprinkle on the seasonings. Add the beans and corn, and pour in the salad dressing. Stir to combine. Cover, and cook on low for 8 to 10 hours. Serve over rice, or shred the chicken and serve in tortillas.

The Verdict

I use frozen chicken pieces with this dish, and have used both bottled and homemade Italian salad dressing. I've even used a balsamic blend that I had in the fridge—go ahead and use whatever you have in the house. This is so simple to throw into the pot, yet consistently gets rave reviews.

ROASTED BELL PEPPER AND BASIL CHICKEN

Serves 4

2	pounds boneless, skinless chicken breast (frozen is fine)
1	(12-ounce) jar roasted bell peppers, undrained
3	garlic cloves, sliced
¼	cup tightly packed fresh basil leaves
¼	cup freshly grated Parmesan cheese
	Hot cooked quinoa or polenta, for serving

Use a 6-quart slow cooker. Place the chicken into the insert. Add the peppers and garlic. Stir in the basil and cheese. Cover, and cook on low for 8 hours, or until the chicken breaks apart easily with a fork. Serve over quinoa or a pile of hot polenta.

 The Verdict

This is fancy-pants lazy chicken—it's pretty much a dump-and-go recipe, but tastes like you worked super hard. I won't tell if you don't!

SESAME HONEY CHICKEN

Serves 4

6	boneless, skinless chicken thighs, cut into 2-inch chunks
1	cup honey
½	cup soy sauce (I use gluten-free)
¼	cup ketchup
6	garlic cloves, minced
2½	teaspoons sesame seeds
1	green onion, thinly sliced
	Hot cooked white rice, for serving

Use a 4-quart slow cooker. Put the chicken into the insert, and add the honey, soy sauce, ketchup, garlic, and 2 teaspoons of the sesame seeds. Stir well. Cover, and cook on low for 5 to 6 hours, or on high for 3 to 4 hours. Stir in the remaining ½ teaspoon sesame seeds and the green onion. Leave the lid off and heat on high for 30 minutes before serving over a bed of white rice.

 The Verdict

Sweet and sticky—just like it should be! My kids could eat this 24/7; it's one of their absolute favorites. I've switched it up and used chopped pecans or almonds instead of the sesame seeds and that also goes over really well.

SLOPPY JOE–STUFFED PEPPERS

Serves 6

1	pound extra-lean ground turkey
1	cup shredded Cheddar cheese
½	red onion, diced
1	stalk celery, diced
¼	cup ketchup
¼	cup mustard
3	garlic cloves, minced
1	tablespoon Worcestershire sauce (I use gluten-free)
6	bell peppers, any color, cored, seeded, and left whole (retain tops)
½	cup warm water

Use a 6-quart slow cooker. In a large bowl, combine the turkey, cheese, onion, celery, ketchup, mustard, garlic, and Worcestershire sauce. Spoon this filling evenly into each of the bell peppers, place the pepper tops back on, and transfer the peppers to the insert. (If you have leftover filling, save it for another day.) Carefully pour water around the base of the peppers. Cover, and cook on low for 6 to 7 hours, or until meat is cooked through, and peppers have begun to wilt and pucker.

 THE VERDICT
THESE ARE SOME FANTASTIC STUFFED PEPPERS. THE SWEETNESS FROM THE KETCHUP REALLY PROVIDES A SLOPPY JOE TASTE!

SLOW-ROASTED TURKEY BREAST

Serves 6

1	**5- to 6-pound bone-in turkey breast, skin removed**
1	**tablespoon chicken bouillon granules**
1	**tablespoon ground cumin**
1	**tablespoon garlic powder**
1	**tablespoon poultry seasoning**
8	**tablespoons (1 stick) butter**
	Hot mashed potatoes and steamed dark green vegetable, for serving

Use a 6-quart slow cooker. Place the turkey into the insert. Sprinkle with all the seasonings, and add the butter. Cover (if the lid doesn't fit completely, make a foil tent to cover the pot securely), and cook on low for 8 to 10 hours. The meat will no longer be pink and will fall easily from the bone when it's ready to serve. Pair with mashed potatoes and a dark green vegetable.

THE VERDICT

WHO SAYS A TURKEY DINNER HAS TO BE COMPLICATED? WE ATE THIS DINNER THE FIRST WEEK OF MAY, AFTER NOT HAVING TURKEY FOR MONTHS AND MONTHS. I FOUND A FRESH HALF-TURKEY AT THE GROCERY STORE FOR AN UNHEARD OF FORTY-SEVEN CENTS A POUND, AND QUICKLY SCOOPED IT UP AND PLOPPED IT INTO THE CROCK. OUR DINNER WAS FABULOUS, AND I DIDN'T EVEN NEED TO PULL OUT THE CHOPPING BOARD!

SPICY APRICOT CHICKEN

Serves 4

- **3 pounds skinless chicken thighs or drumsticks**
- **¾ cup chunky salsa**
- **I onion, chopped**
- **⅓ cup apricot preserves**
- **¼ cup orange juice**
- **Hot cooked rice or quinoa, for serving**

Use a 4-quart slow cooker. Put the chicken into the insert, and top with the salsa, onion, preserves, and orange juice. Toss the chicken with the sauce mixture to distribute—just do the best you can, it will all cook together regardless of how it looks at this stage. Cover, and cook on low for 5 to 6 hours, or on high for about 4 hours. Remove the chicken from the slow cooker, and serve with rice or quinoa with a spoonful of the sauce on top.

The Verdict

The bit of spice from the salsa cuts down the sweet apricot flavor, resulting in a great flavor combination. This is a very customizable recipe—if you worry that the salsa might be too hot for your children, cut down on the salsa and add a bit more apricot preserves (or vice versa if you'd like more heat!).

SPINACH-STUFFED CHICKEN BREASTS

Serves 4

- **4 boneless, skinless chicken breast halves**
- **I cup thawed, drained frozen spinach**
- **I cup shredded Monterey Jack cheese**
- **I teaspoon paprika**
- **I teaspoon garlic powder**
- **½ teaspoon seasoned salt**
- **½ teaspoon ground cumin**
- **½ teaspoon dried Italian seasoning**
- **½ teaspoon cayenne pepper**
- **½ cup dry white wine or chicken broth**
- **Hot cooked pasta or baked potatoes, for serving**

Use a 6-quart slow cooker. Carefully slice each chicken breast in half lengthwise, about three-fourths of the way through—you are creating a pocket inside each chicken breast for the spinach stuffing. Squeeze the spinach well so you don't have soggy stuffing and place in a medium bowl with the cheese and all the seasonings. Using your fingers, push a quarter of the stuffing into each chicken breast half. Place the stuffed pieces into the insert. Pour the wine evenly over the top. Cover, and cook on low for 7 hours, or on high for about 4 hours. Serve with pasta or baked potatoes.

The Verdict

There's a little bit of heat in this stuffing, which provides a fantastic Cajun-style kick. The spinach and cheese cook together to make a delicious gooey sauce. If you have any leftovers, they freeze and reheat well.

SQUASH AND SAUSAGE MEDLEY

Serves 4

1	(16-ounce) package smoked chicken sausage, sliced
1	small butternut squash, peeled, seeded, and cubed
2	sweet potatoes, peeled and cut into 1-inch pieces
1	red onion, sliced into thin rings
4	garlic cloves, diced
1	tablespoon olive oil
1	tablespoon dried rosemary
½	teaspoon kosher salt
¼	teaspoon ground black pepper

Use a 6-quart slow cooker. This is a dump-everything-in recipe. It really doesn't matter how, or in what order. Once everything is in the pot, toss the ingredients to evenly disperse the oil and spices. Do not add any liquid. Cover, and cook on low for 7 hours, or on high for about 4 hours, or until the squash and sweet potato have reached desired tenderness.

 The Verdict

This beautiful harvest dinner tastes like it should be enjoyed outside while on a hayride. This is a bowl full of fall's delights.

STICKY CHICKEN

Serves 4

4	boneless, skinless chicken thighs
1	onion, thinly sliced
4	garlic cloves, chopped
½	cup packed dark brown sugar
½	cup freshly grated Parmesan cheese
3	tablespoons soy sauce (I use gluten-free)
1	tablespoon dried Italian seasoning
	Hot cooked rice and a steamed green vegetable, for serving

Use a 4-quart slow cooker. Place the chicken into the insert. Add the onion and garlic. In a small bowl, combine the sugar, cheese, soy sauce, and Italian seasoning. Pour this mixture evenly on top of the ingredients in the pot. Cover, and cook on low for 6 to 7 hours, or on high for about 4 hours. Serve with rice and a green vegetable.

 The Verdict

I was excited to try this recipe—it came highly recommended to me from Laura in South Dakota who puts this sauce "on everything: from chicken, to pork chops, to beef tips." The ingredients are certainly different; I've never before paired Parmesan cheese with soy sauce, but we do now! This is a GREAT chicken—all three of my kids had double servings. Thank you, Laura!

SWEET-AND-SAVORY CABBAGE ROLLS

Serves 6

12	large green cabbage leaves
1	pound lean ground turkey
½	cup brown rice
⅓	cup dried cranberries
1	large egg
1	tablespoon garlic powder
1	tablespoon smoked paprika
3	cups tomato juice
1	tablespoon ground cinnamon
1	teaspoon ground nutmeg

Use a 6-quart slow cooker. Put the cabbage leaves in a casserole dish with a few tablespoons of water and steam in the microwave for 2 minutes to soften. In a large bowl, combine the turkey, rice, cranberries, egg, garlic powder, and paprika. Mix well—it'll be the consistency of meatloaf. Scoop about ⅓ cup of the meat mixture into each cabbage leaf, and fold the leaf over to create a packet. Put these packets seam-side down into the insert, stacked as needed. In a large measuring cup, combine the tomato juice, cinnamon, and nutmeg. Pour this juice evenly over the top of the cabbage rolls (it's okay if they aren't fully submerged). Cover, and cook on low for 6 to 8 hours, or until meat is cooked through and rice is tender.

 THE VERDICT
THESE CABBAGE ROLLS HAVE A FUN MOROCCAN TWIST TO THEM. I GOT THE IDEA FROM A RECIPE I FOUND ON PINTEREST FROM THE BEVCOOKS.COM WEBSITE. I LOVE THE MIX OF FLAVORS. BEV RECOMMENDS DRINKING WINE WHILE ASSEMBLING THE ROLLS TO MAKE THE TIME GO FASTER— GREAT IDEA!

SWEET-AND-SOUR CHICKEN

Serves 4

½   **cup milk**

1   **large egg, beaten**

¾   **cup panko-style breadcrumbs (I use gluten-free)**

½   **teaspoon seasoned salt**

½   **teaspoon garlic powder**

2   **pounds boneless, skinless chicken breasts, cut into 1-inch cubes**

¾   **cup sugar**

½   **cup apple cider vinegar**

¼   **cup ketchup**

1   **tablespoon soy sauce (I use gluten-free)**

1   **teaspoon kosher salt**
     Hot cooked white rice and steamed broccoli, for serving

Use a 4-quart slow cooker. In a shallow dish, whisk together the milk and egg. In another shallow dish, combine the breadcrumbs, seasoned salt, and garlic powder. Dip each piece of chicken into the egg and milk mixture and then into the breadcrumb mixture. Place the coated chicken pieces into the insert. In a medium bowl, make the sweet-and-sour sauce by whisking together the sugar, vinegar, ketchup, soy sauce, and kosher salt. Pour this sauce evenly over the top of the chicken. Cover, and cook on low for 5 to 6 hours, or until the chicken has fully cooked and the sauce is bubbly. Serve with rice and broccoli.

THE VERDICT

I'VE MADE THIS QUITE A FEW TIMES—MY KIDS LOVE THE SAUCE AND WOULD PROBABLY EAT A TENNIS BALL IF IT HAD THIS SAUCE ON IT. IF YOU'D LIKE THE CHICKEN TO HAVE A CRISPIER TEXTURE, YOU CAN PAN-FRY THE BREADED CHICKEN IN BUTTER BEFORE PLACING INTO THE CROCK. YOU CAN ALSO (GASP!) USE FROZEN CHICKEN NUGGETS OR CUT-UP BREADED CHICKEN PATTIES INSTEAD.

TANGY SWEET-AND-SOUR CHICKEN WITH PINEAPPLE

Serves 4

1½	pounds boneless, skinless chicken, cut into 1-inch pieces
1	onion, thinly sliced
1	(8-ounce) can bamboo shoots, drained
¼	cup seasoned rice wine vinegar
¼	cup soy sauce (I use gluten-free)
2	tablespoons dark brown sugar
1	teaspoon ground ginger
½	teaspoon allspice
1	cup broccoli florets
1	cup baby carrots
1	(8-ounce) can pineapple chunks, drained
1	cup chicken broth
	Hot cooked rice or quinoa, for serving

Use a 4-quart slow cooker. Put the chicken into the insert, and add the onion and bamboo shoots. Add the vinegar, soy sauce, sugar, ginger, and allspice. Stir to evenly coat the chicken with the sauce. Add the broccoli, carrots, and pineapple. Pour the broth over the top. Cover, and cook on low for 6 to 7 hours. Serve over a bed of rice or quinoa.

 The Verdict

Sweet-and-sour chicken, at home, without the grease—score! This is a light, healthy version of sweet-and-sour chicken sure to please both your tongue and your cardiologist.

THAI CHICKEN WITH BASIL

Serves 4

2	pounds boneless, skinless chicken thighs, cut into 1-inch chunks
1	bunch asparagus, chopped into 1-inch pieces
½	cup cashews
¼	cup tightly packed basil leaves, coarsely chopped
¼	cup beer (Redbridge by Anheuser-Busch is gluten-free)
4	garlic cloves, minced
1	jalapeño pepper, thinly sliced
1	tablespoon sugar
1	tablespoon soy sauce (I use gluten-free)
1	tablespoon fish sauce
1	teaspoon sesame oil
	Hot cooked white or brown basmati rice, for serving

Use a 4-quart slow cooker. Place the chicken into the insert. Add the asparagus, cashews, basil, beer, garlic, jalapeño, sugar, soy sauce, fish sauce, and oil. Toss the ingredients until everything is equally distributed. Cover, and cook on low for 5 to 6 hours, or until the chicken is cooked through and has reached desired tenderness. Serve on a bed of rice.

 The Verdict

This recipe is adapted from Jaden Hair's Steamy Kitchen website (steamykitchen.com). I was in the mood for Thai food, but didn't want to order in or try to man the stove during the late-afternoon cranky-kid hour. This worked well in the slow cooker—and was much more cost-effective than takeout. If you'd prefer your asparagus to retain a crunch, don't put it in until the last hour of cooking time.

TROPICAL CHICKEN

Serves 6

3   **pounds boneless, skinless chicken breasts, cut into 1-inch pieces**
1   **cup coconut milk**
½   **cup soy sauce (I use gluten-free)**
½   **cup frozen orange juice concentrate**
2   **tablespoons sesame oil**
    Hot steamed vegetables and cooked rice, for serving

Use a 4-quart slow cooker. Place the chicken into the insert, and add the coconut milk, soy sauce, orange juice concentrate, and oil. Stir well to combine. Cover, and cook on low for 5 to 6 hours, or until the chicken has reached desired tenderness. Serve with a side of steamed fresh vegetables and rice.

 The Verdict

The orange juice and coconut complement each other beautifully. If you'd like, remove the chicken from the pot and cook a pot of brown basmati rice in the drippings.

TURKEY AND VEGETABLE MEATLOAF

Serves 4

1¼ **pounds lean ground turkey**
1   **(16-ounce) bag broccoli slaw, coarsely chopped**
1   **small onion, finely diced**
1   **large egg, beaten**
½   **cup oats (I use certified gluten-free rolled oats)**
½   **cup ketchup**
2   **teaspoons garlic powder**
1   **teaspoon kosher salt**

Use a 6-quart slow cooker with a 9 x 5 x 3-inch loaf pan set in the insert. Coat the loaf pan with cooking spray and set aside. In a large bowl, mix together the turkey, broccoli slaw, onion, egg, and oats. Stir in ¼ cup of the ketchup, the garlic powder, and salt. Mix together to form a gloppy mixture, then press into the prepared loaf pan. Place the loaf pan into the insert (do not add water). Brush on the remaining ¼ cup of the ketchup. Cover, and cook on low for 6 to 7 hours, or until an inserted knife comes out clean. Let sit with the lid off and the slow cooker unplugged for 15 minutes before removing pan.

 The Verdict

My mom found this recipe in a magazine and loved it. I was eager to give it a try in the slow cooker, and was very pleased with the results. The broccoli slaw provides a lovely texture and keeps the turkey nice and moist. Delicious! I served our meatloaf with a baked sweet potato and some roasted asparagus.

TURKEY IN TOMATO SAUCE

Serves 4

4	**turkey thighs, skin removed**
4	**red potatoes, washed and cubed**
2	**onions, cut into wedges**
I	**cup baby carrots**
⅓	**cup water or red wine (see Verdict)**
2	**tablespoons cornstarch**
I	**(8-ounce) can tomato sauce**
2	**tablespoons sugar**
I	**tablespoon garlic powder**
2	**teaspoons dried Italian seasoning**
½	**teaspoon kosher salt**
½	**teaspoon ground black pepper**

Use a 6-quart slow cooker. Put the turkey into the insert and add the potatoes, onions, and carrots. In a medium bowl, whisk together the water and cornstarch. When combined, whisk in the tomato sauce, sugar, garlic powder, Italian seasoning, salt, and pepper. Pour this sauce evenly over the top of the turkey and vegetables. Cover, and cook on low for 7 to 8 hours, or on high for about 4 hours.

 **THE VERDICT**
THE TURKEY MELTS RIGHT OFF THE BONES IN THIS DELICIOUS TOMATO-BASED STEW. IF YOU'D LIKE AN EVEN RICHER DISH, SWAP OUT THE WATER FOR A BIT OF RED WINE.

TURKEY AND STUFFING DINNER

Serves 4 to 6

2	**cups toasted bread cubes or plain croutons (I use gluten-free bread)**
½	**cup diced onion**
¼	**cup chopped celery**
I	**teaspoon ground sage**
½	**teaspoon kosher salt**
¼	**teaspoon ground black pepper**
¼	**teaspoon dried thyme**
I	**tablespoon butter, melted**
4	**turkey drumsticks, skin removed if desired**
½	**cup chicken broth**

Use a 6-quart slow cooker. Spray the insert well with cooking spray. Add the bread cubes, onion, celery, sage, salt, pepper, and thyme. Toss well, pour in the butter, and toss again. Lay the turkey over the top. Pour the broth evenly over the top. Cover, and cook on low for 7 to 8 hours, or on high for about 5 hours.

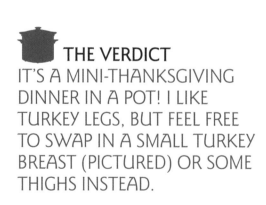 THE VERDICT
IT'S A MINI-THANKSGIVING DINNER IN A POT! I LIKE TURKEY LEGS, BUT FEEL FREE TO SWAP IN A SMALL TURKEY BREAST (PICTURED) OR SOME THIGHS INSTEAD.

WHITE CHICKEN ENCHILADAS

Serves 6 to 8

8   **to 10 corn tortillas**
2   **cups shredded cooked chicken**
2   **cups shredded Monterey Jack cheese**
2   **tablespoons butter**
3   **tablespoons all-purpose flour (I use rice flour)**
I   **cup chicken broth**
I   **cup sour cream**
I   **(4-ounce) can diced green chiles, undrained**

Use a 4-quart slow cooker. Place a layer of tortillas into the bottom of the insert; you may need to tear them to get a good fit. In a large bowl, combine the chicken and cheese. Put a hefty handful of chicken filling on top of the tortillas. Put another layer of tortillas on top. Repeat layers until you've run out of tortillas and chicken filling. In a small saucepan over medium heat, melt the butter. Whisk in the flour to make a roux. Add the broth, sour cream, and chiles. Whisk until sauce is smooth, taking care not to boil. Pour this sauce evenly over the top of the stacked tortillas and chicken. Cover, and cook on low for 4 to 5 hours, or on high for about 2 hours. Your dinner is finished when the tortillas have browned and the cheese is fully melted and bubbly. Let sit, unplugged, with the lid off for 10 minutes before serving.

THE VERDICT

THIS RECIPE WAS ADAPTED FROM ONE AT JOYFUL MOMMA'S KITCHEN (JOYFUL-MOMMAS-KITCHEN.BLOGSPOT.COM) AND IS ABSOLUTELY DELICIOUS. MY KIDS LAPPED UP THE CREAMY CHILE SAUCE—IT'S SMOOTH AND TASTY WITH A LOVELY TANG.

YELLOW CURRIED CHICKEN WITH POTATOES

Serves 4

2	pounds chicken parts, skin removed
2	Yukon Gold potatoes, peeled and cut into 2-inch wedges
1	onion, diced
1	tablespoon curry powder
1	teaspoon ground turmeric
½	teaspoon kosher salt
1	(15-ounce) can chickpeas, drained and rinsed

Use a 4-quart slow cooker. Place the chicken into the insert, and add the potatoes and onion. Add the curry, turmeric, and salt, then pour in the chickpeas. Toss all the ingredients together to distribute the spices. Cover, and cook on low for 5 to 6 hours, or on high for 3 to 4 hours.

The Verdict

The chicken and potatoes cook very nicely without any additional broth in this dish, which makes the curry color and flavor really stand out instead of getting watered down. This is a beautiful mild curry, with no added fat or grease—enjoy!

ZESTY STUFFED BELL PEPPERS

Serves 4

4	bell peppers (any color)
1	pound ground turkey
1	onion, finely diced
1	(10-ounce) can tomatoes and chiles, drained
⅓	cup long-grain white rice, rinsed
2	tablespoons ketchup
½	teaspoon kosher salt
¼	teaspoon ground black pepper
⅓	cup water

Use a 6-quart slow cooker. Core and seed the peppers but retain the tops. In a large bowl, combine the turkey, onion, tomatoes and chiles, rice, ketchup, salt, and black pepper. Stuff this mixture into the cored bell peppers. Stand the stuffed peppers up in the bottom of the insert, and replace the pepper tops. Carefully pour the water around the base of the peppers. Cover, and cook on low for 6 hours, or on high for about 3 hours. Your peppers are done when the meat is no longer pink and the rice is bite-tender.

The Verdict

I'm the only one in the house who eats stuffed peppers, so I share these with my mom and grandma, who also really like them. I prefer to use red or orange peppers, because the green can taste bitter (and remind me of soggy grade-school pizza). The peppers steam perfectly in the slow cooker, and the meat and rice cook in the peppers without drying out the way they sometimes do in the oven.

BEEF & LAMB

5-MINUTE STROGANOFF

Serves 4 to 6

1	(3-pound) beef roast, cut into long strips
1	tablespoon garlic powder
½	teaspoon ground black pepper
1	pound fresh button mushrooms, thinly sliced
2	cups beef broth
1	(8-ounce) package cream cheese, softened (to add later)
1	cup sour cream, at room temperature (to add later) Hot cooked wide flat noodles, for serving (I use gluten-free)

Use a 6-quart slow cooker. Put the meat into the insert, and add the garlic powder and pepper. Add the mushrooms on top, and pour in the broth. Cover, and cook on low for 7 to 8 hours, or until the meat has reached desired tenderness. Carefully remove the beef and mushrooms from the pot with a slotted spoon and set aside. Put the cream cheese and the sour cream into the insert, and cook on high for 15 minutes, or until fully melted. Stir in the meat and mushrooms. Serve over noodles.

 The Verdict

This is what beef stroganoff should taste like. The meat is super tender, breaks apart easily with a fork, and each piece is coated in a velvety cream sauce with just a bit of a peppery taste. Yum.

ALL-AMERICAN POT ROAST

Serves 6

1	tablespoon garlic powder
2	teaspoons dried basil
1	teaspoon kosher salt
½	teaspoon ground black pepper
1	(4-pound) pot roast, trimmed
6	red potatoes, washed and quartered
2	onions, cut into wedges
1	bunch celery, cut into 1-inch pieces
1	cup carrots cut into 1-inch pieces
2	cups beef broth

Use a 6-quart slow cooker. In a small bowl, combine the garlic powder, basil, salt, and pepper. Rub the spices into the meat, taking care to cover all sides. Place the meat into the insert. Nestle all the vegetables around the meat. Pour in the broth. Cover, and cook on low for 8 to 10 hours, or until the meat has relaxed and pulls apart easily with a fork.

 The Verdict

Pot roast is usually one of the first dishes new slow cooker owners prepare. If you find that the meat isn't quite as tender as you'd like near dinnertime, remove it from the pot, and cut it into a few pieces before returning it to the pot for a while longer. A dry or tough pot roast means that it hasn't cooked long enough.

ALL-DAY SPAGHETTI

Serves 10 to 12

2	**pounds ground beef**
2	**onions, diced**
6	**garlic cloves, minced**
3	**(14.5-ounce) cans diced tomatoes, drained**
3	**(8-ounce) cans tomato sauce**
2	**(6-ounce) cans tomato paste**
⅓	**cup sugar**
2	**tablespoons dried oregano**
I	**tablespoon dried basil**
2	**teaspoons dried marjoram**
I	**teaspoon kosher salt**
½	**teaspoon ground black pepper**
I	**pound spaghetti (I use gluten-free)**
	Freshly grated Parmesan cheese, for serving

Use a 6-quart slow cooker. In a large skillet over medium heat, add the beef, onion, and garlic and cook, stirring, until the beef is browned. Drain off any accumulated grease, and pour the mixture into the insert. Add the tomatoes, tomato sauce, and tomato paste. Now add the sugar, oregano, basil, marjoram, salt, and pepper. Stir well to combine the ingredients. Cover and cook on low for 8 to 10 hours. Meanwhile, cook the spaghetti according to package directions. Serve the sauce over the hot pasta with a sprinkle of cheese.

 THE VERDICT
THIS RECIPE COMES FROM LAURA, WHO WRITES THE REAL MOM KITCHEN BLOG (REALMOMKITCHEN.COM). MY FAMILY AND I LOVED EVERYTHING ABOUT THIS PASTA SAUCE—IT'S THICK, HEARTY, AND HAS JUST A HINT OF KID-PLEASING SWEETNESS TO IT. THIS SAUCE FREEZES AND REHEATS WELL (IF YOU ARE ABLE TO SAVE ANY OF THE LEFTOVERS; THEY'LL GO FAST!).

ANCHOVY AND CAPER BEEF

Serves 4 to 6

1	**(3-pound) beef chuck roast, trimmed**
½	**cup chopped fresh flat-leaf parsley**
1	**lemon, juiced**
1	**tablespoon capers, drained**
2	**anchovies, chopped**
½	**teaspoon kosher salt**
½	**teaspoon ground black pepper**

Use a 4-quart slow cooker. Place the roast into the insert. In a small bowl, combine the parsley, lemon juice, capers, anchovies, salt, and pepper to create a paste. Smear this mixture all over the meat. Cover and cook on low for 6 to 7 hours, or until the meat has relaxed and begun to lose its shape.

THE VERDICT

THIS IS A MEAL FOR ADVENTUROUS PALATES. IF YOU'RE NOT A FAN OF ANCHOVIES OR CAPERS, I'M NOT GOING TO CHANGE YOUR MIND, BUT I LOVE THIS DINNER. I LIKE TO SERVE THE MEAT SLICED OVER A BED OF FRESH SPINACH WITH A SPOONFUL OF BROTH FROM THE CROCK.

BANGERS AND MASH

Serves 6

4	baking potatoes, washed and cut into 2-inch chunks
6	smoked sausages, thickly sliced
2	onions, sliced into thin rings
I	cup chopped baby carrots
I	cup chopped celery
I	tablespoon garlic powder
½	teaspoon kosher salt
½	teaspoon ground black pepper
I	cup beef broth

Use a 6-quart slow cooker. Put the potatoes into the insert, and add the sausage, onions, carrots, and celery. Sprinkle in the garlic powder, salt, and pepper. Stir to combine. Pour the broth evenly over the top. Cover, and cook on low for 7 to 8 hours.

 The Verdict

Bangers and mash is a traditional British comfort food. I like how cooking the potatoes with the vegetables and sausage in the slow cooker causes them to break apart and mash all on their own. This super-easy (and inexpensive!) meal is a regular in our monthly meal rotation.

BARBACOA BEEF

Serves 4 to 6

I	(3-pound) beef chuck roast
I	tablespoon ground chipotle chile
I	tablespoon ground cumin
I	tablespoon dried oregano
½	teaspoon ground cloves
½	teaspoon kosher salt
I	onion, sliced into thin rings
I	cup beef broth
I	lime, juiced
	Warmed corn tortillas, for serving
	Suggested toppings: shredded Cheddar cheese, sour cream, lime wedges

Use a 4-quart slow cooker. Place the roast into the insert. In a small bowl, combine the chipotle, cumin, oregano, cloves, and salt. Rub this mixture on all sides of the meat, and top with the onion rings. Add the broth and lime juice. Cover, and cook on low for 8 hours or on high for 4 to 5 hours. Shred the meat and serve in tortillas with desired toppings.

 The Verdict

My friend Kathy sent me this recipe. She makes it as a copycat of the Chipotle Mexican Grill's barbacoa beef. I love how the heat of the ground chipotle interacts with the tang of the lime—delicious. Canned chipotle in adobo sauce contains gluten, which is why we opted to go with the dried powder.

BEEF BRISKET WITH MANGO BARBECUE SAUCE

Serves 6

1	(4-pound) beef brisket
4	ripe tomatoes, quartered
2	mangoes, peeled, pitted, and coarsely chopped
¼	cup chopped fresh flat-leaf parsley
¼	cup tightly packed fresh basil leaves
2	limes, juiced
4	garlic cloves, peeled
1	tablespoon olive oil
1	teaspoon kosher salt

Use a 6-quart slow cooker. Place the brisket into the insert. In a food processor or blender, combine the rest of the ingredients and pulse until they create a sauce—it's up to you how chunky or smooth you'd like it to be. Pour this sauce evenly over the top of the brisket. Cover, and cook on low for 8 to 10 hours, or until the meat easily falls apart when poked with a fork.

 The Verdict

This homemade mango barbecue sauce is sweet with a great fresh flavor you just don't get from a bottled sauce. You'll really enjoy it!

BEEF DAUBE WITH MUSTARD SAUCE

Serves 6 to 8

2	pounds beef stew meat
2	onions, sliced into thin rings
1	(16-ounce) can plum tomatoes, undrained
6	garlic cloves, thinly sliced
2	tablespoons Dijon mustard
1½	cups dry white wine
1½	cups chicken broth
4	sprigs fresh thyme
2	bay leaves
	Salt and ground black pepper, to taste
	Baked potatoes or hot cooked rice, for serving

Use a 6-quart slow cooker. Place the beef into the insert, along with the onions, tomatoes, and garlic. In a large measuring cup, whisk the mustard into the wine and broth until it's completely dissolved. Pour evenly over the ingredients in the insert. Float the thyme and bay leaves on top and add salt and pepper to taste. Cover, and cook on low for 8 hours, or until meat breaks apart easily with a fork. Remove the thyme sprigs and bay leaves and serve with a baked potato or over rice.

The Verdict

Thank you to Sarah V., for sending along this recipe. She adapted it to the slow cooker after finding it in *Joy of Cooking*. We both appreciate that the beef cooks and tenderizes all day long with no additional fat or oil. The Dijon mustard and wine make a luscious gravy—if you'd like, you can thicken it with a cornstarch slurry.

BEEF GYROS

Serves 4 to 6

1   (3-pound) beef chuck roast, cut into thin strips
1   onion, diced
4   garlic cloves, minced
2   lemons, juiced
2   teaspoons dried oregano
1   teaspoon paprika
1   teaspoon dried dill
1   teaspoon kosher salt
     Pita bread or corn or brown rice tortillas, for serving

FOR THE YOGURT SAUCE
1   small cucumber, peeled, seeded, and diced
1   cup plain nonfat yogurt
1   lemon, juiced
1   tablespoon olive oil
2   tablespoons chopped fresh mint leaves

Use a 4-quart slow cooker. Place the beef in the insert along with the onion, garlic, lemon juice, oregano, paprika, dill, and salt. Toss the meat strips to get them fully coated with the seasoning. Cover, and cook on low for 8 hours, or until the meat is super tender. While the meat is cooking, combine the sauce ingredients in a medium bowl. Serve in pita bread or tortillas with a dollop of the yogurt sauce.

 THE VERDICT
I LOVE THE TANGY FLAVOR OF THIS MEAT—IT'S PERFECT. I'VE USED THIS SAME RECIPE WITH LAMB SHANK—IT WORKS JUST AS WELL, BUT I PREFER THE BEEF CHUCK PRICE POINT. THE YOGURT SAUCE WITH THE CUCUMBER GIVES A LOVELY CRUNCH AND I HIGHLY RECOMMEND IT.

BEEF SHORT RIBS IN RED WINE

Serves 6

5	pounds beef short ribs
1	large onion, sliced into thin rings
1	head garlic, peeled (about 10 cloves)
1	(8-ounce) bottle oil-packed sun-dried tomatoes, drained
1	tablespoon dried rosemary
½	teaspoon kosher salt
½	teaspoon ground black pepper
1	(750-ml) bottle dry red wine

Use a 6-quart slow cooker. Put the ribs into the insert, and add the onion and garlic. Place the sundried tomatoes on top. Add the rosemary, salt, and pepper. Pour in the entire bottle of wine. Cover, and cook on low for 8 hours. Serve alongside roasted potatoes and a green salad.

THE VERDICT

FOOD FIT FOR A KING. EVERYTHING ABOUT THIS DISH WORKS: THE SUN-DRIED TOMATOES ADD TARTNESS, THE ROSEMARY AND WINE PAIR BEAUTIFULLY TO FORM A RICH, DARK, GRAVY, AND THE GARLIC CLOVES PROVIDE A SOMEWHAT NUTTY AND MELLOW GARLIC FLAVOR TO EVERY BITE. DELICIOUS.

BEEF SHORT RIBS WITH DRIED PLUMS

Serves 4

4	to 6 pounds beef short ribs (see Verdict below)
I	onion, sliced into thin rings
4	garlic cloves, chopped
I	teaspoon ground cumin
I	teaspoon kosher salt
I	teaspoon ground black pepper
2	cups dried plums (prunes)
I	cinnamon stick
½	cup dry white wine or apple juice

Use a 4-quart slow cooker. Place the ribs into the insert. Add the onion and garlic. Sprinkle in the cumin, salt, and pepper. Toss the meat a few times to disperse the spices, onion, and garlic. Toss in the prunes and cinnamon stick, and pour in the wine. Cover, and cook on low for 7 to 8 hours, or on high for 4 to 5 hours. The meat will be quite tender, and the prunes will break down while cooking to create a delicious sweet sauce. Discard the cinnamon stick before serving.

The Verdict

My kids ate so much of this meat, Adam and I hardly got any. There's plenty of sauce here—if you have big eaters, go ahead and up the poundage. The rule of thumb is approximately ½ pound of meat per person, but sometimes that just doesn't work out!

BEER-BRAISED BRISKET

Serves 4

I	(3- to 4-pound) beef chuck or pot roast
5	garlic cloves, chopped
2	tablespoons dark brown sugar
I	tablespoon paprika
I	tablespoon ground cumin
I	tablespoon instant coffee granules
I	teaspoon kosher salt
I	onion, sliced into thin rings
I	(12-ounce) bottle beer (Redbridge by Anheuser-Busch is gluten-free)
	Hot mashed potatoes, for serving

Use a 4-quart slow cooker. Put the roast into the insert. In a small bowl, combine the garlic, sugar, paprika, cumin, coffee, and salt. Rub this paste on all sides of the meat. Separate the onion rings and place on top of the meat. Pour in the beer. Cover, and cook on low for 8 to 10 hours, or until the meat is fork-tender. Serve on top of a bed of mashed potatoes.

The Verdict

The hearty velvety flavor of this gravy is fantastic, and it has a nice dark color. If I wasn't trying to be a good role model for the kids, I'd like to pour it into a mug and drink it straight. If you'd like to thicken the gravy a bit, remove the meat from the pot, then slowly whisk in some cornstarch, a teaspoon at a time.

BRAISED BEEF WITH SUN-DRIED TOMATOES

Serves 4

2   pounds beef stew meat
1   cup sun-dried tomato halves (not oil-packed)
1   onion, cut into wedges
4   garlic cloves, chopped
1   tablespoon dark brown sugar
1   tablespoon Worcestershire sauce (I use gluten-free)
2   sprigs fresh rosemary or 1 teaspoon dried rosemary
½   teaspoon kosher salt
½   teaspoon ground black pepper
2   cups beef broth
1   cup dry red wine or grape juice
    Hot mashed potatoes or cooked polenta, for serving

Use a 4-quart slow cooker. Place the beef into the insert, and toss in the sun-dried tomato halves (no need to reconstitute, they'll do so in the pot). Add the onion, garlic, and sugar. Now add the Worcestershire sauce, rosemary, salt, and pepper. Pour in the broth and wine. Cover, and cook on low for 7 to 8 hours, or until the meat is fully tender and can pull apart with a fork. Serve over a bed of mashed potatoes or polenta.

 The Verdict

This is a great use for the stew meat you bought "buy 1, get 1 free" last July and forgot about in the freezer. The sun-dried tomatoes, rosemary, and wine give what could be a rather ordinary Tuesday night beef dinner a new feel. This freezes and reheats quite well.

CHERRY COKE AND JALAPEÑO MEATBALLS

Serves 4 to 6

2   pounds store-bought or homemade meatballs, cooked (frozen is fine; check for gluten if purchasing)
½   cup packed dark brown sugar
½   cup Cherry Coke
1   teaspoon kosher salt
½   teaspoon ground black pepper
1   teaspoon paprika
3   jalapeño peppers (don't cut)

Use a 6-quart slow cooker. Place the meatballs into the insert. In a medium bowl, whisk together the sugar, Cherry Coke, salt, pepper, and paprika. Pour this evenly over the meatballs. Toss the meatballs to get a nice coating of the sauce. Place the jalapeños on top. Cover, and cook on low for 5 to 6 hours, or until the meatballs are heated throughout. Discard the jalapeños before serving.

The Verdict

These meatballs were inspired by the Kayotic Kitchen website (kayotic.nl)—they make an excellent appetizer for entertaining, although I end up eating so much that it turns into dinner. Aidells makes a gluten-free meatball, and so does Coleman Natural.

CHILI CON CARNE (NO-BEAN CHILI)

Serves 6

- 1 **pound ground beef**
- 1 **large onion, diced**
- 6 **garlic cloves, diced**
- 1 **(28-ounce) can crushed tomatoes, undrained**
- 2 **tablespoons chili powder**
- 1 **teaspoon dried oregano**
- 1 **teaspoon ground cumin**
- 1 **teaspoon Tabasco sauce or more to taste**
- 2 **tablespoons red wine vinegar**
  Cornbread, for serving
  Suggested toppings: shredded Cheddar cheese, sour cream

Use a 6-quart slow cooker. In a large skillet over medium heat, cook the beef, onion, and garlic, stirring, until the meat is browned. Drain off any accumulated fat. Transfer the meat mixture to the insert. Add the tomatoes, and stir in the chili powder, oregano, and cumin. Add the Tabasco sauce and vinegar, and stir well to combine. Cover, and cook on low for 8 to 10 hours. Serve with cornbread and topped with cheese and sour cream, if desired.

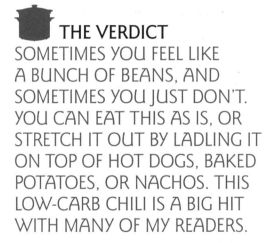 **THE VERDICT**

SOMETIMES YOU FEEL LIKE A BUNCH OF BEANS, AND SOMETIMES YOU JUST DON'T. YOU CAN EAT THIS AS IS, OR STRETCH IT OUT BY LADLING IT ON TOP OF HOT DOGS, BAKED POTATOES, OR NACHOS. THIS LOW-CARB CHILI IS A BIG HIT WITH MANY OF MY READERS.

CHINESE POT ROAST WITH SNOW PEAS

Serves 6

1	**(3- to 4-pound) pot roast, trimmed**
2	**onions, sliced into thin rings**
½	**cup soy sauce (I use gluten-free)**
½	**cup packed dark brown sugar**
1	**teaspoon ground ginger**
1	**(10-ounce) package frozen snow peas, thawed**
	Hot cooked white rice, for serving

Use a 4-quart slow cooker. Put the roast into the insert, and add the onions. Pour in the soy sauce, and add the sugar and ginger. Flip the roast a few times to get it coated on all sides with the sauce. Cover, and cook on low for 8 hours, or until the meat has relaxed and can shred easily with a fork. If the meat isn't tender enough after 8 hours, cut it into a few pieces and return to the pot for further cooking. Before serving, stir in the snow peas and serve over hot rice.

 THE VERDICT

I MADE THIS POT ROAST ON A NIGHT THAT BOTH OF MY OLDER GIRLS HAD SLEEPOVER GUESTS, AND ALL THE CHILDREN HAPPILY ATE THEIR DINNERS, EVEN ALL THE SNOW PEAS!

CHUCK ROAST TACOS

Serves 6 to 8

I	**(3- to 4-pound) beef chuck roast (frozen is fine)**
I	**onion, sliced into thin rings**
I	**(10-ounce) can tomatoes and chiles, undrained**
I	**tablespoon garlic powder**
I	**teaspoon ground cumin**
I	**teaspoon chili powder**
½	**teaspoon kosher salt**
I	**cup beer (Redbridge by Anheuser-Busch is gluten-free)**
I	**tablespoon Worcestershire sauce (I use gluten-free)**
	Corn tortillas or taco shells, for serving
	Suggested toppings: shredded Cheddar cheese, sliced avocado, sour cream

Use a 6-quart slow cooker. Put the roast into the insert. Add the onion and tomatoes and chiles. Add the garlic powder, cumin, chili powder, and salt. Pour in the beer and Worcestershire sauce. Cover, and cook on low for 10 hours, or until the meat shreds easily with a fork. Stir well, and serve with a slotted spoon into taco shells or tortillas and add your favorite taco toppings.

THE VERDICT

I LOVE THAT I CAN THROW THIS ON EARLY IN THE MORNING WITH A FROZEN HUNK OF MEAT AND HAVE IT COOK ALL DAY WITH PANTRY STAPLES. MY KIDS ARE HUGE FANS OF ANYTHING TACO, AND WILL EAT TONS. IF YOU'D PREFER TO SKIP THE BEER, USE BEEF BROTH INSTEAD.

ENCHILADA STACK

Serves 6

2	pounds shredded cooked beef or lamb (see page 174)
1	(14.5-ounce) can diced tomatoes, drained
8	corn tortillas
4	cups shredded Mexican blend cheese
1	(10-ounce) can red or green enchilada sauce
	Suggested toppings: sour cream, sliced black olives

Use a 4-quart slow cooker. Coat the insert with cooking spray. In a large bowl, combine the meat and the tomatoes and set aside. Put a layer of tortillas into the bottom of the insert (you may need to tear them to get even coverage). Scoop a layer of the meat mixture on top. Add a handful of the cheese. Repeat the layers until you run out of ingredients. Top with another handful of cheese, and pour the enchilada sauce evenly over the top. Cover, and cook on low for 4 to 5 hours or until meat is hot, the cheese is melty, and the tortillas have begun to brown on the edge. Serve with sour cream and olives, if desired.

 The Verdict

This is a great way to use up leftover meat from a roast without having to serve the same exact meal two nights in a row. My kids love Mexican food (I think it's the gobs of cheese), and love it when I make enchiladas in the slow cooker.

EVERYDAY MEATLOAF

Serves 4 to 6

1	pound lean ground beef
1	onion, grated
½	cup breadcrumbs (I use gluten-free)
2	large eggs
6	cloves garlic, chopped
1	tablespoon dried Italian seasoning
1	tablespoon Worcestershire sauce (I use gluten-free)
¼	cup ketchup

Use a 6-quart slow cooker and a glass or metal baking pan. Spray the baking pan with cooking spray, and set aside. In a large bowl, combine the beef with the onion, breadcrumbs, eggs, garlic, Italian seasoning, and Worcestershire sauce. I usually use my hands—you want everything fully incorporated. Put the meat mixture into the prepared baking pan and push down with your hands to make it fit. Spread the ketchup evenly over the top. Place the pan into the slow cooker insert (do not add water), and cover. Cook on low for 7 to 8 hours, or on high for 4 hours.

 The Verdict

This is a beautiful, delicious, and moist meatloaf. My kids like to dip their meat into barbecue sauce, and Adam loves it best the next day, cold, in a meatloaf sandwich. If you'd like, you may nestle washed baking potatoes around the meatloaf pan for a complete meal.

INDIAN-STYLE SEEKH LAMB

Serves 4

1	**pound lean ground lamb**
1	**large onion**
¼	**cup fresh mint leaves**
¼	**cup fresh cilantro leaves**
1	**(1-inch) piece fresh ginger, peeled**
2	**small green chile peppers, stems removed**
1	**teaspoon ground cumin**
1	**teaspoon ground coriander**
1	**teaspoon kosher salt**
½	**teaspoon cayenne pepper**
	Lavash, pita bread, or hot cooked rice, for serving
	Tzatziki Sauce, for serving (recipe follows)

Use a 4-quart slow cooker. Place a wire rack into the insert. (If you do not have a rack, you can make one by weaving together aluminum foil "worms" in a waffle pattern.) Put the lamb into a large bowl and set aside. In a food processor, pulse together the rest of the ingredients, except the tzatziki sauce, until they are well blended and mixed together. Stir this mixture into the lamb (or use your hands) until you have a large lamb meatball. Pinch off tennis ball–size pieces of meat, and press gently to create elongated meatballs. Place these into the insert, on top of the rack—it's okay if they overlap a bit. Cover, and cook on low for 7 hours, or on high for about 4 hours. Serve in lavash, pita bread, or over rice with tzatziki sauce.

TZATZIKI SAUCE

1	**cup plain yogurt**
1	**cucumber, peeled, seeded, and diced**
1	**garlic clove, minced**
1	**teaspoon dried dill**
1	**tablespoon olive**
½	**lemon, juiced**

In a bowl, combine all the ingredients, and store any leftovers in the fridge.

THE VERDICT

TRADITIONALLY, GROUND LAMB IS WRAPPED AROUND A WOODEN SKEWER AND GRILLED OVER AN OPEN FLAME. SINCE I'M PETRIFIED OF THE GRILL, I WANTED TO FIGURE OUT HOW TO MAKE THEM (SAFELY!) IN MY TRUSTY SLOW COOKER. NOT ONLY DID IT WORK, THE MEAT TASTED JUST AS GOOD AS IT DOES WHEN COOKED OUTDOORS. IF YOU'D LIKE MORE HEAT, USE MORE CHILES AND CAYENNE—THESE MEASUREMENTS ARE FOR A SLOW, MILD HEAT.

GREEK SPICED POT ROAST

Serves 4

1   (3- to 4-pound) beef chuck or rump roast
1   onion, sliced into thin rings
8   garlic cloves, smashed
1   teaspoon kosher salt
1   teaspoon ground black pepper
½   teaspoon fennel seed
½   teaspoon anise seed
1   teaspoon ground cumin
1   teaspoon ground cinnamon
¼   cup packed dark brown sugar
1   tablespoon honey
1   lemon, juiced

Use a 4-quart slow cooker. Put the roast into the insert, and add the onion and garlic. In a small bowl, combine the salt, pepper, and spices with the sugar and honey. Smear this paste onto the top of the roast. Pour in the lemon juice. Cover, and cook on low for 8 to 10 hours, or until the meat breaks apart easily with a fork.

🍲 The Verdict

Contrary to an old-school belief, you do not need to drown the meat in liquid to have it cook properly in the slow cooker. This meat cooks in its own juices and is perfectly seasoned. If your cooker seems to release a lot of steam while it cooks, place a layer of foil under the lid to trap in valuable condensation and heat.

JEN'S FAMOUS ITALIAN MEATLOAF

Serves 6

2   pounds lean ground beef
1   cup breadcrumbs (I use gluten-free)
1   onion, diced
4   ounces Parmesan cheese, freshly grated
1   cup prepared pasta sauce, divided
⅓   cup milk
2   large eggs
1   teaspoon kosher salt
¼   teaspoon ground black pepper
    Hot baked or mashed potatoes, for serving

Use a 6-quart oval slow cooker with a glass or metal 9 x 5 x 3-inch loaf pan. In a large bowl, combine the beef, breadcrumbs, onion, cheese, ⅓ cup of the pasta sauce, the milk, eggs, salt, and pepper. Combine well (I use my hands) and press the mixture into the loaf pan. Pour the remaining ⅔ cup pasta sauce evenly over the top. Place the loaf pan into the insert (do not add water). Cover, and cook on low for 7 hours, or on high for about 4 hours. The meatloaf is finished when it's brown on top and has begun to pull away from the sides. Let it sit, cooling, for 15 minutes before slicing. Serve with baked or mashed potatoes.

🍲 The Verdict

This is my friend Jen, The Cocktail Lady's (cocktail365. blogspot.com) meatloaf. I first had it at her house, cold, and couldn't keep myself from cutting little slices "to even it up." It's moist, packed with flavor, and makes amazing next-day sandwiches. Thank you for sharing your recipe, Jen!

LAZY SUNDAY POT ROAST

Serves 6 to 8

I	**(3- to 4-pound) pot roast, trimmed**
I	**pound fresh cremini mushrooms, thinly sliced**
I	**onion, sliced**
4	**garlic cloves, chopped**
I	**(26-ounce) jar prepared pasta sauce (retain jar)**
¼	**cup beef broth or water**
I	**tablespoon dried Italian seasoning**
	Hot baked potatoes or buttered pasta (I use gluten-free), for serving

Use a 6-quart slow cooker. Put the pot roast into the insert, and add the mushrooms, onion, and garlic. Pour the pasta sauce evenly over the top. Put the broth into the empty pasta jar and seal. Shake well, pour this liquid into the pot, and stir in the Italian seasoning. Cover, and cook on low for 8 to 10 hours, or until the meat has reached desired tenderness. Serve with baked potatoes or pasta.

 **THE VERDICT**

THIS IS A GREAT SUNDAY NIGHT DINNER TO SERVE TO GUESTS. THE MEAT IS TENDER AND JUICY, AND CAN SIMMER ALL DAY WHILE YOU ARE OUT OF THE HOUSE. SERVE WITH CRUSTY BREAD (WE USE GLUTEN-FREE) AND A GREEN SALAD.

LEG OF LAMB WITH GARLIC AND HONEY

Serves 6

8   garlic cloves, chopped
2   tablespoons honey
2   tablespoons prepared brown mustard
1   teaspoon kosher salt
½   teaspoon ground black pepper
1   (4- to 5-pound) lamb roast, trimmed
1   (14-ounce) can fire-roasted diced tomatoes, undrained
½   cup dry white wine or apple juice

Use a 6-quart slow cooker. In a small bowl, combine the garlic, honey, mustard, salt, and pepper. Rub this mixture on all sides of the lamb (remove any string or netting). Place the lamb into the insert. Pour in the tomatoes, and add the wine. Cover, and cook on low for 8 hours, or until the lamb pulls apart easily with a fork.

 The Verdict

Growing up, I thought people only ate lamb on Easter Sunday. I am now happy to serve lamb throughout the year—the entire family loves it, and I appreciate how naturally lean and flavorful it is. Stock up when it goes on sale in the spring months to freeze for future use. We like to serve lamb with brussels sprouts and asparagus.

LOUISIANA POT ROAST

Serves 6

2   tablespoons dark brown sugar
1   teaspoon ground white pepper
1   teaspoon garlic powder
1   teaspoon cayenne pepper
1   teaspoon smoked paprika
1   teaspoon kosher salt
1   (3-pound) beef chuck roast
2   onions, sliced into thin rings
6   red potatoes, washed and quartered
1   cup baby carrots
4   ripe tomatoes, quartered

Use a 6-quart slow cooker. Combine the sugar, white pepper, garlic powder, cayenne pepper, paprika, and salt in a small bowl, and rub the spice mixture all over the roast, taking care to get all sides. Place the meat into the insert. Add the onions, potatoes, and carrots, and top with the tomatoes. Cover, and cook on low for 8 to 10 hours, or until the meat has begun to lose shape and can pull apart easily with a fork.

 The Verdict

It's not a mistake that there isn't any liquid added to this pot roast—the meat and vegetables create their own sauce while cooking. The meat has a beautiful smoky heat to it—which you can customize by adding more (or less!) of the cayenne pepper.

MINT-GLAZED LEG OF LAMB

Serves 6 to 8

1	onion, sliced into thin rings
1	(4- to 5-pound) boneless leg of lamb
⅓	cup mint jelly
4	garlic cloves, chopped
3	sprigs fresh mint
1	tablespoon fresh rosemary
1	teaspoon kosher salt
1	teaspoon ground black pepper
	Hot mashed potatoes, for serving

Use a 6-quart slow cooker. Separate the onion rings with your fingers and place in the insert. Put the lamb on top. In a small bowl, combine the jelly, garlic, mint, rosemary, salt, and pepper. Smear this mixture on all sides of the meat. Cover, and cook on low for 7 hours, or until the lamb is fully cooked and begins to relax and lose its shape. Serve with mashed potatoes and a spoonful of the accumulated gravy.

 THE VERDICT

I HAVE ALWAYS SHIED AWAY FROM MINT JELLY—IT LOOKS LIKE LIME JELL-O TO ME, AND I COULDN'T FIGURE OUT WHY LAMB WAS SUPPOSED TO BE PAIRED WITH SOMETHING THAT SMELLED LIKE DOUBLEMINT GUM, UNTIL I TRIED THIS! LAMB AND MINT ARE MEANT TO GO TOGETHER! THIS SWEET, SALTY, AND MINTY GLAZE CANNOT BE BEAT. I CAN'T WAIT TO SERVE THIS THE NEXT TIME WE ARE TOGETHER FOR A BIG FAMILY MEAL SO I CAN IMPRESS MY GUESTS.

MEAT LOVER'S CHILI

Serves 8

4 pounds mixed ground meat (combination beef, turkey, and pork)
2 onions, diced
1 head garlic, peeled and diced (about 10 cloves)
1 green bell pepper, seeded and diced
2 stalks celery, thinly sliced
1 jalapeño pepper, diced (wear gloves!)
1 (14.5-ounce) can stewed tomatoes, undrained
½ (6-ounce) bottle of beer (I use gluten-free beer)
2 tablespoons tomato paste
1 tablespoon ground cumin
1 tablespoon chili powder
1 tablespoon kosher salt
1 teaspoon ground black pepper
   Suggested toppings: sliced pickled jalapeño peppers, shredded Cheddar cheese, sour cream

Use a 6-quart slow cooker. In a large skillet over medium heat, add the meat, onions, and garlic and cook, stirring, until the meat is browned. Drain off most of the accumulated fat (save a little for flavor), and transfer the meat mixture to the insert. Add the bell pepper, celery, and jalapeño. Pour in the tomatoes. Fill the tomato can with water and pour that into the insert. Add the beer and tomato paste. Stir in the seasonings. Cover, and cook on low for 8 to 10 hours. Serve with the desired toppings.

 The Verdict

I grew up believing all chili should have beans; I never before had a chili without them. My mind has been changed. Thick, spicy, delicious, and packed with meat, you will not be missing beans after eating a bowl.

MEXICAN STUFFED PASTA SHELLS

Serves 4 to 6

1 (8-ounce) package large pasta shells (I use gluten-free)
1 pound lean ground beef or turkey
1 (1-ounce) packet taco seasoning (for homemade, see page 28)
1 (8-ounce) package cream cheese, softened
1 (16-ounce) bottle prepared mild salsa
2 cups shredded Cheddar cheese
   Suggested toppings: sliced olives, sour cream, tortilla chips

Use a 6-quart slow cooker sprayed well with cooking spray. Rinse the pasta shells with hot water, and set aside. In a skillet over medium heat, add the meat, and cook, stirring, until browned. Drain off any accumulated grease. Stir in the taco seasoning and cream cheese until well incorporated. Use a spoon to stuff the creamy meat mixture into each pasta shell. Place the stuffed shells into the insert—stacking and overlapping as needed. Pour the entire bottle of salsa evenly over the top and add the cheese. Cover, and cook on low for 6 to 7 hours, or on high for about 4 hours. Serve with your favorite toppings, or eat as is.

The Verdict

I was super excited to find gluten-free pasta shells (Tinkyada), and love having a new way to make casseroles in the slow cooker. If you have a hard time finding the shells, you can layer in penne or rigatoni pasta or use uncooked lasagna noodles.

MONGOLIAN BEEF TAKEOUT FAKE OUT

Serves 4

2	to 3 pounds flank steak, cut into long strips
1	tablespoon cornstarch
¾	cup packed dark brown sugar
½	cup soy sauce (I use gluten-free)
4	garlic cloves, minced
1	teaspoon grated fresh ginger
3	green onions, thinly sliced
	Hot cooked white rice, for serving

Use a 4-quart slow cooker. Place the steak into a zippered plastic bag with the cornstarch. Shake the bag to evenly coat the meat, and dump the bag contents into the insert. Add the sugar, soy sauce, garlic, ginger, and two-thirds of the green onions. Stir to combine. Cover, and cook on low for 4 to 5 hours, or until the meat is cooked through and tender. Add the remaining green onion to the pot, and serve over rice.

 **THE VERDICT**
I KNOW THERE'S A LOT OF SUGAR IN THIS DISH—BUT THIS IS THE RIGHT AMOUNT TO RECREATE A COPYCAT DISH AT HOME. THE MEAT IS SWEET, STICKY, AND DELICIOUS—DON'T FORGET THE CHOPSTICKS!

NOT YOUR MOTHER'S MEATBALLS

Makes 24 meatballs

¼ cup chopped fresh flat-leaf parsley
1½ pounds lean ground beef
4 slices applewood-smoked bacon, diced
¼ cup freshly grated Parmesan cheese
¼ cup panko-style breadcrumbs (I use gluten-free)
2 large eggs
2 tablespoons dried minced onion
1 tablespoon garlic powder
½ teaspoon kosher salt
½ teaspoon ground black pepper
1 cup all-purpose flour (I use rice flour)
2 cups chicken or beef broth
1 (6-ounce) can tomato paste
Hot cooked pasta or rice, for serving (optional)

Use a 6-quart slow cooker. In a large bowl, combine the parsley, beef, and bacon. Add in the cheese, breadcrumbs, eggs, and all the seasonings. Combine well (I use my hands). After the meat is mixed, line a cookie sheet with parchment paper or nonstick aluminum foil. Pour the flour into a shallow dish (a pie pan works great). Roll the meat into golf ball–size balls, and then lightly dust each meatball with the flour before placing on the lined cookie sheet. When all the meat is used, put the whole sheet into the freezer for 1 hour, or until completely frozen. It's okay to freeze overnight, if you'd like to do this over 2 days (put in sealed container if freezing for longer).

Once the meatballs are frozen, place them one by one (this means don't dump!) into a lightly greased slow cooker. It's okay to stack them. In a small bowl, whisk together the broth and tomato paste to create a gravy. Pour this evenly over the meatballs. Cover, and cook on low for 5 hours, or until the meatballs have browned and are fully cooked. They are hearty, and can remain in the slow cooker set on warm for up to 4 additional hours. Serve with pasta or rice, or all on their own. These are filling!

THE VERDICT

YOU WILL LOVE THESE. THESE MEATBALLS HAVE BEEN WELL REVIEWED ON MY WEBSITE, AND HAVE BEEN MADE IN HUNDREDS OF KITCHENS ALL OVER THE WORLD. THE FLOUR-AND-FREEZING TRICK IS SUCH A FANTASTIC TECHNIQUE TO KEEP THE MEAT TOGETHER, AND THE FLOUR DREDGE PROVIDES A BIT MORE OF A "CRUSTY" TEXTURE AND THICKENS THE TOMATO GRAVY BEAUTIFULLY.

MUSHROOM BEEF STROGANOFF

Serves 6

2	pounds beef stew meat (frozen is fine)
2	pounds fresh button mushrooms, thinly sliced
1	large fresh tomato, diced
3	green onions, thinly sliced
4	garlic cloves, minced
¼	cup minced fresh flat-leaf parsley
1	teaspoon dried oregano
½	teaspoon paprika
½	teaspoon dried thyme
1	cup beef broth
¼	cup dry red wine
2	tablespoons cold water
1½	tablespoons cornstarch
1	cup sour cream
	Hot cooked pasta, rice, or baked potatoes, for serving

Use a 4-quart slow cooker. Put the beef into the insert. Add the mushrooms, tomato, green onions, and garlic. Then add the parsley, oregano, paprika, and thyme. Stir in the broth and wine (if you'd prefer not to use wine, just add more broth). Cover, and cook on low for 8 hours, or until the meat has reached desired tenderness. In a small bowl, combine the water and cornstarch to make a slurry. Scoop out 1 cup of hot liquid from the cooker, and whisk it into the slurry. Stir back into the pot and add the sour cream. Cook on high for 20 to 30 minutes, or until the sour cream has completely dissolved. Serve over pasta, rice, or potatoes.

 THE VERDICT

BETTY ANN WROTE TO ME AND SHARED HER FAMILY'S FAVORITE STROGANOFF RECIPE. WE ALL LOVED IT, AND I APPRECIATE THAT IT USES FRESH INGREDIENTS. THIS IS A WONDERFUL DINNER, AND WILL BE A NEW STAPLE IN OUR HOME.

OVERNIGHT POT ROAST

Serves 6

1   (5-pound) beef chuck roast
1   tablespoon dried or 3 sprigs fresh rosemary
1   teaspoon kosher salt
1   teaspoon ground black pepper
1   head garlic, peeled (about 10 cloves)
    Hot mashed potatoes and green vegetable,
    for serving

Use a 6-quart slow cooker. Place the roast into the insert, and rub the rosemary, salt, and pepper all over the outside of the meat. Toss in the garlic cloves. Cover, and cook on low for 16 to 20 hours. Please make sure the cooker seals well—you should see a lot of built-up condensation on the lid. If your cooker doesn't seal nicely, lay down a length of foil to trap in steam and moisture, then place the lid on top. Serve with mashed potatoes and green vegetable of your choice.

 The Verdict

This is the most tender pot roast you'll ever have—the meat cuts easily with a spoon after cooking in its own juices for so long. The garlic breaks down and creates a smooth, nutty gravy with the rosemary.

PASTA BAKE

Serves 6

1   (16-ounce) bag or box of rigatoni, penne, or fusilli pasta (I use gluten-free)
1   pound lean ground beef
1   onion, diced
4   cloves garlic, chopped
1   (26-ounce) jar prepared pasta sauce
2   cups shredded mozzarella cheese

Use a 6-quart slow cooker. Coat the insert with cooking spray. Rinse the pasta under running water (this is just to add a bit of moisture to the cooker), then add to the insert. In a large skillet over medium heat, add the beef, onion, and garlic, and cook, stirring, until the meat is browned and the onion is translucent. Drain off any accumulated fat, and add the pasta sauce to the skillet. Stir well, and pour this meat mixture over the pasta in the slow cooker. Stir to combine. Top with cheese. Cover, and cook on low for 5 to 6 hours, or until pasta has reached desired tenderness.

 The Verdict

This is an incredibly easy way to have a complete pasta dinner at the end of a busy day. Feel free to add mushrooms, bell pepper, or even sliced pepperoni to the mix to change it up a bit to suit your family's taste.

PIZZA LASAGNA

Serves 8

1	pound lean ground beef or lamb
1	(26-ounce) jar prepared pasta sauce (retain jar)
1	(10-ounce) package lasagna noodles (I use gluten-free)
1	(16-ounce) container ricotta cheese
1	tablespoon dried Italian seasoning
1	pound fresh button mushrooms, thinly sliced
1	green bell pepper, seeded and thinly sliced
24	pepperoni slices
4	cups shredded mozzarella cheese
¼	cup warm water

Use a 6-quart slow cooker. Coat the insert with cooking spray, and set aside. Add the meat to a large skillet over medium heat, and cook, stirring, until browned. Drain off any accumulated grease. Pour the pasta sauce into the meat, and stir. Add a large spoonful of the meat mixture into the bottom of the insert. Add a layer of lasagna noodles (you may need to break them to get a good fit). In a small bowl, combine the ricotta cheese with the Italian seasoning. Smear a spoonful of this cheese mixture onto the dry lasagna noodles. Add a handful of the mushrooms, bell peppers, and pepperoni. Top with 1 cup of the cheese. Now add another large spoonful of meat and sauce, and repeat layers until you run out of ingredients and the slow cooker is full. Add the water to the empty pasta sauce jar, seal, and shake. Pour this liquid evenly over the top of the assembled lasagna. Cover, and cook on low for 6 to 7 hours, or until the casserole is bubbly, the cheese has melted, and the pasta is bite-tender. Let it sit with the lid off for about 10 minutes before serving.

🍲 The Verdict

I made this for a sleepover and all four kids asked for seconds. This is a very customizable lasagna—if you aren't a fan of mushrooms, add olives or a handful of spinach, instead.

PIZZA PASTA BAKE

Serves 6 to 8

3	cups cooked pasta, such as penne (I use gluten-free)
1	pound lean ground beef or turkey
1	onion, diced
3	garlic cloves, minced
1	(26-ounce) jar prepared pasta sauce
¾	teaspoon dried Italian seasoning
½	teaspoon dried oregano
20	pepperoni slices
8	ounces fresh button mushrooms, thinly sliced
½	cup canned sliced black olives
2	cups shredded mozzarella cheese

Use a 6-quart slow cooker. Spray the insert well with cooking spray. Press the pasta into the bottom of the cooker—this will become the pizza "crust." Add the meat, onion, and garlic to a large skillet over medium heat and cook until the meat is browned and the onion is translucent. Drain off any accumulated grease, and stir in the pasta sauce, Italian seasoning, and oregano. Pour the meat sauce over the top of the pasta. Count out 20 pieces of pepperoni (and then eat the rest of the package!) and dot the pieces over the top, along with the mushrooms and olives. Top with handfuls of the cheese. Cover, and cook on high for 4 hours, or until the cheese topping has fully melted and begun to brown on top.

🍲 The Verdict

Pizza in a pot! In order for our family and friends to eat pizza, we need to order at least two. After delivery and tip we're out about $40—this is such a more economical way to enjoy pizza and satisfies any and all cravings.

RED WINE AND PLUMS BEEF STRIPS

Serves 4

2	to 3 pounds beef stew meat or tri-tip strips
2	cups dry red wine
1	cup dried pitted plums (prunes)
1	tablespoon dried or 3 sprigs fresh rosemary
1	tablespoon soy sauce (I use gluten-free)
½	teaspoon ground black pepper
	Hot mashed potatoes or polenta, for serving

Use a 4-quart slow cooker. Place the beef into the insert, and add the wine and dried plums. Add the rosemary, soy sauce, and pepper. Cover, and cook on low for 8 hours, or on high for about 5 hours. Serve over mashed potatoes or polenta.

 **THE VERDICT**
OUR SEVEN-YEAR-OLD NEIGHBOR INVITED HIMSELF OVER FOR DINNER WHEN HE SMELLED THIS COOKING. HE ATE TWO PLATEFULS, WHICH WAS GREAT PEER PRESSURE FOR OUR THREE GIRLS, WHO FOLLOWED SUIT. EVERYTHING ABOUT THIS DISH WORKED, IT'S A KEEPER.

RED WINE BRISKET

Serves 6

1	**(5-pound) beef brisket, trimmed**
1	**tablespoon herbes de Provence**
1	**tablespoon garlic powder**
1	**teaspoon kosher salt**
½	**teaspoon ground black pepper**
1	**tablespoon tomato paste**
2	**cups dry red wine**

Use a 6-quart slow cooker. Place the brisket into the insert. In a small bowl, combine the seasonings with the tomato paste. Smear this paste on your hunk of meat—taking care to get all sides. Pour in the wine. Cover, and cook on low for 8 to 10 hours—the meat should be quite tender and cut easily with a fork.

THE VERDICT

THIS IS ONE OF MY FAVORITE WAYS TO BRING A FROSTBITTEN ROAST BACK TO LIFE. I ALWAYS HAVE THESE INGREDIENTS ON HAND, AND PULL THIS RECIPE INTO THE ROTATION WHEN I'M FEELING UNINSPIRED TO GET TO THE STORE. IT MAKES EVERYBODY HAPPY, AND I DON'T HAVE TO CHANGE OUT OF MY JAMMY PANTS!

REUBEN IN A POT

Serves 6

2   cups diced cooked corned beef
1   (32-ounce) package fresh sauerkraut, drained
     and rinsed
1   tablespoon caraway seeds
2   cups shredded Swiss cheese
1   cup Thousand Island dressing

Use a 4-quart slow cooker. Put the beef into the bottom of the insert, and add the sauerkraut. Add the caraway seed, and then use kitchen tongs to fluff up the sauerkraut and disperse the caraway seeds. Sprinkle the cheese on top, and pour the salad dressing over the whole thing. Cover and cook on low for 6 hours, or until hot and bubbly.

The Verdict

Before we went gluten-free my husband liked to order Reuben sandwiches from a neighborhood deli. This casserole satisfies any Reuben cravings, and is a fun way to use up any leftover St. Patrick's Day corned beef.

SALISBURY STEAK

Serves 4 to 6

2   pounds lean ground beef
1   (1-ounce) packet onion soup mix (for homemade,
     see page 109)
2   teaspoons garlic powder
1   pound fresh button mushrooms, thinly sliced
2   cups beef broth
1   tablespoon A1 Steak Sauce
     Hot mashed potatoes, for serving

Use a 6-quart slow cooker, sprayed with cooking spray. In a large bowl, combine the beef, onion soup mix, and garlic powder. Form into 4 to 6 large hamburger patties and place them in the insert (it's okay to overlap a bit). In a separate large bowl, combine the mushrooms, broth, and steak sauce. Pour the mushroom mixture evenly over the top of the meat patties in the insert. Cover, and cook on low for 5 to 6 hours, or on high for 3 to 4 hours. Serve with mashed potatoes.

The Verdict

If you've only had Salisbury steak in your elementary school's cafeteria, you don't know what you're missing. My kids loved their meal, although only one actually ate the mushrooms.

SHREDDED KOREAN BEEF SOFT TACOS

Serves 6

1	(3- to 4-pound) beef chuck roast, trimmed if desired
½	cup packed dark brown sugar
⅓	cup soy sauce (I use gluten-free)
1	head garlic, peeled (about 10 cloves)
½	onion, diced
1	(1-inch) piece fresh ginger, peeled and grated
2	tablespoons seasoned rice wine vinegar
1	tablespoon sesame oil
1	jalapeño pepper, seeded and diced (be careful, use gloves!)
	Soft corn or flour tortillas, Shredded Cabbage Slaw (recipe follows), and white or brown rice, for serving

Use a 6-quart slow cooker. This truly can't be any easier. I don't brown the meat, but I do trim off the visible fat. I can make these directions complicated and tell you to add this or that first, but it honestly doesn't matter. This is going to cook on low all day long, and the ingredients will distribute just fine all on their own. Throw in the beef, sugar, soy sauce, garlic, onion, ginger, vinegar, oil, and jalapeño however you'd like. Cover, and cook on low for 8 to 10 hours or until the meat has fully shredded (you can help it out by cutting the meat into pieces an hour or so before serving time). Serve in tortillas with the cabbage slaw and rice.

SHREDDED CABBAGE SLAW

1	(16-ounce) bag shredded coleslaw
1	tablespoon soy sauce (I use gluten-free)
2	tablespoons seasoned rice vinegar
	Salt and ground black pepper, to taste

In a bowl, toss everything together and serve immediately (it wilts if you make it early in the day).

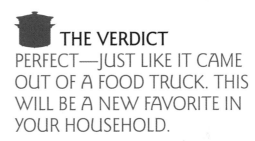

THE VERDICT
PERFECT—JUST LIKE IT CAME OUT OF A FOOD TRUCK. THIS WILL BE A NEW FAVORITE IN YOUR HOUSEHOLD.

SALSA MEATLOAF

Serves 4

2	pounds lean ground beef
2	cups shredded Mexican blend cheese
2	large eggs
I	cup breadcrumbs (I use gluten-free)
I	(1-ounce) packet of taco seasoning (for homemade, see page 28)
I	(8-ounce) jar of your favorite salsa
	Hot cooked beans and rice, for serving

Use a 6-quart oval slow cooker and a glass or metal 9 x 5 x 3-inch loaf pan. In a large bowl, combine the meat, cheese, eggs, breadcrumbs, and taco seasoning. Combine well (I use my hands) and press the mixture into the loaf pan. Pour the salsa over the top (just pour in enough to cover the loaf, not so much it drips over the sides of the pan). Place the loaf pan into the insert. Cover, and cook on low for 7 hours, or on high for about 4 hours. The meatloaf is finished when it's brown on top and has begun to pull away from the sides. Let it cool for 15 minutes before slicing. Serve with a side of beans and rice.

 The Verdict

Oh my gracious—this is all the good parts of a taco without the messy fingers and drippy forearms. If I was into calling things "deconstructed," I'd call this a deconstructed taco. But I'm not that trendy.

SHREDDED BEEF FOR SOFT TACOS, ENCHILADAS, OR TAMALES

Serves 12

I	(4-pound) beef chuck roast, trimmed
2	large onions, diced
6	garlic cloves, chopped
2	teaspoons kosher salt
I	teaspoon ground black pepper
I	tablespoon ground cumin
2	(4-ounce) cans diced green chiles, undrained
I	cup beef broth

Use a 4- or 6-quart slow cooker. Put the roast into the insert, and add the onions and garlic. Sprinkle the salt, pepper, and cumin over the top and add the chiles. Pour in the broth. Cover, and cook on low for 8 to 10 hours, or until the meat shreds easily with a fork. Shred completely and serve.

 The Verdict

It's wonderful to have a bunch of cooked and seasoned meat tucked away in the freezer or refrigerator for quick weekend lunches or a busy weeknight dinner. One of my kids' favorite afternoon snacks is a shredded beef quesadilla. Easy, filling, and homemade! You can also use it as a soft taco filling, in enchiladas (page 174), or in tamales (page 180).

SLOW COOKER COWBOY COOKOUT

Serves 4

	Aluminum foil
4	**hamburger patties (frozen is fine)**
I	**onion, sliced into thin rings**
I	**(16-ounce) can baked beans**
I	**red bell pepper, seeded and thinly sliced**
½	**cup barbecue sauce**

Use a 6-quart slow cooker. Spread out 4 long sheets of aluminum foil on the countertop. Place a hamburger patty in the center of each piece. Separate the onion rings with your fingers and place a few rings onto each patty. Spoon equal amounts of the baked beans on top, and add a few bell pepper slices. Top each stack with a spoonful of the barbecue sauce. Fold the foil over and crimp the sides to create a fully enclosed packet. Place these packets into the insert. Cover, and cook on low for 6 to 7 hours, or on high for 4 hours. Your meal is finished when the meat is no longer pink in the middle and the onion has reached desired tenderness.

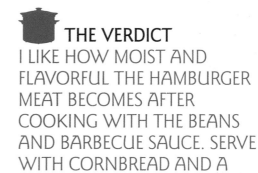 **THE VERDICT**
I LIKE HOW MOIST AND FLAVORFUL THE HAMBURGER MEAT BECOMES AFTER COOKING WITH THE BEANS AND BARBECUE SAUCE. SERVE WITH CORNBREAD AND A GREEN SALAD FOR A FULL MEAL.

SLOW COOKER SPANISH RICE

Serves 8 to 10

2	pounds lean ground beef or turkey
1	large onion, diced
4	garlic cloves, chopped
2	green bell peppers, seeded and diced
1	(28-ounce) can diced tomatoes, undrained
1	(8-ounce) can tomato sauce
2	teaspoons Worcestershire sauce (I use gluten-free)
3	teaspoons chili powder
1	teaspoon kosher salt
1	teaspoon ground black pepper
1	cup converted rice (see Note below)
1	cup water
	Suggested toppings: shredded Cheddar cheese, sour cream, chopped fresh chives

Use a 6-quart slow cooker. Add the meat, onion, and garlic to a large skillet over medium heat, and cook, stirring, until the meat is browned and the onion is translucent. Drain off any accumulated fat, and pour the meat mixture into the insert. Add the bell peppers, tomatoes, tomato sauce, Worcestershire sauce, chili powder, salt, and black pepper. Stir in the rice and water. Cover and cook on low for 6 to 7 hours, or on high for about 3 hours. Serve with a handful of shredded cheese, a dollop of sour cream, and sprinkle of chives, if desired.

Note: Converted rice is simply brown rice that has had the hull removed after being steamed, which keeps it from getting gummy in the pot.

THE VERDICT

SPANISH RICE WAS A SLEEPOVER STANDARD WHEN I SPENT THE NIGHT AT MY GRANDPARENTS' HOUSE. GRANDMA DIDN'T ADD WORCESTERSHIRE SAUCE OR FRESH BELL PEPPER, BUT SHE HAS TASTE-TESTED AND APPROVED THIS RECIPE. SO HAVE MY KIDS, WHO ADD SHREDDED CHEESE AND SOUR CREAM TO THE TOP.

SMOKY BRISKET WITH BAKED SWEET POTATOES

Serves 8

> **Aluminum foil**
> 1   **(4-pound) beef brisket, halved lengthwise**
> 1   **teaspoon celery seed**
> 1   **tablespoon garlic powder**
> 2   **teaspoons kosher salt**
> ¼   **cup liquid smoke**
> 4   **large sweet potatoes, washed and halved lengthwise**

Use a 6-quart slow cooker. Spread a length of aluminum foil out on your kitchen counter. Place the brisket in the middle of the foil. Sprinkle the celery seed, garlic powder, salt, and liquid smoke into the middle of the meat. Fold the meat together, and gather the edges of the foil to create a tight packet. Place into the insert. Wrap each sweet potato half in foil, and nestle each packet around the roast. Do not add water. Cover, and cook on low for 8 hours. Carefully remove the packets from the pot and open away from your face—the steam will be hot!

The Verdict

I love layered dinners such as this one. If you prefer not to use aluminum foil, you can make packets out of parchment paper, it'll work the same way. The leftover meat makes amazing sandwiches the next day!

SNOW PEAS BEEF

Serves 6

> 2   **pounds fajita meat (thinly sliced beef)**
> 1   **onion, sliced into thin rings**
> 2   **red bell peppers, seeded and thinly sliced**
> 6   **garlic cloves, thinly sliced**
> ½   **cup packed dark brown sugar**
> ½   **cup soy sauce (I use gluten-free)**
> ¼   **cup dry white wine or apple juice**
> 2   **tablespoons cold water**
> 1   **tablespoon cornstarch**
> 1   **(10-ounce) package frozen snow peas, thawed and drained**
> 2   **green onions, thinly sliced**
>   **Hot cooked white rice, for serving**

Use a 6-quart slow cooker. Place the meat into the insert, and add the onion, separating the rings with your fingers. Add the bell peppers and garlic. Stir in the sugar, soy sauce, and wine. Cover, and cook on low for 5 to 6 hours, or on high for about 3 hours. In a small bowl, whisk together the water and cornstarch to make a slurry, then stir the mixture into the insert to thicken the juice. Add the snow peas and green onions. Cover, and cook on high for 45 minutes, or until the snow peas are fully hot and have begun to slightly wilt. Serve over rice.

The Verdict

I can't wait to make this again. It tastes just like our favorite restaurant's version of this dish, but without being loaded down with oil or gluten. We like to eat this on a blanket in front of the TV in true takeout fashion.

SUNDAY BEEF BRISKET

Serves 6

I	**(4-pound) beef brisket**
¼	**cup packed dark brown sugar**
2	**tablespoons paprika**
2	**tablespoons onion powder**
I	**tablespoon ground cumin**
I	**tablespoon chili powder**
I	**tablespoon kosher salt**
½	**teaspoon ground black pepper**
I	**red onion, cut into thin rings**
4	**baking potatoes, peeled and cut into chunks**
3	**large carrots, cut into 2-inch chunks**
3	**stalks celery, cut into 2-inch chunks**

Use a 6-quart slow cooker. Place the brisket into the insert. In a small bowl, prepare the spice rub by combining the sugar, paprika, onion powder, cumin, chili powder, salt, and pepper. Rub this evenly all over the meat—flipping it over a few times to get good coverage. Add all the vegetables on top. Do not add water. Cover, and cook on low for 8 to 10 hours, or until the meat breaks apart easily with a fork.

 The Verdict

This smoky meat will quickly become a family favorite. I like to prepare the spice rub and cut the vegetables the night before, then plop it all into the slow cooker before leaving the house for the day.

SWEET-AND-SOUR POT ROAST

Serves 6

I	**(4 -pound) beef rump or chuck roast**
2	**onions, sliced into thin rings**
I	**(14.5-ounce) can diced tomatoes, undrained**
½	**cup ketchup**
¼	**cup packed dark brown sugar**
¼	**cup soy sauce (I use gluten-free)**
4	**garlic cloves, diced**
	Hot mashed or baked potatoes, for serving

Use a 6-quart slow cooker. Put the roast into the insert, and add the onions, separated into rings. In a medium bowl, combine the tomatoes, ketchup, sugar, soy sauce, and garlic. Pour this sauce evenly over the top of your roast. Cover, and cook on low for 8 hours, or until the meat has relaxed and begun to lose shape. Serve with mashed or baked potatoes.

 The Verdict

My kids love the tangy sauce that this roast is cooked in. It tastes like a chunky sweet barbecue sauce—the kids use their fingers to lick it up. If you'd like your whole meal cooked in the pot, feel free to add quartered potatoes and some cut carrots.

TACO CASSEROLE

Serves 6

1	**pound lean ground beef or lamb**
½	**cup of water**
1	**(1-ounce) packet taco seasoning (for homemade, see page 28)**
4	**to 6 corn tortillas**
1	**(15-ounce) can refried beans**
⅓	**cup sliced pickled jalapeño peppers**
3	**cups shredded Mexican blend cheese**
	Salsa or taco sauce, for serving (optional)

Use a 4-quart slow cooker. Add the meat to a large skillet over medium heat and cook, stirring, until the meat is browned. Drain off any accumulated fat. Add the water and the taco seasoning to the skillet and stir well. Add a large spoonful of the seasoned meat into the insert. Top with a layer of tortillas (you may need to tear them to get a full layer). Smear on some of the refried beans, sprinkle on a few jalapeño slices, and add a handful of the cheese. Repeat the layers until you run out of ingredients. Cover, and cook on low for 5 hours, or on high for about 3 hours. Unplug the cooker and let it sit with the lid off for about 10 minutes before serving. Top with salsa or taco sauce, if desired.

 THE VERDICT
THIS IS A GREAT KID-PLEASING MEAL. I USE MILD JALAPEÑOS, WHICH AREN'T TOO SPICY FOR MY KIDS. IF YOU ARE NERVOUS ABOUT THE HEAT, YOU CAN LEAVE THEM OUT AND USE SLICED OLIVES INSTEAD.

TAMALES IN CORN HUSKS

Makes about 20

20   **large dried corn husks (available at Mexican grocers)**
4   **cups masa harina (corn flour; naturally gluten-free)**
2½ **cups beef broth**
1⅓ **cups vegetable shortening**
2   **teaspoons baking powder**
1   **teaspoon kosher salt**
     Shredded Beef (see page 174) or your own favorite filling, cooled

Use a 6-quart slow cooker. Soften the corn husks by submerging them in a bowl of hot water until they are pliable. Beat the masa, broth, shortening, baking powder, and salt in a large bowl with a handheld mixer until the dough is light and fluffy. Check the dough by pinching off a small ball and dropping it into a glass of water. If the dough floats, it is done. If your dough doesn't float, continue beating with the hand mixer.

Take a golf ball–size piece of dough and spread it into a wet corn husk. The dough should be about ¼ inch thick—you should not be able to see the husk through the dough. Add a spoonful of the meat filling, and carefully fold the corn husk in half until the masa meets together to form an enclosed packet. Fold the rest of the corn husk around the tamale, and place it seam-side down into the insert. (As an option, you can use a thin strand of the corn husks to tie the tamale closed, as we did in the photograph.) Repeat the filling and folding process until you run out of ingredients.

Cover, and cook on high for 4 to 6 hours, or until a tester tamale looks and tastes done (it'll be brown and fully baked). I begin checking my tamales at 4 hours and then recheck every 30 to 45 minutes (it's okay to unwrap and rewrap the same one to check).

THE VERDICT

I FEEL VERY DOMESTIC MAKING HOMEMADE TAMALES. THE KIDS LIKE TO HELP, AND ALTHOUGH MASA GETS TRACKED ALL THROUGH THE HOUSE, IT'S A FUN ACTIVITY TO DO TOGETHER. IF YOU'D LIKE TO MAKE A BIG BATCH AND FREEZE YOUR TAMALES, WRAP THEM TIGHTLY IN WAXED PAPER, AND THEN IN PLASTIC WRAP TO KEEP FROM GETTING FREEZER BURN. REHEAT IN THE MICROWAVE.

TANDOORI BEEF WITH SWEET POTATO

Serves 6 to 8

2	medium sweet potatoes, peeled and cut into 1-inch chunks
1	red onion, cut into wedges
4	pounds beef stew meat
8	garlic cloves, coarsely chopped
1	teaspoon ground coriander
1	teaspoon ground cumin
1	teaspoon ground allspice
1	teaspoon kosher salt
½	teaspoon ground cinnamon
¼	to ½ teaspoon cayenne pepper
1	cup plain yogurt
	Hot cooked white or brown basmati rice, for serving

Use a 6-quart slow cooker. Put the sweet potatoes and onion into the insert. In a large zippered plastic bag, toss the beef, garlic, and all the seasonings until the meat is fully coated. Pour the contents of the bag into the insert. Cover, and cook on low for 7 to 8 hours, or on high for 4 to 5 hours. The meat is finished when it is fork-tender, and begins to lose its shape. Stir in the plain yogurt before serving over rice.

 THE VERDICT

IT'S TAKEOUT AT HOME! THIS MEAL HAS ALL THE FLAVOR AND CONVENIENCE OF A TAKEOUT DINNER FOR ABOUT A SIXTH OF THE PRICE.

TEXAS-STYLE BRISKET

Serves 6

FOR THE MARINADE

1	(5- to 6-pound) beef brisket
½	cup beef broth
¼	cup Worcestershire sauce (I use gluten-free)
3	garlic cloves, minced
1	tablespoon chili powder
1	teaspoon kosher salt
1	teaspoon ground black pepper

FOR THE SAUCE

1	onion, sliced into thin rings
1	cup ketchup
½	cup molasses
4	garlic cloves, thinly sliced
2	tablespoons apple cider vinegar
1	teaspoon ground mustard
1	teaspoon chili powder
1	teaspoon paprika

Use a 6-quart slow cooker. Cut your brisket in half, and place both pieces in a large zippered plastic bag or sealable container. Add the broth, Worcestershire sauce, garlic, chili powder, salt, and pepper. Shake to evenly coat the meat, and refrigerate overnight, or for at least 6 hours. In the morning, dump the contents of the bag into the insert. Add all the sauce ingredients and stir to combine. Cover, and cook on low for 10 to 12 hours, or until the meat easily pulls apart with a fork.

 The Verdict

This tender, delicious brisket is full of flavor thanks to the overnight marinating. It then becomes even more juicy and delicious by simmering all day in the thick, yummy barbecue sauce.

THAI GLAZED MEATBALLS

Makes 24 meatballs

1	tablespoon olive oil
1½	pounds lean ground beef or turkey
8	garlic cloves, minced
¼	cup chopped fresh basil leaves
1	large egg
2	tablespoons dried minced onion
½	teaspoon ground black pepper
1	cup all-purpose flour (I use rice flour)
1	cup beef broth
¼	cup soy sauce (I use gluten-free)
1	lime, juiced
1	teaspoon crushed red pepper flakes

Use a 6-quart slow cooker. Rub the oil in the insert—you want it to glisten. In a large bowl, combine the meat, garlic, basil, egg, dried onion, and black pepper. Combine well—I always use my hands. Make golf ball–size meatballs and dredge in flour. Freeze the meatballs on a parchment-lined cookie sheet as outlined in the Not Your Mother's Meatballs (page 164).

After the meatballs have set in the freezer, place them one by one into the insert (don't just dump them in). In a glass measuring cup, whisk together the broth, soy sauce, lime juice, and red pepper flakes and pour this evenly over the top of the meatballs. Cover and cook on low for 5 hours, or until the meatballs have browned and are fully cooked.

The Verdict

I serve these tasty meatballs for dinner with a scoopful of sticky white rice, but they would also make an excellent appetizer for a dinner party.

TRADITIONAL CORNED BEEF AND CABBAGE

Serves 8

1	(4-pound) corned beef brisket with seasoning packet, trimmed
¼	cup packed dark brown sugar
¼	cup yellow mustard
6	red potatoes, washed and quartered
6	carrots, cut into 2-inch pieces
1	head cabbage, cut into wedges
4	stalks celery, cut into 1-inch pieces
1	cup water

Use a 6-quart slow cooker. Place the brisket into the insert. Empty the contents of the seasoning packet (peppercorns, bay leaf, coriander seeds) into a small bowl, and add the sugar and mustard. Stir to combine, and spread this mixture evenly over the top of the corned beef. Nestle all the vegetables on top and around the beef. Pour in the water. Cover, and cook on low for 8 hours, or on high for about 5 hours. The meat should pull apart easily with a fork.

 The Verdict

My husband really likes his cabbage and vegetables cooked with the beef for added flavor and authenticity. If you would prefer your vegetables to have more of an al dente texture, add the carrots, celery, and cabbage during the last 2 hours of slow cooking on low, or the last hour of slow cooking on high.

TRIPLE-THREAT CRANBERRY BRISKET

Serves 8 to 10

1	(5-pound) beef brisket
1	onion, diced
4	garlic cloves, minced
1	(16-ounce) can whole-berry cranberry sauce
½	cup cranberry juice cocktail
¼	cup soy sauce (I use gluten-free)
¼	cup dried cranberries
	Hot mashed potatoes, for serving

Use a 6-quart slow cooker. Place the brisket into the insert. Add the onion and garlic. In a medium bowl, mix together the cranberry sauce, juice, soy sauce, and dried cranberries. Pour this combination evenly over the top of the meat. Cover, and cook on low for 8 to 10 hours, or on high for about 6 hours. The meat is finished when it has begun to lose its shape and can pull apart easily with a fork. Serve over mashed potatoes with a spoonful of the sauce.

 The Verdict

I came up with this recipe because I was doing an ad campaign for cranberry juice. I served this meat at a dinner party, and all the guests (six adults, nine children) loved the meat. We also made totally awesome cranberry martinis—but you're going to have to e-mail me for that recipe. . . .

ZESTY HORSERADISH MEATLOAF

Serves 6

1	**pound ground beef**
1	**pound ground pork**
1	**onion, diced**
1	**green bell pepper, seeded and diced**
1	**cup rolled oats (I use a certified gluten-free variety)**
1	**large egg**
2	**tablespoons prepared horseradish**
¼	**cup ketchup**

Use a 6-quart slow cooker with an inserted 9 x 5 x 3-inch metal or glass loaf pan. This is a 2-day process. The night before you'd like to cook the meatloaf, combine the beef, pork, onion, bell pepper, oats, egg, and horseradish in a large bowl (I use my hands) until fully mixed. Coat the inside of your baking pan with cooking spray, and press the meat mixture into the loaf pan. Use a pastry brush to paint the top of the meatloaf with the ketchup. Wrap with plastic wrap, and place the pan into the refrigerator overnight—or for 6 to 8 hours. In the morning, unwrap the loaf pan and place it into the insert. Cover, and cook on low for 6 to 8 hours, or on high for 3 to 5 hours. Test for doneness with a knife—it should come out clean (or check with a meat thermometer to ensure the meat has reached an internal temperature of at least 145°F).

 **THE VERDICT**
THIS MEATLOAF WAS E-MAILED TO ME BY A READER WHO PREFERS TO STAY ANONYMOUS. SHE WRITES THAT THE OVERNIGHT MARINATING IS WHAT REALLY MAKES THE HORSERADISH FLAVOR "POP." I AGREE! I LOVED EVERYTHING ABOUT THIS MEATLOAF, AND WILL BE TRYING THE MARINATING OVERNIGHT TRICK AGAIN. IT ALSO MAKES THE EARLY MORNING "QUICK-THROW-SOMETHING-IN-THE-SLOW-COOKER-BECAUSE-THE-AFTERNOON-IS-GOING-TO-BE-BONKERS" MORE MANAGEABLE!

PORK

APPLE HAM (CROCK) POT PIE

Serves 4

2   cups diced cooked ham
2   Granny Smith apples, peeled and diced
I   large sweet potato, peeled and diced
2   tablespoons dark brown sugar
I   teaspoon curry powder
½   teaspoon kosher salt
I   cup pancake mix (I use gluten-free)
I   cup milk
2   tablespoons butter, melted
½   teaspoon ground mustard
½   teaspoon ground ginger

Use a 4-quart slow cooker. In the insert, toss together the ham, apples, sweet potato, sugar, curry powder, and salt. In a medium bowl, combine the pancake mix, milk, butter, mustard, and ginger. Pour the batter over the top of the ingredients in the slow cooker. Cover, and cook on low for 6 hours, or on high for about 3½ hours. Uncover, and cook on high for 20 to 30 minutes to release condensation. The pot pie is finished when the baked topping is puffed and golden brown.

 The Verdict

I was eager to try this recipe—I had never heard of a ham pot pie before, and adapted a recipe I found on the Taste of Home website. The curry mixed with the apple, ham, and sweet potato is such a great flavor; you'll love it!

APPLE CHOPS

Serves 4

4   boneless pork chops
2   Granny Smith apples, peeled and sliced
½   cup packed dark brown sugar
¼   cup soy sauce (I use gluten-free)
¼   cup raisins
I   tablespoon ground cinnamon
½   teaspoon ground ginger

Use a 4-quart slow cooker. Place the chops into the insert. In a medium bowl, combine the apples, sugar, soy sauce, raisins, cinnamon, and ginger. Spoon this mixture evenly over the top of the chops. Cover, and cook on low for 6 to 7 hours, or on high for 3 to 4 hours.

 The Verdict

The apples break down a bit during slow cooking, which creates a beautiful sweet-and-salty sauce that has bursts of additional sweetness from the plump raisins. Delicious.

AU GRATIN POTATOES WITH HAM OR TURKEY

Serves 10

6   baking potatoes, such as Idaho or Russet, peeled and
    sliced ¼ inch thick
2   cups diced cooked ham or turkey
2   cups half-and-half
1½ cups 1% milk
1   cup shredded Cheddar cheese
½   cup butter, melted
1   white onion, diced
4   teaspoons ground mustard
2   teaspoons ground thyme
1½ teaspoons kosher salt
1   teaspoon ground black pepper
¼   teaspoon ground white pepper

Use a 6-quart slow cooker. Coat the insert well with
cooking spray. Put a third of the potato slices into the
insert, and add a handful of the meat. In a large bowl,
combine the remaining ingredients. Pour a third of this
mixture onto the meat and potatoes. Add another layer of
potatoes and repeat layers until you run out of ingredients.
Cover, and cook on low for 8 hours, or on high for about
5 hours. Uncover, and continue to cook on high for an
additional 30 minutes to release condensation.

 THE VERDICT
THIS IS A GREAT WAY TO USE
UP THE EXTRA LEFTOVER MEAT
FROM A HOLIDAY MEAL—IT
FEEDS AN ENTIRE HOUSEFUL
OF COMPANY, BUT DOESN'T
FEEL LIKE "LEFTOVERS." THE
INSPIRATION FOR THIS DISH
COMES FROM TWITTER
FOLLOWER @NANCYGEIZ WHO
WROTE THAT SHE AND HER
HUSBAND ARE FOODIES AND
LOVED THE CREAMY SAUCE.
WE DO, TOO!

AUTUMN HARVEST PORK LOIN

Serves 6

½   **cup packed dark brown sugar**
¼   **teaspoon ground cinnamon**
¼   **teaspoon dried thyme**
¼   **teaspoon ground sage**
I   **(2-pound) pork tenderloin**
2   **Granny Smith apples, peeled and thickly sliced**
I   **large butternut squash, peeled, seeded, and cubed**
I   **cup apple cider**

Use a 4-quart slow cooker. In a small bowl, combine the sugar, cinnamon, thyme, and sage. Rub this mixture evenly on all sides of the pork tenderloin. Place the meat into the insert. Nestle the apples and butternut squash around the meat. Pour on the apple cider. Cover, and cook on low for 6 to 7 hours. Remove the pork from cooker, and let it stand on a cutting board before slicing into ½-inch-thick pieces. Serve each slice topped with a spoonful of apples and squash.

 THE VERDICT

THIS DELICIOUS FALL DISH COMES FROM NIKKI IN COLUMBUS, OHIO. THANK YOU, NIKKI, FOR SHARING THE PORK RECIPE; IT'S PHENOMENAL. I LOVE HOW THE SQUASH GIVES THE MEAT A BEAUTIFUL AND SUBTLE BUTTERY FLAVOR.

BACON AND CARAMEL–STUFFED ACORN SQUASH

Serves 4

2	acorn squash, halved and seeded
½	pound bacon, diced
1	small onion, diced
½	cup packed dark brown sugar
½	cup chopped walnuts (optional)
2	tablespoons all-natural maple syrup
1	tablespoon butter, melted
½	teaspoon ground cinnamon
½	cup water

Use a 6-quart slow cooker. Place the acorn halves flesh-side up into the insert. In a large skillet over medium heat, add the bacon and onion and cook, stirring, until the bacon is crisp and the onion is translucent. Drain off the accumulated grease, and pour the bacon and onion into a medium bowl. Add the sugar, walnuts (if using), maple syrup, butter, and cinnamon. Stir to combine. Spoon the mixture evenly into each squash half. Pour the water around the base of the squash halves in the insert. Cover and cook on low for 5 hours, or on high for about 2½ hours.

 The Verdict

I got the idea for this dish by watching an episode of *Worst Cooks in America*. Bobby Flay told his team to think outside the box when it comes to flavor combinations and went on to wrap crisp bacon around a soft caramel. The smoky saltiness of the bacon works incredibly well with the sweet sugar and acorn squash. This dish is just as good with crumbled bulk sausage.

BACON RISOTTO

Serves 4

6	slices thick-cut bacon, diced
1	white onion, diced
2	garlic cloves, chopped
1½	cups Arborio rice, rinsed
4	cups chicken broth
½	cup freshly grated Parmesan cheese (to add at the very end)

Use a 4-quart slow cooker. In a large skillet over medium heat, add the bacon, onion, and garlic and cook, stirring until the bacon is crisp and the onion and garlic are translucent. Drain off most of the accumulated grease (retaining about 1 tablespoon) and pour the mixture into the insert. Add the rice, and swirl it around until the rice is nicely coated in oil. Pour in the broth. Cover, and cook on high for 2 to 4 hours, or until the rice is tender (check after 2 hours; it usually takes 2 hours, 45 minutes in my machine). Stir well, and add the cheese. Turn off the cooker, and let the risotto sit with the lid off for 10 minutes before serving.

 The Verdict

Bacon makes everything better and this risotto is no different. I love making risotto in the slow cooker—it turns out beautifully every time, and I'm free to wander out of the kitchen, an impossibility when making it on the stovetop.

BARBECUED COUNTRY-STYLE RIBS

Serves 6

5   to 6 pounds boneless country-style pork ribs
I   teaspoon kosher salt
I   teaspoon ground black pepper
I   teaspoon ground mustard
I   teaspoon ground ginger
I   (20-ounce) can crushed pineapple
½   cup ketchup
½   cup packed dark brown sugar
I   tablespoon Worcestershire sauce (I use gluten-free)

Use a 6-quart slow cooker. Place the ribs into the insert and rub the salt, pepper, mustard, and ginger into the meat. In a medium bowl, combine the pineapple, ketchup, sugar, and Worcestershire sauce. Pour this sauce evenly over the top of the ribs. Cover, and cook on low for 8 hours, or on high for about 5 hours. The meat should be quite tender at serving time—if it's not, cook for an hour or so longer.

 The Verdict

I love how lean country-style ribs are and this sauce can't be beat. Pair these ribs with fresh corn on the cob for a great picnic meal.

BARBECUED PORK AND CORNBREAD CASSEROLE

Serves 4

I   (1-pound) pork tenderloin, cut into thin strips
I   sweet potato, peeled and thinly sliced
I   (16-ounce) can creamed corn
2   cups barbecue sauce
1¼   cups all-purpose flour (I use a gluten-free flour mixture)
I   cup milk
¾   cup cornmeal
I   large egg, lightly beaten
I   teaspoon baking powder

Use a 4-quart slow cooker. Spray the insert well with cooking spray. Add the pork, sweet potato, creamed corn, and barbecue sauce, and stir well to combine the ingredients. In a large bowl, whisk together the flour, milk, cornmeal, egg, and baking powder. Spread this topping evenly over the top of the filling. Cover, and cook on low for 6 to 7 hours. The casserole is finished when the cornbread is set in the center and has begun to brown and pull away from the sides.

 The Verdict

Although I've included instructions to make a brand-new filling for this casserole, you can certainly use any leftover pulled pork you might have from a previous meal, or bring back to life pulled pork that has been hanging out in the depths of your freezer.

BREAKFAST FOR DINNER QUICHE

Serves 4

1 **pound bulk sausage, crumbled**
1 **onion, diced**
1 **red bell pepper, seeded and diced**
2 **potatoes, peeled and diced**
1 **cup milk**
1 **cup shredded Cheddar cheese**
½ **cup baking mix (I use a gluten-free baking mix)**
2 **large eggs**
¼ **teaspoon ground black pepper**

Use a 4-quart slow cooker. In a large skillet over medium heat, add the sausage and onion and cook, stirring, until the sausage is no longer pink, and the onion has become translucent. Drain off the accumulated fat, and pour the sausage mixture into the insert. Add the bell pepper and potatoes. In a large bowl, whisk together the milk, cheese, baking mix, eggs, and black pepper. Pour this evenly over the top of the ingredients in the cooker. Cover, and cook on low for 7 hours, or until casserole has set and browned on top and has begun to pull away from the sides. Uncover, and let sit for 10 to 15 minutes in the cooling slow cooker.

 **THE VERDICT**
THIS QUICK AND EASY CASSEROLE IS A FAMILY FAVORITE. MY KIDS CALL IT A QUICHE, AND ADAM DOUSES HIS IN SALSA AND AVOCADO SLICES. I HAVE MADE THIS AT ALL TIMES OF THE DAY, BUT LIKE TO CHOOSE THIS WHEN WE HAVE A BREAKFAST-FOR-DINNER NIGHT BECAUSE I DON'T NEED TO TURN INTO A SHORT-ORDER COOK!

BRATS IN BEER

Serves 12

1	dozen fresh bratwurst sausages (about 3 pounds)
2	red onions, cut into wedges
1	green bell pepper, seeded and thinly sliced
1	red bell pepper, seeded and thinly sliced
2	(12-ounce) bottles of beer (Redbridge by Anheuser-Busch is gluten-free)
2	cups water
12	hoagie rolls or French rolls, for serving (I use-gluten free)
	Suggested toppings: ketchup, brown mustard, sauerkraut, pickle relish

Use a 6-quart slow cooker. Put the sausages into the insert, and add the onions and bell peppers. Pour in the beer and water. Cover, and cook on low for 6 to 8 hours. Remove the brats from the pot, and grill lightly on an outdoor barbecue or indoor grill pan. Scoop the onion and pepper out of the pot, and place into a large skillet. Cook the onions and peppers, stirring occasionally, until they have begun to sweat and caramelize. Serve the brats on the rolls, topped with the onion and peppers and desired condiments.

THE VERDICT

ABI, ONE OF MY READERS, LIKES TO COOK THESE BRATS ON FATHER'S DAY, AND SAYS THEY ARE MELT-IN-YOUR-MOUTH DELICIOUS. YES, THEY MOST CERTAINLY ARE, THANKS ABI! THIS IS A GREAT WAY TO MAKE A BUNCH OF BRATS AT ONCE WITHOUT HEATING UP YOUR KITCHEN ON A HOT SUMMER DAY.

BROCCOLI AND SAUSAGE CASSEROLE

Serves 6

2	(16-ounce) packages frozen broccoli florets, thawed and drained
1	pound smoked sausage, thickly sliced
2	cups shredded Cheddar cheese
1	cup milk
4	large eggs, lightly beaten
⅓	cup baking mix (I use a gluten-free baking mix)
1	teaspoon kosher salt
½	teaspoon ground black pepper

Use a 4-quart slow cooker. Mix the broccoli and sausage together in the insert. In a large bowl, whisk together the cheese, milk, eggs, baking mix, salt, and pepper. Pour this mixture evenly over the top of the broccoli and sausage. Cover, and cook on high for 3 to 4 hours, or until casserole has browned on top and begun to pull away from the sides. Uncover, and continue to cook on high for an additional 20 minutes to release condensation.

 **THE VERDICT**
THIS QUICK AND EASY CASSEROLE COMES TOGETHER IN JUST MINUTES USING EVERYDAY INGREDIENTS.

BROWN SUGAR PORK LOIN WITH MUSTARD

Serves 4 to 6

I	(2- to 3-pound) pork tenderloin
½	cup packed dark brown sugar
¼	cup spicy brown mustard
I	teaspoon sea or kosher salt
⅓	cup lemon-lime soda

Use a 4-quart slow cooker. Place the tenderloin into the insert, and add the sugar, mustard, and salt. Flip the meat over a few times to evenly coat it with the sauce. Pour in the soda, and marvel at the bubbles. Cover, and cook on low for 6 to 8 hours, or on high for about 4 hours. I like to cook the meat for a very long time and cut it into long, tender, fall-apart strips.

The Verdict

This is a super-easy way to tenderize and flavor a sometimes-can-be-boring pork tenderloin. The flavors work well together and please picky palates. This is an excellent candidate for a slow cooker TV dinner, as described on page 10. If you like, throw in a few foil-wrapped regular or sweet potatoes on top of the tenderloin to create a full meal-in-a-pot.

BUTTERMILK BUTTON MUSHROOM CHOPS

Serves 4

4	boneless pork chops
2	tablespoons all-purpose flour
I	tablespoon chicken bouillon granules
I	teaspoon kosher salt
I	teaspoon ground black pepper
I	teaspoon dried basil
I	teaspoon dried thyme
I	pound fresh button mushrooms, halved
I	cup buttermilk
½	cup dry white wine

Use a 4-quart slow cooker. Put the chops into a large zippered plastic bag and toss with the flour, bouillon, salt, pepper, basil, and thyme. Once the chops are coated, place them into the insert. Put the mushrooms on top, and pour in the buttermilk and wine. Cover, and cook on low for 8 hours.

The Verdict

Not only is it fun to say the name (try it five times fast!), it's a fun dinner to eat. This is a great busy-weeknight meal, and the leftovers freeze beautifully. Serve with hot buttered noodles (I use gluten-free) and a green salad.

CHILI AND MAPLE GLAZED PORK TENDERLOIN

Serves 4

2	pounds pork tenderloin, quartered
2	tablespoons all-natural maple syrup
I	tablespoon prepared chili pepper sauce (sambal oelek)
I	teaspoon five-spice powder
½	teaspoon kosher salt
¼	teaspoon ground black pepper
2	green onions, thinly sliced

Use a 4-quart slow cooker. Put the pork into the insert. Add the maple syrup, chili sauce, five-spice powder, salt, and pepper. Stir well to disperse the spices. Toss in the green onions. Cover, and cook on low for 7 to 8 hours, or until the pork has reached desired tenderness.

 THE VERDICT
THIS MOIST, SWEET PORK HAS A TINY BIT OF LINGERING HEAT FROM THE CHILI PEPPER SAUCE. PORK TENDERLOIN HAS A TENDENCY TO DRY OUT, BUT COOKING IN THE SLOW COOKER REALLY TRAPS IN VALUABLE STEAM. IF YOU FIND THAT YOUR COOKER RELEASES A LOT OF STEAM WHILE COOKING, YOU CAN WRAP THE PORK IN A PIECE OF ALUMINUM FOIL TO KEEP IT NICE AND JUICY.

CHUTNEY CHOPS

Serves 6

6   bone-in pork chops
1   green apple, peeled and diced
1   cup diced dried apricot
1   onion, diced
2   stalks celery, thinly sliced
½   cup apple juice
½   cup packed dark brown sugar
1   tablespoon soy sauce (I use gluten-free)
    Cornstarch slurry made with 1½ tablespoons
    cornstarch and 2 tablespoons cold water (optional)
    Hot mashed potatoes or cooked rice, for serving

Use a 6-quart slow cooker. Place the chops into the insert. In a large bowl, combine the apple, apricots, onion, celery, apple juice, sugar, and soy sauce. Pour the chutney evenly onto the chops. Cover, and cook on low for 6 hours, or on high for about 4 hours. If you'd like, remove the meat from the pot and strain the fruit and vegetables, retaining the broth. Whisk your cornstarch slurry into the retained broth to thicken, if desired. Return the meat and the retained chutney to the pot and drizzle the broth over the top. Serve with mashed potatoes or over a bed of rice.

 The Verdict

Longtime reader Susan R. sent me her family's favorite pork chop recipe. She reports that she will use the same recipe but sometimes swap out the chops for a pork loin and shred the meat before serving. The meat is sweet and tangy—a great combination.

CITRUS DIJON PORK SHOULDER

Serves 8

1   (5-pound) pork butt or shoulder
½   cup Dijon mustard
¼   cup honey
1   tablespoon ground cumin
1   tablespoon dried oregano
1   orange, juiced
2   limes, juiced
    Hot cooked brown rice and lime wedges, for serving

Use a 6-quart slow cooker. Put the pork into the insert. In a small bowl, combine the mustard, honey, cumin, and oregano. Spread the mixture evenly over the top of the roast. Pour the juice of the orange and limes over the roast; no other liquid is required. Cover, and cook on low for 8 to 10 hours. Shred the meat with 2 large forks. Serve over rice with a lime wedge.

 The Verdict

Not only is the meat delicious as is over rice, it makes fabulous soft taco or enchilada filling the next day. You can add a dash of taco sauce or Tabasco if you'd like a peppery punch, or sprinkle on a few pickled jalapeño peppers. Yum.

CRANBERRY AND PEAR PORK ROAST

Serves 6

1	tablespoon olive oil
2	onions, cut into wedges
6	red potatoes, washed and quartered
1	cup baby carrots
3	tablespoons dark brown sugar
1	teaspoon five-spice powder
1	teaspoon kosher salt
1	(3-pound) pork tenderloin
2	pears, sliced (I don't peel, it's up to you)
½	cup sweetened dried cranberries
¼	cup honey
¼	cup soy sauce (I use gluten-free)
1	tablespoon apple cider vinegar

Use a 6-quart slow cooker. Add the oil to the insert, and add the onion, potatoes, and carrots. Swirl the vegetables around in the oil so they are well coated. In a small bowl, combine the sugar, five-spice powder, and salt. Rub this mixture on all sides of the pork. Place the pork on top of the vegetables in the insert. Sprinkle the pear and cranberries on top, and drizzle on the honey, soy sauce, and vinegar. Cover, and cook on low for 7 to 8 hours. Remove the pork and let it stand for 10 minutes before slicing. Serve with the vegetables from the pot and a spoonful of the accumulated sauce.

 THE VERDICT

THANK YOU TO ELIZABETH M. FOR SHARING THIS GREAT PORK RECIPE! THIS IS A FANTASTIC ALL-IN-ONE-POT MEAL. THE VEGETABLES COOK BELOW THE PORK, WHICH ALLOWS THE PORK TO RETAIN ITS SHAPE AND SLICE NICELY FOR SERVING. I LOVE HOW THE FIVE-SPICE POWDER AND CRANBERRIES WORK TOGETHER TO FLAVOR THE MEAT AND VEGETABLES.

DRY-RUB RIBS WITH BAKED APPLE CHUTNEY

Serves 4

1   rack baby back ribs (about 3 pounds)
1   tablespoon ground nutmeg
1   tablespoon paprika
1   tablespoon ground ginger
1   tablespoon kosher salt
1   teaspoon ground cinnamon
1½   teaspoons ground black pepper
4   Granny Smith apples, peeled and diced

Use a 6-quart slow cooker. Place the ribs into the insert (you may need to cut them in half to get them to fit completely). In a small bowl combine the nutmeg, paprika, ginger, salt, cinnamon, and pepper. Rub this spice blend evenly over all sides of the ribs. Dump the apple on top. Cover, and cook on low for 6 to 7 hours. Serve the ribs with a spoonful of cooked apple on top.

THE VERDICT

BAKED APPLES AND RIBS ARE A NATURAL PAIRING, AND THIS RECIPE COMBINES TWO FAVORITES IN ONE POT. RIB PURISTS WILL FIND THE PORK IS BEAUTIFULLY SEASONED WITHOUT NEEDING ADDITIONAL SAUCE. BUT IT'S UP TO YOU—IF YOU LIKE SAUCE, FEEL FREE TO SERVE YOUR OWN FAVORITE BARBECUE SAUCE.

EASY BRATS AND CORN DINNER

Serves 5

- I (10-ounce) package bratwurst sausage (about 5 links)
- I onion, diced
- I green bell pepper, seeded and diced
- I (16-ounce) package frozen white corn
- I tablespoon paprika

Use a 4-quart slow cooker. Add the bratwurst to a large skillet over medium heat and cook with the onion and bell pepper, stirring occasionally, until the meat is browned. While the brats are cooking, coat the inside of a 4-quart insert with cooking spray. Pour in the corn and paprika and stir well. Once the sausage has browned, pour the contents of the skillet onto the corn. Cover, and cook on low for 8 hours.

 The Verdict

Lindy K. wrote to me and shared her favorite way to cook bratwurst. The smokiness from the sausage really flavors the corn beautifully. This is a wonderful summertime dinner—we all love it. If you are gluten-free, take care to read the sausage ingredients carefully and do not purchase the "beer" bratwurst.

EJ'S PORK ADOBO

Serves 8

- I (5-pound) boneless pork shoulder
- I onion, thinly sliced
- 6 garlic cloves, smashed
- I cup soy sauce (I use gluten-free)
- I cup white vinegar
- 2 teaspoons oyster sauce
- 1½ teaspoons sugar
- I teaspoon black peppercorns
- 2 bay leaves
  Hot cooked white rice, for serving

Use a 6-quart slow cooker. Place the pork into the insert, and add the onion and garlic. In a medium bowl, whisk together the soy sauce, vinegar, oyster sauce, sugar, and peppercorns. Pour this sauce evenly over the top of the meat. Drop in the bay leaves. Cover, and cook on low for 10 to 12 hours, or until the pork shreds easily with a fork. Discard the bay leaves, and serve the meat over a pile of rice.

The Verdict

Our neighbor, EJ, is to thank for this fabulous adobo recipe. I love the minimal prep work and the huge flavor that comes from slow cooking all day in an amazing sauce. This is a great party dish—it can stretch to feed a bunch by supplying corn tortillas or taco shells.

FENNEL AND SAUSAGE SCRABBLE

Serves 4 to 6

1	pound smoked sausage, thickly sliced
1	red onion, diced
1	fennel bulb, diced
8	garlic cloves, peeled
4	red potatoes, washed and cubed
1	cup thinly sliced carrots
1	tablespoon dried Italian seasoning
½	cup chicken broth
¼	cup balsamic vinegar

Use a 6-quart slow cooker. Put the sausage into the insert, and add the onion, fennel, and garlic. Add the potato, carrots, and Italian seasoning. Stir in the broth and vinegar. Cover, and cook on low for 8 hours, or on high for about 5 hours. Serve in bowls—it'll be juicy!

 The Verdict

The fun tart twist of the vinegar is a nice surprise in this dish. The sausage and vegetables give off quite a bit of juice—serve with crusty bread or homemade rolls to sop up the yummy broth.

FUNERAL POTATOES

Serves 12

1	(26-ounce) bag frozen hash browns
1	onion, diced
2	cups diced cooked ham
2	cups shredded Cheddar cheese
1	cup frozen peas
1	cup milk
1	cup chicken broth
1	teaspoon kosher salt
1	teaspoon ground black pepper
1	teaspoon dried thyme
½	teaspoon ground mustard

Use a 6-quart slow cooker. Coat the insert with cooking spray. Pour in the hash browns. Add the onion, and stir well to combine. In a very large bowl, combine the ham, cheese, peas, milk, broth, salt, pepper, thyme, and mustard. Stir well, and pour evenly over the top of the potatoes in the cooker. Cover, and cook on low for 7 hours, or until cooked through. Take the lid off, and cook on high for an additional 20 to 30 minutes to release steam and allow the potatoes on top to brown.

 **The Verdict**

I've never had funeral potatoes, but gave them a try at the urging of one of my readers, Kathy, who says that she eats them at weddings, too. This is a great potluck dish; it feeds a lot and can stay on the "warm" setting for quite a while.

GARLIC PORK ROAST WITH BALSAMIC VINEGAR

Serves 6 to 8

3	**pounds pork tenderloin**
2	**tablespoons olive oil**
8	**garlic cloves, minced**
2	**tablespoons balsamic vinegar**
2	**teaspoons kosher salt**
½	**teaspoon ground black pepper**

Use a 6-quart slow cooker. Place the tenderloins in the middle of a large piece of aluminum foil (I place them together, but you can make 2 bundles if you prefer). In a small bowl, combine the oil, garlic, vinegar, salt, and pepper to create a paste. Spread this paste evenly over the tenderloins. Fold the foil over and crimp the sides tightly to form a fully enclosed packet. Place this foil bundle into the insert. Cover, and cook on low for 7 hours, or on high for 4 to 5 hours. Carefully remove the foil packets from the cooker and place on a cutting board. Let the meat sit for 10 minutes before unwrapping and slicing.

 THE VERDICT
THIS PORK WAS ADAPTED FROM A RECIPE ON KITCHENCONFIDANTE.COM AND WORKS BEAUTIFULLY IN THE SLOW COOKER. THE FOIL WRAP SEALS IN THE JUICE AND I LOVED HOW THE VINEGAR AND GARLIC FLAVORED THE MEAT. SERVE WITH ROASTED OR MASHED POTATOES.

GINGER ALE HAM
(OR HONEY CITRUS HAM)

Serves 8

1	**(6- to 7-pound) bone-in spiral-cut smoked ham**
¼	**cup honey**
¼	**cup spicy brown mustard**
¼	**teaspoon ground ginger**
¼	**teaspoon ground cloves**
¼	**teaspoon ground cinnamon**
1	**orange, juiced**
1	**lemon, juiced**
1	**lime, juiced**
1	**cup ginger ale**

Use a 6-quart slow cooker. Unwrap the ham, and discard the flavor packet. Place the ham into the insert. In a small bowl, combine the honey, mustard, ginger, cloves, and cinnamon. Smear this paste on top of the ham, allowing some to drip in between the slices. Pour the juice and add a bit of the pulp of the orange, lemon, and lime into the same bowl and swirl around to get the last of the "good stuff." Pour this into the insert, and top with the ginger ale. Cover, and cook on low for 6 hours, or on high for about 3 hours.

THE VERDICT

OH GOSH, THIS IS A GREAT HAM. THE HONEY MIXED WITH THE MUSTARD AND CITRUS PULP REALLY MAKES IT SPECIAL—I REALLY LIKE HOW IT'S NOT GREASY OR OVERLY SWEET. WE SERVED THIS HAM TO SEVEN CHILDREN, AND THEY ALL LOVED IT! SAVE THE HAM BONE FOR SPLIT PEA SOUP (PAGE 45).

GARLIC TOMATO PORK CHOPS

Serves 4

4	bone-in pork chops
I	(6-ounce) can tomato paste
I	tablespoon Worcestershire sauce (I use gluten-free)
I	tablespoon apple cider vinegar
I	tablespoon dried Italian seasoning
½	teaspoon crushed red pepper flakes
I	head garlic, peeled (about I0 cloves)

Use a 4-quart slow cooker. Place the chops into the insert. In a small bowl, combine the tomato paste, Worcestershire sauce, vinegar, Italian seasoning, and red pepper flakes. Smear this mixture on top of the chops (it will be quite thick). Toss in the garlic cloves. Cover, and cook on low for 6 to 7 hours, or on high for about 4 hours.

 THE VERDICT

THERE IS VERY LITTLE MOISTURE IN THIS DISH, BUT DON'T LET IT DETER YOU. NEWER SLOW COOKERS WORK WELL TO TRAP ALL THE STEAM AND CONDENSATION, RESULTING IN JUICY, FLAVORFUL CHOPS THAT DON'T NEED TO BATHE IN LIQUID ALL DAY LONG. THESE CHOPS WERE A HIT IN OUR HOUSE! SERVE WITH BAKED POTATOES AND A SIDE SALAD.

HAM AND POTATO BAKE

Serves 8

8   potatoes, washed and sliced ¼ inch thick
1   onion, diced
1   pound cooked ham, cubed
3   cups shredded Cheddar cheese
2   tablespoons butter
¼   cup all-purpose flour (I use rice flour)
1   cup milk
1   cup chicken broth
½   teaspoon kosher salt
½   teaspoon ground black pepper

Use a 6-quart slow cooker. Spread a layer of the potato slices onto the bottom of the insert, and sprinkle with a bit of the onion. Add a handful of ham, and top with ½ cup of the cheese. Continue stacking layers until you run out of potatoes, onion, ham, and cheese. In a small saucepan over low heat, melt the butter, and then stir in the flour to make a roux. Whisk in the milk, broth, salt, and pepper until fully combined. Pour this evenly over the top of the ingredients in the slow cooker. Cover, and cook on low for 6 to 7 hours, or until potatoes are brown on the edges, and bite-tender. Let sit, uncovered and unplugged, for 10 minutes before serving.

 The Verdict

This is a great meal-in-a-pot. I love how creamy and delicious the potatoes become and how I can control the fat content by using low or nonfat milk. This is marvelous comfort food, and a great potluck candidate.

HAPPY KID CHOPS

Serves 4

4   bone-in pork chops
1   onion, thinly sliced
4   garlic cloves, minced
½   cup soy sauce (I use gluten-free)
¼   cup honey
¼   cup chili sauce (in the ketchup aisle)
1   teaspoon curry powder

Use a 4-quart slow cooker. Place the chops into a zippered plastic bag, and add all the remaining ingredients. Seal the bag well and shake. Pour the contents of the bag into the insert. Cover, and cook on low for 5 hours, or on high for about 3½ hours.

 The Verdict

The little bit of curry powder gives these chops a smoky and exotic flavor—it's just present enough to cause you to take notice. My kids and their friends love these chops. I've taken to just calling them "your favorite pork chops."

HOT AND SPICY HAM

Serves 10 to 12

1	**(7- to 8-pound) bone-in spiral-cut ham**
½	**cup packed dark brown sugar**
¼	**cup prepared horseradish**
1½	**teaspoons kosher salt**
1	**teaspoon ground ginger**
1	**(12-ounce) can cola**

Use a 6-quart or larger slow cooker. Put the ham into the insert. In a small bowl, combine the sugar, horseradish, salt, and ginger. Rub this mixture evenly over the top of the ham. Carefully pour the soda around the base of the ham, taking care not to "wash" away the paste on top. Cover, and cook on low for 6 to 8 hours. Let the ham rest on a cutting board for 15 to 20 minutes before carving.

The Verdict

The horseradish and ginger do a great job of balancing out the sweet ham. This is a great change of pace from an over-the-top sweet ham; I loved it. Save a pound of your cooked meat for a Ham and Potato Bake (page 209)!

HUNGARIAN GOULASH (SLASH JAMBALAYA)

Serves 8

1	**pound pork or beef stew meat, cut into 1-inch cubes**
1	**pound smoked kielbasa sausage, thickly sliced**
2	**tablespoons Hungarian paprika**
1	**tablespoon olive oil**
1	**teaspoon caraway seed**
1	**teaspoon kosher salt**
½	**teaspoon ground black pepper**
2	**Yukon Gold potatoes, washed and diced**
1	**onion, chopped**
4	**garlic cloves, diced**
8	**ounces fresh button mushrooms, thinly sliced**
6	**cups chicken broth**
½	**cup chopped fresh flat-leaf parsley**
2	**tablespoons tomato paste**

Use a 6-quart slow cooker. Place the stew meat and kielbasa into the insert and toss with the paprika, oil, caraway seed, salt, and pepper. Add the vegetables. In a large bowl, whisk together the broth, parsley, and tomato paste. Pour this evenly over the meat and vegetables. Cover, and cook on low for 8 to 10 hours.

The Verdict

Long-time reader Dawn sent along her goulash recipe, and says that "it's more of a goulash/jambalaya, since we don't like green peppers and really like kielbasa, but now it's a family staple and is made about once a month, even if it's not the most authentic." Dawn, your goulash/jambalaya rocks. Thank you for sharing it.

ITALIAN SAUSAGE LASAGNA

Serves 6

1	**pound bulk Italian sausage, crumbled**
1	**onion, diced**
4	**garlic cloves, minced**
1	**(26-ounce) jar prepared pasta sauce (retain jar)**
½	**teaspoon fennel seed, crushed**
½	**teaspoon crushed red pepper flakes**
1	**(10-ounce) box lasagna noodles (I use brown rice noodles)**
1	**(15-ounce) container ricotta cheese**
8	**ounces fresh button mushrooms, thinly sliced**
1	**yellow bell pepper, seeded and thinly sliced**
1	**orange bell pepper, seeded and thinly sliced**
8	**ounces mozzarella cheese, sliced**
4	**cups shredded Italian blend cheese**
¼	**cup hot water**

Use a 6-quart slow cooker. In a large skillet over medium heat, add the sausage, onion, and garlic and cook, stirring, until the meat is browned. Drain off any accumulated fat. Stir in the pasta sauce (save the unrinsed jar!), fennel seed, and red pepper flakes. Scoop a spoonful of this meat mixture into the bottom of the insert. Add a layer of lasagna noodles (you may need to break a few to get a good fit). Smear ricotta cheese onto the noodles, and add a handful of the mushrooms and bell peppers and then a few slices of mozzarella cheese. Repeat the layers until you run out of ingredients. Top with the shredded Italian blend cheese. Add the water to the empty pasta sauce jar. Seal the jar, and shake well. Pour this saucy liquid evenly over the top. Cover, and cook on low for 6 to 7 hours, or until noodles are bite-tender and the cheese has fully melted and has begun to brown and pull away from the sides. Uncover, and let sit in the cooling cooker for 15 minutes before cutting.

 **THE VERDICT**

BETTER THAN A RESTAURANT'S—THIS LASAGNA IS MY ABSOLUTE FAVORITE. IT'S LOADED WITH CHEESE, VEGGIES, AND HAS A NICE SURPRISING HEAT FROM THE SAUSAGE AND PEPPER FLAKES THAT I MISS IN OTHER LASAGNAS.

KALUA PULLED PORK

Serves 6

4	**pounds pork butt or shoulder**
1	**tablespoon sea or Hawaiian salt**
1	**tablespoon liquid smoke**
	Warmed tortillas, toasted buns (I use gluten-free), or hot cooked rice, for serving

Use a 6-quart slow cooker. Put the pork into the insert and sprinkle the salt on top. Pour in the liquid smoke. Flip the meat over a few times with kitchen tongs to get the salt and liquid smoke on all sides. Cover and cook on low for 10 hours, or until the meat completely falls apart. Shred well, and serve in tortillas, on buns, or over a bed of rice.

 **THE VERDICT**
I ALWAYS MISTAKENLY THOUGHT KALUA PORK HAD KAHLÚA LIQUEUR IN IT, AND WAS SURPRISED THAT THE READER RECIPES I WAS SENT DIDN'T HAVE THE DRINK LISTED. AFTER GOOGLING, I LEARNED THAT IN HAWAIIAN, KALUA MEANS TO "COOK UNDERGROUND IN AN OVEN." YOU LEARN SOMETHING NEW EVERY DAY!

LEMON PORK CHOPS

Serves 4 to 6

- 1   onion, sliced into thin rings
- 4   to 6 pork chops
- 2   lemons, juiced
- ¼   cup packed dark brown sugar
- ¼   cup ketchup
- ½   teaspoon kosher salt
- ¼   teaspoon ground black pepper
       Hot mashed potatoes or cooked brown rice, for serving

Use a 4-quart slow cooker. Separate the onion rings and place into the insert. Place the meat on top. In a small bowl, combine the lemon juice, sugar, ketchup, salt, and pepper. Pour this sauce evenly over the top. Cover, and cook on low for 5 to 6 hours, or on high for 3 to 4 hours. Serve with mashed potatoes or rice.

🍲 The Verdict

This is a simple, kid-pleasing pork chop recipe. If you'd like even more of a pronounced lemon flavor, you can squeeze on a bit more at the table, but we like it just as it is.

LEMON PORK TENDERLOIN

Serves 4 to 6

- 1   (2-pound) pork tenderloin
- 2   lemons, juiced
- ¼   cup soy sauce (I use gluten-free)
- 6   garlic cloves, minced
- 2   tablespoons Worcestershire sauce (I use gluten-free)
- 1   tablespoon extra-virgin olive oil
       Cornstarch slurry: 1 teaspoon cornstarch whisked into 2 teaspoons cold water (optional)
       Hot cooked rice, for serving

Use a 4-quart slow cooker. Place the pork into a zippered plastic bag, and add the lemon juice, soy sauce, garlic, Worcestershire sauce, and oil. Seal, and refrigerate overnight (6 to 8 hours). In the morning, dump the bag contents into the insert, and cook on low for 7 to 8 hours. If you'd like to thicken the crock drippings before serving, you can whisk in the cornstarch slurry. Slice the meat thinly and serve with rice.

🍲 The Verdict

I really liked the light, lemony flavor of this pork tenderloin. I served it with quinoa pilaf, made in the rice cooker by replacing the water with chicken broth, and added a handful of slivered almonds.

MAPLE-COFFEE PULLED PORK

Serves 8

1	**(4- to 5-pound) pork shoulder or butt**
2	**onions, sliced into thin rings**
2	**tablespoons ground coffee (not instant)**
2	**tablespoons dark brown sugar**
1	**tablespoon garlic powder**
2	**teaspoons chili powder**
2	**teaspoons kosher salt**
	Hot cooked rice or toasted buns, for serving

FOR THE MAPLE-COFFEE BARBECUE SAUCE

½	**cup ketchup**
½	**cup apple cider vinegar**
½	**cup all-natural maple syrup**
½	**cup cold brewed coffee**
2	**tablespoons Tabasco sauce**
2	**tablespoons spicy brown mustard**
½	**teaspoon kosher salt**

Use a 6-quart slow cooker. Put the pork into the insert, and add the onions. In a small bowl, combine the coffee, sugar, garlic powder, chili powder, and salt, and then smear the mixture on all sides of the meat. Cover, and cook on low for 8 to 10 hours, or until the pork has lost shape and can be shredded easily with a fork. Meanwhile, in a medium bowl, stir together all the barbecue sauce ingredients. Drain the accumulated liquid from the cooker, and stir in the barbecue sauce. Reheat on high for 30 minutes, or until fully hot. Serve over a bed of rice or on buns.

 The Verdict

I got this recipe from Susan Russo, who writes the blog Food Blogga (foodblogga.blogspot.com). She shared this recipe with www.porkknifeandspoon.com, which is the recipe site run by the National Pork Board. I love how the meat cooks in the spice rub with no added liquid, then gets a huge blast of flavor from the awesome homemade barbecue sauce. Delicious!

MEMPHIS-STYLE DRY-RUB RIBS

Serves 4

4	**pounds baby back ribs**
2	**tablespoons dark brown sugar**
1	**tablespoon ground cumin**
1	**tablespoon paprika**
1	**teaspoon dried oregano**
1	**teaspoon kosher salt**
½	**teaspoon ground black pepper**
½	**teaspoon cayenne pepper**

Use a 6-quart slow cooker. Cut the racks in half to ensure a nice fit in the insert. In a small bowl, combine the sugar, cumin, paprika, oregano, salt, black pepper, and cayenne pepper. Rub this mixture into the ribs, and wrap the ribs tightly in aluminum foil. If you have time to do so, refrigerate this foil bundle overnight, or for about 8 hours. Place the foil packet into the insert. Cover, and cook on low for 8 hours.

The Verdict

I love the ease of these ribs. If you would prefer to forgo the foil and cook directly in the crock—that's fine, too. The foil helps to keep the steam and moisture close to the meat for extra tenderness, but it's not necessary—you'll still have phenomenal ribs without!

MEXICAN PULLED PORK

Serves 8

1	(3-pound) boneless pork butt or shoulder
2	tablespoons tomato paste
1	tablespoon ground cumin
1	tablespoon dried oregano
1	teaspoon kosher salt
½	teaspoon ground black pepper
2	onions, sliced into thin rings
1	(10-ounce) can tomatoes and chiles, undrained
1	(15-ounce) can corn, drained
1	(15-ounce) can black beans, drained and rinsed
1	cup chicken broth or beer
	Hot cooked rice or warmed corn tortillas, for serving
	Suggested toppings: sour cream, lime wedges, shredded Cheddar cheese

Use a 6-quart slow cooker. Put the pork into the insert. In a small bowl, stir together the tomato paste, cumin, oregano, salt, and pepper. Smear this concoction on all sides of the meat. Add the onions, tomatoes and chiles, corn, and beans. Stir in the broth. Cover, and cook on low for 8 to 10 hours, or until the pork pulls apart easily with a large fork. Serve as is with desired toppings, or serve over rice or wrapped in tortillas.

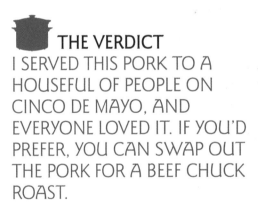 THE VERDICT
I SERVED THIS PORK TO A HOUSEFUL OF PEOPLE ON CINCO DE MAYO, AND EVERYONE LOVED IT. IF YOU'D PREFER, YOU CAN SWAP OUT THE PORK FOR A BEEF CHUCK ROAST.

MOO SHOO PORK

Serves 6

1	**(2-pound) boneless pork loin, cut into 4 pieces**
1	**cup hoisin sauce (see recipe below for gluten-free version)**
3	**garlic cloves, minced**
3	**green onions, thinly sliced, plus extra for garnish**
2	**teaspoons ground ginger**
1	**(16-ounce) package coleslaw mix**
3	**tablespoons rice wine vinegar**
2	**tablespoons brown sugar**
	Small tortillas or hot cooked white rice, for serving

Use a 4-quart slow cooker. Put the pork into the insert and add the hoisin sauce, garlic, green onions, and ginger. Toss each piece of pork a few times to fully coat with the sauce and spices. Cover and cook on low for 8 to 9 hours, or until the pork shreds easily with a fork. Meanwhile, in a large bowl combine the coleslaw with the vinegar and sugar. (As an option, you can briefly stir-fry the slaw in a skillet over medium heat, to combine the flavors.) Shred the pork completely, and serve in tortillas with a spoonful of the slaw and a tad more hoisin sauce, or spoon on top of a bed of white rice. Garnish with sliced green onions, if desired.

GLUTEN-FREE HOISIN SAUCE

¼	**cup gluten-free soy sauce**
2	**tablespoons creamy peanut butter**
1	**tablespoon honey**
2	**teaspoons rice wine vinegar**
2	**teaspoons sesame oil**
1	**teaspoon Asian hot sauce**

In a small bowl, whisk the ingredients together.

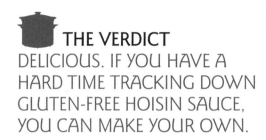

THE VERDICT
DELICIOUS. IF YOU HAVE A HARD TIME TRACKING DOWN GLUTEN-FREE HOISIN SAUCE, YOU CAN MAKE YOUR OWN.

NOT ANOTHER BORING COLA ROAST

Serves 6

1	**(3- to 4-pound) pork shoulder or butt**
1	**(7-ounce) can fire-roasted diced green chiles**
1	**(6-ounce) can tomato paste**
⅓	**cup packed dark brown sugar**
1	**tablespoon ground cumin**
1	**tablespoon garlic powder**
1	**teaspoon kosher salt**
½	**teaspoon ground chipotle chile**
1	**cup cola**

Use a 6-quart slow cooker. Put the pork into the insert. In a medium bowl, combine the chiles and tomato paste. Add the sugar, cumin, garlic powder, salt, and chipotle. Stir to combine, and spread this mixture on all sides of the pork roast. Pour in the cola. Cover, and cook on low 7 to 8 hours, or until the pork has begun to relax and fall apart.

THE VERDICT

I USED A PORK TENDERLOIN AND SLICED THE MEAT, BUT THIS SAUCE WOULD ALSO CREATE A MEAN PULLED PORK IF YOU USED A SHOULDER OR BUTT. THERE IS A BIT OF HEAT FROM THE CHIPOTLE POWDER, WHICH WAS THE PERFECT AMOUNT FOR OUR FAMILY. I SERVED OURS WITH MASHED POTATOES AND A CAESAR SALAD, AND MADE COLD SANDWICHES WITH THE LEFTOVERS THE NEXT DAY.

PEANUT BUTTER–GLAZED HAM

Serves 8

1   (6- to 7-pound) bone-in spiral-cut ham
¼   cup creamy peanut butter
¼   cup honey
2   tablespoons soy sauce (I use gluten-free)
3   garlic cloves, chopped
1   lime, juiced

Use a 6-quart slow cooker. Place the ham in the insert. In a small bowl, combine the peanut butter, honey, soy sauce, garlic, and lime juice. Smear this paste all over the ham. Lay a large piece of aluminum foil over the top of the ham, and push down the sides to cover the ham as best you can. Put the lid on, and cook on low for 6 hours, or until heated through. Carefully remove the foil. Let the ham sit for 20 minutes before carving.

 The Verdict

I first heard of putting peanut butter and ham together from watching an episode of Paula Deen's cooking show. I've done peanut butter pork chops and tenderloin, but this was the first time with a ham. We liked it! The salty peanut butter and soy sauce complement the sweet smoky ham quite nicely.

PEANUT BUTTER PORK CHOPS

Serves 4 to 6

1   onion, sliced into thin rings
4   garlic cloves, chopped
¾   cup creamy peanut butter
⅓   cup honey
⅓   cup soy sauce (I use gluten-free)
2   tablespoons seasoned rice wine vinegar
4   to 6 pork chops

Use a 4-quart slow cooker. Separate the onion rings and place in the insert. In a small bowl, combine the garlic, peanut butter, honey, soy sauce, and vinegar. Smear this mixture on top of the chops—it'll be pretty thick. Add the chops to the insert, cover, and cook on low for 5 to 6 hours, or on high for about 3 to 4 hours.

The Verdict

This recipe comes from Sandy, who shares that her three children "each eat their weight in these chops"—and I'd agree! All three of my own children really enjoyed their dinner. Adam added a bit of red chile pepper flakes to his own serving, and I enjoyed the leftover sauce on top of a bed of rice the next day for lunch.

PEANUT BUTTER THAI PORK

Serves 4 to 6

2   **pounds pork stew meat**
2   **red bell peppers, seeded and thinly sliced**
2   **green onions, thinly sliced**
4   **garlic cloves, thinly sliced**
⅓   **cup creamy peanut butter**
2   **limes, juiced**
¼   **cup soy sauce (I use gluten-free)**
¼   **cup packed dark brown sugar**
I   **tablespoon white wine vinegar**
     Hot cooked basmati rice, for serving

Use a 4-quart slow cooker. Place the pork into the insert, and add the bell peppers, green onions, and garlic. In a small bowl, whisk together the peanut butter, lime juice, soy sauce, sugar, and vinegar. Pour this sauce (it will be thick) evenly over the meat and vegetables. Cover, and cook on low for 7 to 8 hours. When the pork has reached desired tenderness (I like it to pull apart with a fork), stir well and serve over rice.

🍲 The Verdict

Put away your wallet, and stay away from the phone. There's no need to order in tonight, make this instead! If you'd like more of a crunch, or to dress up the plate for serving, you can add chopped peanuts, a lime wedge, and a few more green onion pieces before serving, but it's really not necessary.

PINEAPPLE-CRANBERRY PORK ROAST

Serves 6

4   **garlic cloves, minced**
I   **teaspoon ground allspice**
I   **teaspoon kosher salt**
½   **teaspoon ground black pepper**
I   **(4-pound) pork tenderloin or butt**
I   **(15-ounce) can cranberry sauce**
I   **(20-ounce) can crushed pineapple, drained**
     Hot mashed potatoes, for serving

Use a 6-quart slow cooker. Combine the garlic, allspice, salt, and pepper in a small bowl. Rub this spice mix evenly on all sides of the pork, and place the pork in the insert. In a large bowl, stir together the cranberry sauce and pineapple. Now pour this evenly over the top of the pork. Cover, and cook on low for 8 hours. Slice the meat and serve with mashed potatoes and a scoopful of the sauce.

🍲 The Verdict

The allspice, cranberry, and pineapple work together to create an awesome autumn-spiced pork. This freezes and reheats well.

PORK ROAST WITH APPLES

Serves 4

1	**(2- to 3-pound) boneless pork roast**
2	**tablespoons dark brown sugar**
1	**tablespoon herbes de Provence**
1	**tablespoon dried thyme**
½	**teaspoon kosher salt**
½	**teaspoon ground black pepper**
3	**Granny Smith apples, peeled and cubed**
4	**green onions, thinly sliced**
	Hot cooked rice or potatoes, for serving

Use a 4-quart slow cooker. Put the pork into the insert. In a small bowl, combine the sugar, herbes de Provence, thyme, salt, and pepper. Rub this mixture on the meat, covering all sides. Nestle the apples and green onions around the meat. Cover, and cook on low for 6 to 7 hours, or on high for about 4 hours. Slice the meat and serve with rice or potatoes with the cooked apples spooned over the top.

 **THE VERDICT**
THIS RECIPE COMES FROM MELONY, WHO WRITES THAT IT'S HER VERSION OF A "FANCIFIED PORK AND APPLESAUCE" ROAST. I LOVE THAT THE MEAT SIMMERS IN ITS OWN JUICES WITH THE FRESH APPLE. MAKE SURE THE COOKER SEALS WELL FOR THIS DISH—IF YOU DON'T HAVE BEADED UP CONDENSATION ON THE LID, PLACE A LAYER OF FOIL UNDER THE LID TO TRAP THE VALUABLE STEAM AND MOISTURE.

RANCH PACKET PORK CHOPS

Serves 4

4   pork chops (bone-in or boneless)
1   (1-ounce) packet ranch salad dressing mix
     (for homemade, see page 256)
1   tablespoon butter
3   tablespoons all-purpose flour
½   cup milk
½   cup chicken broth
¼   teaspoon kosher salt
¼   teaspoon ground black pepper
     Hot mashed potatoes or corn on the cob, for serving

Use a 4-quart slow cooker. Place the chops into the insert, and sprinkle with the salad dressing mix. Flip the chops over a few times to get the seasoning on all sides. In a small saucepan over medium heat, melt the butter and stir in the flour to make a roux. Whisk in the milk, broth, salt, and pepper. When your sauce ingredients are fully combined, pour evenly over the top of the chops. Cover, and cook on low for 6 to 7 hours, or on high for about 4 hours. Serve with mashed potatoes or corn on the cob.

THE VERDICT

MY KIDS COULD TRULY EAT THIS EVERY SINGLE DAY. THE ORIGINAL RECIPE THAT'S PRINTED ON THE SIDE OF THE SEASONING PACKET BOX CALLS FOR A CAN OF CREAM-OF-CHICKEN SOUP, BUT I LIKE OUR HOMEMADE VERSION BETTER. IT TASTES GREAT, IT'S QUICK TO WHIP TOGETHER, AND DOESN'T HAVE ANY UNPRONOUNCEABLE INGREDIENTS. IF YOU'D PREFER TO USE A HOMEMADE RANCH MIX, THE RECIPE IS ON PAGE 256.

SAUCY PORK CHOPS

Serves 4

4	**pork chops (bone-in or boneless)**
I	**onion, sliced into thin rings**
4	**garlic cloves, chopped**
¼	**cup barbecue sauce**
¼	**cup packed dark brown sugar**
¼	**cup ketchup**
2	**tablespoons soy sauce (I use gluten-free)**

Use a 4-quart slow cooker. Place the chops into the insert. Separate the onion rings and place on top. Add the garlic, barbecue sauce, sugar, ketchup, and soy sauce. Flip the chops over a few times to coat evenly with the sauce. Cover, and cook on low for 6 hours, or on high for about 3 hours.

The Verdict

This is such an easy and delicious sauce—I've used it on chicken thighs and beef strips successfully, as well. This is a great candidate for a slow cooker TV dinner: Assemble all the ingredients into a plastic zippered bag, then freeze. Thaw overnight in the fridge, then dump into the insert in the morning for an easy meal on a busy day. Serve this with mashed potatoes and a green salad.

SAUSAGE BALLS

Serves 4 for dinner; 8 as an appetizer

I	**pound bulk hot sausage**
I	**(8-ounce) package cream cheese, at room temperature**
I¼	**cups baking mix (I use a gluten-free baking mix)**

Use a 4-quart slow cooker. In a large bowl, combine all the ingredients until fully incorporated. Pinch off a 1-inch piece, and roll it into a ball. Place into the insert, and continue until you run out. It's okay to stagger-stack the meatballs; they will still cook. Cover, and cook on low for 6 hours, or on high for about 3 hours. Remove the meatballs with a large spoon and let them rest on a layer of paper towels for 10 to 15 minutes before serving. Serve hot, cold, or at room temperature.

The Verdict

Dan from Ontario e-mailed me this recipe last fall and declared it "the best crockpot thing ever." Dan shares that he has tripled this recipe and made enough of the meatballs to fill an 8-quart slow cooker. They're really good—I can see why you like them, Dan!

SMOKY BARBECUE COUNTRY RIBS

Serves 4

3   pounds baby back ribs or beef or boneless short ribs
½   cup packed dark brown sugar
1   teaspoon chili powder
1   teaspoon kosher salt
1   teaspoon ground black pepper
1   onion, thinly sliced
4   garlic cloves, chopped
1   (12-ounce) bottle chili sauce (in the ketchup aisle)
¼   cup balsamic vinegar
2   tablespoons Worcestershire sauce (I use gluten-free)
½   teaspoon Tabasco sauce
¼   teaspoon liquid smoke

Use a 6-quart slow cooker. Put the ribs in the insert. In a small bowl, combine the sugar, chili powder, salt, and pepper. Rub this mixture on all sides of the ribs. Toss in the onion and garlic. In the same small bowl, combine the chili sauce, vinegar, Worcestershire sauce, Tabasco, and liquid smoke. Pour evenly over the top. Cover, and cook on low for 8 hours, or until the meat is tender and pulls easily from the bone.

🍲 The Verdict

These are award-winning ribs. My friend Janet served these ribs at her work's annual potluck cook-off, and they took the top prize and earned an extra vacation day! There's a perfect combination of smoke, sweet, and spice—these ribs are finger-licking good.

SPAGHETTI BOLOGNESE

Serves 10

2   pounds ground beef
1   pound ground pork
2   yellow onions, diced
8   to 10 garlic cloves, minced
2   (15-ounce) cans diced tomatoes, undrained
2   (15-ounce) cans tomato sauce
1   pound fresh button mushrooms, thinly sliced
1½   tablespoons dried Italian seasoning
1   teaspoon kosher salt
½   teaspoon ground black pepper
2   pounds spaghetti (we use gluten-free corn or brown rice spaghetti)

Use a 6-quart slow cooker. In a large skillet over medium heat, add the beef, pork, onions, and garlic and cook, stirring, until the meat is browned. Drain off any accumulated fat, and pour the meat mixture into the insert. Add the tomatoes, tomato sauce, and mushrooms. Stir in the Italian seasoning, salt, and pepper. Cover, and cook on low for 8 to 10 hours. When the sauce is almost done, cook the spaghetti according to package directions until it is al dente. Serve the sauce over the hot spaghetti.

🍲 The Verdict

Yup, this is what spaghetti should taste like. The sauce is thick and rich with lots of chunks of meat and mushrooms. This makes a lot, and freezes very well.

SPICE-RUBBED PORK ROAST

Serves 4

1	**onion, sliced into thin rings**
1	**(2- to 3-pound) boneless pork roast**
2	**tablespoons dark brown sugar**
1	**tablespoon ground coriander**
1	**tablespoon paprika**
1	**teaspoon ground cumin**
1	**teaspoon anise seed**
1	**teaspoon kosher salt**
½	**teaspoon ground black pepper**
	Lime wedges, for serving (optional)

Use a 4-quart slow cooker. Separate the onion rings and place them into the insert. Place the meat directly on top. In a small mixing bowl combine the sugar, coriander, paprika, cumin, anise, salt, and pepper. Rub this mixture on all sides of the meat. Cover, and cook on low for 5 to 6 hours, or on high for about 4 hours. Your meat is finished when it shreds easily with a large fork. Squeeze a bit of lime onto each serving, if desired.

 THE VERDICT

THE PORK ROAST BAKES BEAUTIFULLY IN THE SLOW COOKER WITH NO LIQUID INGREDIENTS REQUIRED. IF YOU'D LIKE A COMPLETE MEAL IN THE CROCK, USE A LARGER MODEL AND ADD WHOLE POTATOES, WRAPPED IN FOIL. I LOVE THIS SPICE RUB—IT WOULD MAKE A HIKING BOOT TASTE GOOD. MY CHILDREN DIPPED THEIR MEAT INTO BARBECUE SAUCE, BUT THEY ALWAYS DO.

SPICY STICKY MUSTARD RIBS

Serves 4

3   to 4 pounds beef or pork ribs
¼   cup soy sauce (I use gluten-free)
¼   cup molasses
¼   cup prepared yellow mustard
¼   cup red wine vinegar
2   teaspoons Tabasco sauce

Use a 6-quart slow cooker. Put the ribs into the insert. In a small mixing bowl, combine the soy sauce, molasses, mustard, vinegar, and Tabasco sauce. Pour the sauce mixture evenly over the top of the ribs. Cover, and cook on low for 7 to 8 hours, or on high for about 4 hours. Your ribs are ready when they are no longer pink and the meat pulls easily from the bone.

 The Verdict

I love this tangy sauce—these ribs are not overly sweet, and pair well with baked sweet or brown potatoes.

TANDOORIED PORK CHOPS

Serves 4

4   pork chops
I   tablespoon ground cumin
I   teaspoon ground ginger
I   teaspoon ground coriander
I   teaspoon kosher salt
¼   teaspoon cayenne pepper
¼   teaspoon ground cloves
¼   teaspoon ground cardamom
I   (14.5-ounce) can diced tomatoes, undrained
I   cup plain yogurt

Use a 4-quart slow cooker. Place the pork chops into the insert. In a small bowl, combine the cumin, ginger, coriander, salt, cayenne pepper, cloves, and cardamom, and rub this mixture evenly into each chop. Pour the entire can of tomatoes evenly over the top. Cover, and cook on low for 6 to 7 hours, or until the chops are fully cooked and are bite-tender. Remove the chops from the cooker and set aside to keep warm. Stir in the plain yogurt, and recover. Heat on high for 30 minutes or until the sauce is hot. Serve the chops with a ladleful of sauce over the top.

 **The Verdict**

I was worried that this seasoning would be too spicy for my kids, but I shouldn't have worried—they each ate a good amount. The tomato-yogurt sauce provided the perfect amount of tang to stamp out the bit of fire from the spice rub.

TWICE-CROCKED STUFFED POTATOES

Serves 2

4	baking potatoes, such as Russet or Yukon Gold
½	cup diced cooked bacon or ⅓ cup imitation bacon bits
¼	cup milk
2	green onions, thinly sliced
2	tablespoons butter, melted
I	teaspoon Dijon mustard
I	cup shredded sharp Cheddar cheese
½	teaspoon kosher salt
¼	teaspoon ground black pepper
¼	teaspoon paprika

Use a 6-quart slow cooker. Coat the insert well with cooking spray. Scrub the potatoes well with a brush, and slice in half. Place flesh-side up into the prepared insert. Cover, and cook on low for 8 hours, or on high for about 5 hours. While the potatoes are cooking, mix the remaining ingredients together in a large bowl, and refrigerate. When the potatoes are finished, carefully remove from the cooker, and scrape out the flesh, leaving the skin. Combine the cooked potato with the refrigerated ingredients. Spoon this mixture back into the potato skins, and place the stuffed potatoes back into the slow cooker. Cover, and cook on high for I hour, or until the potato is fully hot, and the cheese is melted.

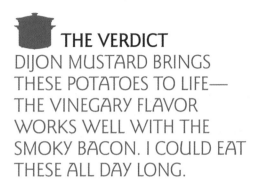

THE VERDICT
DIJON MUSTARD BRINGS THESE POTATOES TO LIFE— THE VINEGARY FLAVOR WORKS WELL WITH THE SMOKY BACON. I COULD EAT THESE ALL DAY LONG.

TAMARIND AND HONEY GLAZED RIBS

Serves 4

5	pounds baby back ribs (cut so they fit into the insert)
½	cup honey
¼	cup ketchup
2	tablespoons soy sauce (I use gluten-free)
2	teaspoons tamarind concentrate or I teaspoon lime juice mixed with I teaspoon sugar
½	teaspoon crushed red pepper flakes

Use a 6-quart slow cooker. Spread a large length of aluminum foil onto your countertop. Place the ribs in the center of the foil. In a small bowl, combine the honey, ketchup, soy sauce, tamarind concentrate, and red pepper flakes. Brush the sauce all over the ribs. Fold the foil over and crimp the sides to make a fully enclosed packet (you may need to have a few packets in order for the ribs to fit inside the insert). Cover, and cook on low for 7 to 8 hours, or on high for 4 to 5 hours. Remove the foil packet, and carefully unwrap—the steam will shoot out, so be careful!

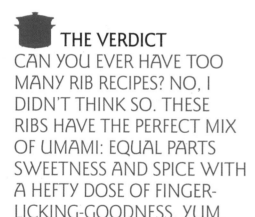 **THE VERDICT**

CAN YOU EVER HAVE TOO MANY RIB RECIPES? NO, I DIDN'T THINK SO. THESE RIBS HAVE THE PERFECT MIX OF UMAMI: EQUAL PARTS SWEETNESS AND SPICE WITH A HEFTY DOSE OF FINGER-LICKING-GOODNESS. YUM.

SANDWICHES

AMERICAN FOOTBALL BARBECUE BEEF SANDWICHES

Serves 12

1   (4-pound) beef chuck roast
1   (20-ounce) bottle ketchup
1   (15-ounce) can tomato sauce
1   cup brewed coffee, at room temperature
1   onion, diced
⅓   cup packed dark brown sugar
2   tablespoons soy sauce (I use gluten-free)
1   cup sweet pickle relish
12   soft hamburger buns (I use gluten-free)
8   ounces Cheddar cheese, thinly sliced (optional)

Use a 6-quart slow cooker. Put the roast into the insert, and add the ketchup, tomato sauce, coffee, onion, sugar, and soy sauce. Stir in the relish. Cover, and cook on low for 8 to 10 hours, or until the meat shreds easily with a fork. Shred completely, and serve in the buns, topped with slices of cheese, if desired.

 The Verdict

These sandwiches are the best part of the game (any game) for me. Kathy from South Carolina sent me this recipe and I was blown away by the ingredient list. This is a great sandwich! Our seven-year-old friend up the street said, "You should make sure to tell the cooker people how good these are."

BARBECUE CHICKEN AND RICE LETTUCE WRAPS

Serves 6

2   pounds boneless, skinless chicken breasts, cut into strips
1   cup wild rice, rinsed
1   onion, diced
1   red bell pepper, seeded and diced
½   cup barbecue sauce
2   cups chicken broth
12   large romaine lettuce leaves

Use a 4-quart slow cooker. Place the chicken into the insert, and add the rice. Add the onion, bell pepper, and barbecue sauce. Stir in the broth. Cover, and cook on low for 6 hours, or until the rice is bite-tender. Serve scooped into the lettuce leaves.

 The Verdict

Lettuce wraps are a wonderful way to liven up your dinner table. The crunch is satisfying, and it's fun to stuff the leaves. They're a tad messy, so keep a stack of napkins close by!

BIG BATCH MEATBALL SUBS

Serves 15 to 20

- **5   pounds frozen meatballs**
- **2   onions, thinly sliced**
- **6   garlic cloves, chopped**
- **1   (26-ounce) jar pasta sauce**
- **1   tablespoon dried Italian seasoning**
- **15   to 20 hoagie rolls (I use gluten-free)**
- **2   cups shredded mozzarella cheese**

Use a 6-quart or larger slow cooker. Put the meatballs into the insert, and add the onions and garlic. Toss well to distribute. Pour in the pasta sauce and stir in the Italian seasoning. Cover, and cook on low for 5 hours, or on high for about 3 hours, stirring every hour or so. Serve the meatballs on the rolls with a handful of the cheese.

The Verdict

You can feed a large group with these simple meatball subs, and everyone will be full and happy. Have lots of napkins on hand; the sandwiches can get drippy! If you are using store-bought meatballs, be sure to read labels carefully for gluten.

BUILD-YOUR-OWN CABBAGE ROLLS

Serves 6

- **1   pound lean ground turkey**
- **1   onion, grated**
- **3   garlic cloves, minced**
- **2   tablespoons dark brown sugar**
- **1   tablespoon apple cider vinegar**
- **1   teaspoon ground cinnamon**
- **½   teaspoon kosher salt**
- **¼   teaspoon ground nutmeg**
- **¼   teaspoon ground black pepper**
- **2   (8-ounce) cans tomato sauce**
- **1   head green cabbage, cored, leaves separated**

Use a 4-quart slow cooker. Place the meat into the insert. Add the onion, garlic, and sugar. Now add the vinegar, cinnamon, salt, nutmeg, and pepper. Stir in the tomato sauce until everything is well combined. Cover, and cook on low for 6 to 7 hours, or on high for about 4 hours. Stir again, and scoop with a slotted spoon into the cabbage leaves. Wrap the edges of the leaves to create a packet, and eat with your hands.

The Verdict

Instead of sloppy joes, it's sloppy cabbage! This sweet and-at-the-same-time-savory meat tastes marvelous and stuffing the cabbage leaves is fun, and will bring a smile to everyone's face.

CHEESE-STUFFED BARBECUE BURGERS

Serves 4

1	**pound lean ground beef**
½	**cup shredded sharp Cheddar cheese**
¼	**cup barbecue sauce**
1	**teaspoon seasoned salt**
½	**teaspoon onion powder**
½	**teaspoon garlic powder**
4	**hamburger buns, toasted (I use gluten-free)**

Use a 4- or 6-quart slow cooker. In a large bowl, combine the beef with the cheese, barbecue sauce, seasoned salt, onion powder, and garlic powder. Divide the mixture into 4 balls and flatten each with your hands to create 4 patties. Place the patties into the insert, using a rack if you wish (you can make one by weaving together foil "worms" in a waffle pattern). Otherwise, just place the patties into the insert, stagger-stacking if need-be. Cover, and cook on low for 6 to 7 hours, or on high for about 3½ hours. Serve on the buns with your favorite toppings.

 **THE VERDICT**

I LOVE MAKING HAMBURGER PATTIES IN THE SLOW COOKER FOR LUNCH DURING THE HOT SUMMER MONTHS. THE KIDS AND THEIR FRIENDS LOVE EATING OUT BY THE WADING POOL, AND I LOVE NOT HEATING UP THE HOUSE OR SCARING MYSELF WITH THE BARBECUE GRILL.

CHICKEN CAESAR SALAD SANDWICHES

Serves 10

4   **pounds boneless, skinless chicken breast**
¼   **cup warm water**
1   **(16-ounce) bottle Caesar salad dressing**
2   **cups shredded romaine lettuce**
½   **cup freshly grated Parmesan cheese**
¼   **cup chopped fresh flat-leaf parsley**
10   **hamburger buns**

Use a 4-quart slow cooker. Place the chicken into the insert and add the water. Cover, and cook on low for 5 to 6 hours, or until the chicken is fully cooked and tender. Remove the chicken and place onto a cutting board. Pour out any accumulated liquid from the insert. Shred the chicken with a knife and fork and return to the cooker. Add the salad dressing, lettuce, cheese, and parsley. Stir well to combine. Serve as is on the hamburger buns, or if you prefer a hot sandwich, reheat on high for 1 hour until the contents are heated through and the lettuce has wilted.

THE VERDICT

WHAT A FUN, CRISP CHICKEN SALAD SANDWICH! I PREFER MY LETTUCE TO RETAIN A CRUNCH, BUT MY FRIEND REPORTS BACK THAT HER BUNCO GROUP ALL LIKE IT BETTER HOT, AFTER THE INGREDIENTS "GET GLOPPY." IT'S YOUR CHOICE! SERVE WITH FRENCH FRIES.

CHICKEN QUESADILLAS

Makes 6

2	pounds boneless, skinless chicken breast (frozen is fine)
I	(10-ounce) can diced tomatoes and chiles, undrained
I	(8-ounce) package cream cheese
12	corn tortillas
I	cup shredded mozzarella cheese
2	tablespoons butter

Use a 6-quart slow cooker. Put the chicken into the insert, and add the tomatoes and chiles and the cream cheese. Cover, and cook on low for about 7 hours, or until the chicken shreds easily with a fork. Scoop a spoonful of the chicken mixture into a tortilla, and sprinkle with some of the mozzarella. Top with another tortilla, creating a quesadilla. In a large skillet over medium heat, melt the butter, and pan-fry each quesadilla until crispy and golden on each side. (If you'd prefer, you can brown the quesadillas on a sheet pan in a 375°F oven for about 8 minutes, flipping once.)

 The Verdict

My kids would eat quesadillas around the clock if I let them. I like that this is an easy dump-it-all-in recipe, yet still has protein and bit of a vegetable component. This is a great after-school snack when you end up with a few extra kids in the house. Full bellies make tackling homework easier!

CONEY ISLAND DOGS

Serves 8

I	pound lean ground beef
I	onion, diced
I	(15-ounce) can tomato sauce
2	tablespoons Worcestershire sauce (I use gluten-free)
I	teaspoon garlic powder
I	teaspoon ground mustard
I	teaspoon chili powder
½	teaspoon kosher salt
¼	teaspoon ground black pepper
I	tablespoon Tabasco sauce (optional)
8	hot dogs
8	hot dog buns (I use gluten-free)
	Suggested toppings: diced raw onion, relish, shredded Cheddar cheese

Use a 6-quart slow cooker. In a large skillet over medium heat, cook the beef and onion, stirring, until the meat is browned. Drain off any accumulated fat. Transfer the meat mixture to the slow cooker, and add the tomato sauce, Worcestershire sauce, garlic powder, mustard, chili powder, salt, and pepper. It's up to you if you'd like to add the Tabasco sauce—I like it, but understand that some don't! Stir well, and add the hot dogs. Cover, and cook on low for 5 to 6 hours, or until the flavors have melded and the hot dogs are fully hot. Remove the hot dogs with tongs and serve in the buns with a scoop of the meat sauce on top and your desired toppings.

 The Verdict

A reader sent me this recipe to try out—she found it online, and said that growing up, she had very fond memories of eating Coney dogs on family vacations. I love that the dogs cook in the seasoned sauce—not only is it an easy cleanup, the flavor permeates the hot dog skin and creates amazing flavor.

CURRIED CHICKEN PITA POCKETS

Serves 4

2	pounds boneless, skinless chicken thighs
½	red onion, diced
6	garlic cloves, minced
I	tablespoon curry powder
I	teaspoon garam masala (for homemade, see page 264)
½	cup chicken broth
4	pita pockets, for serving (I use gluten-free brown rice tortillas)

FOR THE APPLE YOGURT SAUCE

I	green apple, peeled and grated
½	cup plain yogurt
¼	cup sliced celery
½	teaspoon kosher salt
¼	teaspoon ground black pepper

Use a 4-quart slow cooker. Place the chicken into the insert and add the onion, garlic, curry powder, and garam masala. Stir well to combine. Pour the broth over the top and cover. Cook on low for 6 to 7 hours, or until the onion is translucent and chicken is tender. While the chicken is cooking, combine all the sauce ingredients in a medium bowl and let chill in the refrigerator. Serve the chicken in the pita pockets with a scoop of the apple yogurt sauce.

 THE VERDICT

THESE PITA POCKETS WILL BE YOUR NEW ABSOLUTE FAVORITE. THE CURRY AND GARAM MASALA FLAVORS THE CHICKEN IN SUCH A BEAUTIFUL WAY, AND THE CRISP AND TART COMBINATION FROM THE YOGURT SAUCE IS EXCEPTIONAL. DOUBLE YUM.

DR PEPPER SLOPPY JOES

Serves 6

- 1   pound extra-lean ground turkey
- 1   onion, grated
- 1   red bell pepper, seeded and diced
- 2   stalks celery, diced
- 1   tablespoon all-purpose flour (I use rice flour)
- ½   cup ketchup
- 2   tablespoons yellow mustard
- 1   tablespoon Worcestershire sauce (I use gluten-free)
- 1   cup Dr Pepper soda
- 6   hamburger buns, toasted (I use gluten-free)

Use a 4-quart slow cooker. Put the turkey into the insert, and add the onion, bell pepper, celery, and flour. Stir in the ketchup, mustard, and Worcestershire sauce until all the ingredients are well mixed. Pour the Dr Pepper over the top. Cover, and cook on low for 7 to 8 hours. Stir well and serve in the hamburger buns.

THE VERDICT

I MUST ADMIT, I'M A COMPLETE AND TOTAL SUCKER FOR DR PEPPER. MY TONGUE STARTS WATERING JUST AT THE THOUGHT OF CRACKING OPEN AN ICE-COLD CAN. THIS IS A RIDICULOUSLY FUN SANDWICH, AND DEFINITELY WORTH TESTING OUT. THE MEAT HAS A SLIGHT SWEET AND TANGY FLAVOR, AND I LIKE THAT THE LEAN MEAT CAN COOK IN THE POT WITHOUT HAVING TO DIRTY UP THE STOVETOP AND A SKILLET.

HOT DOGS FOR A CROWD

Serves 60

60 hot dogs
60 hot dog buns (I use gluten-free)
   Suggested toppings: diced raw onion, relish,
   shredded Cheddar cheese

Use a 6-quart slow cooker. You can just pile the hot dogs into the insert, or you can get fancy and stand them upright. No need to add water, they will release liquid all on their own. Cover, and cook on low for 4 hours, high for 2 hours, or until all the dogs are heated throughout. The dogs can stay on the "warm" setting indefinitely. Remove the dogs with kitchen tongs and serve in the buns with your preferred toppings.

THE VERDICT
FEEDING THE WHOLE SECOND GRADE LUNCH? OR ARE YOU RUNNING THE CONCESSION STAND AT THE LITTLE LEAGUE FIELD? THIS IS A SUPER SIMPLE WAY TO COOK A BUNCH OF HOT DOGS AT ONCE WITHOUT NEEDING TO WORRY ABOUT BOILING WATER OR STAFFING A BARBECUE GRILL. ALL YOU NEED IS AN OUTLET, AND YOU'RE GOOD TO GO!

HOT PASTRAMI SANDWICHES

Serves 14

2   pounds sliced deli pastrami
2   pounds sliced deli corned beef
1   onion, sliced into thin rings
4   garlic cloves, minced
2   cups beef broth
1   tablespoon Worcestershire sauce (I use gluten-free)
1   teaspoon ground mustard
1   teaspoon ground cumin
28 slices bread, toasted
1   pound Swiss cheese, thinly sliced

Use a 6-quart slow cooker. Place the deli meats into the insert. Add the onion and garlic, and fluff with tongs to disperse with the meat slices. In a large glass measuring cup, whisk together the broth, Worcestershire sauce, mustard, and cumin. Pour this broth evenly over the top of the meat slices. Cover, and cook on low for 5 hours, or on high for about 3 hours. Serve on the bread with cheese, and a small bowl of the accumulated broth for dipping.

The Verdict

Slow cooking in a flavorful broth really wakes up the deli meat, and gives a nice surprise to your guests in the buffet line. I recommend going to the deli counter and ensuring the meat is lean and freshly cut, rather than using prepackaged sandwich meat. Serve alongside a scoop of coleslaw or potato salad.

ITALIAN BEEF SANDWICHES

Serves 8

1   (3- to 4-pound) beef rump roast (frozen is fine)
1   onion, sliced into thin rings
2   tablespoons dried oregano
2   tablespoons dried basil
1   teaspoon cayenne pepper
1   teaspoon kosher salt
½   teaspoon anise seed
1   (14.5-ounce) can whole tomatoes, undrained
1   (12-ounce) bottle beer (Redbridge by Anheuser-Busch is gluten-free)
8   hoagie rolls, toasted (I use gluten-free)
8   slices mozzarella cheese

Use a 6-quart slow cooker. Put the roast into the insert (frozen is okay). Top with the onion, oregano, basil, cayenne pepper, salt, and anise seed. It will seem like there are way too many herbs—try not to worry. Add the tomatoes and beer. Cover and cook on low for 8 hours, or until the meat shreds easily with a fork. Shred the meat completely, and stir well. Serve on the rolls topped with a slice of the cheese.

The Verdict

Having a party? This is a fantastic potluck meal, or game-day feast. The resulting meat is fall-apart tender and nicely seasoned. The cayenne provides a bit of a kick, but not enough to bother sensitive palates. If you'd like more heat, sliced pickled jalapeño peppers work great as an additional sandwich topping.

ITALIAN DIPPED BEEF SANDWICHES

Serves 8

1   (3-pound) beef chuck roast, trimmed
1   (16-ounce) jar pepperoncini peppers, drained,
    plus extra pepperoncini, sliced, for adding to the
    sandwich (optional)
3   tablespoons dried Italian seasoning
2   cups beef broth
8   sandwich rolls, toasted (I use gluten-free)
8   ounces Swiss cheese (optional)

Use a 6-quart slow cooker. Place the roast into the insert, and add the whole pepperoncini peppers and Italian seasoning. Pour in the broth. Cover, and cook on low for 10 hours, or until the meat shreds easily with a fork. Shred completely, and serve in the rolls with the cheese and sliced pepperoncini, if desired. Dip the sandwich into a bowl of juice from the crock before each bite.

 THE VERDICT

I'VE ADAPTED REE DRUMMOND'S (THEPIONEERWOMAN.COM) SANDWICHES TO MAKE THEM SLOW-COOKER FRIENDLY. THIS IS A GREAT TAILGATING PARTY OR POKER NIGHT RECIPE. BE AWARE THAT IF YOU GIVE KIDS A BOWL OF MEAT JUICE, SOMEONE WILL EVENTUALLY KNOCK IT OVER. MAYBE SERVE THE KIDS OUTSIDE?

ITALIAN SLOPPY JOES

Serves 6

1½	pounds extra-lean ground turkey
1	onion, chopped
6	garlic cloves, minced
8	ounces fresh button mushrooms, chopped
2	tablespoons dried Italian seasoning
1	tablespoon sugar
2	cups tomato sauce
6	hamburger buns, toasted (I use gluten-free)
6	slices mozzarella cheese

Use a 4-quart slow cooker. Place the turkey into the insert and stir in the onion and garlic. Add the mushrooms, Italian seasoning, and sugar. Stir in the tomato sauce. Cover, and cook on low for 7 to 8 hours, or on high for 4 hours. Stir very well and serve on the hamburger buns topped with a slice of the cheese.

The Verdict

Gina from www.moneywisemoms.com sent me this recipe, and it's a definite keeper. I usually have everything this meal calls for on hand in the freezer or fridge, and I like how easy it is to stretch if we have extra kids in the house for dinner. Thank you, Gina!

MEXICAN BARBECUE SANDWICHES

Serves 10

1	(5-pound) beef chuck roast or pork shoulder
2	onions, sliced into thin rings
8	garlic cloves, minced
1	(1-ounce) packet taco seasoning
1	cup barbecue sauce
10	hoagie rolls, toasted (I use gluten-free)
8	ounces Cheddar cheese, thinly sliced

Use a 6-quart slow cooker. Place the roast into the insert and add the onion, separating the rings with your fingers. Add the garlic, and sprinkle in the taco seasoning. Add the barbecue sauce. Cover, and cook on low for 10 to 12 hours, or until the meat shreds easily with a fork. Serve on a roll topped with a slice of cheese.

The Verdict

This is a reader recipe from Dawn, in Wisconsin. She makes this "secret family" sandwich every year and serves four generations out of one pot. The taco seasoning provides a fun and different tangy kick to the barbecue sauce. Thank you, Dawn!

OLD-FASHIONED BARBEQUED PULLED PORK SANDWICHES

Serves 10

1	(5-pound) boneless pork butt or shoulder roast
¼	cup packed dark brown sugar
1	tablespoon garlic powder
1	tablespoon onion powder
1	tablespoon ground cumin
1	tablespoon paprika
1	teaspoon ground cinnamon
1	teaspoon cayenne pepper
1	(12-ounce) bottle beer (Redbridge by Anheuser-Busch is gluten-free)
1	(18-ounce) bottle barbecue sauce
10	soft hamburger buns (I use gluten-free)
	Suggested toppings: sliced Cheddar cheese, pickles, jalapeño slices

Use a 6-quart slow cooker. Put the roast into the insert and add the sugar, garlic powder, onion powder, cumin, paprika, cinnamon, and cayenne pepper. Rub the spice mixture into the meat. Pour in the beer. Cover, and cook on low for 10 to 12 hours, or until the meat easily shreds with a fork. Drain the liquid, and stir in the barbecue sauce. Cover, and heat on high for 20 to 30 minutes, or until heated through. Serve on the hamburger buns with your favorite toppings.

 THE VERDICT

EVERY TIME I MAKE PULLED PORK, IT'S SLIGHTLY DIFFERENT. THIS IS MY NEW CURRENT FAVORITE RECIPE, AND I THINK YOU'LL REALLY ENJOY IT. THE CINNAMON ADDS A FUN TWIST, AND THE BROWN SUGAR BALANCES OUT THE CAYENNE PEPPER. I ADD SLICED CHEDDAR CHEESE AND JALAPEÑO TO MY SANDWICH.

PORK AND BLACK BEAN LETTUCE WRAPS WITH MANGO SALSA

Serves 6

1   (1½-pound) pork tenderloin, cut into 4 pieces
1   tablespoon dark brown sugar
1   tablespoon garlic powder
1   tablespoon chili powder
1   tablespoon ground cumin
1   teaspoon kosher salt
1   teaspoon dried oregano
½   teaspoon cayenne pepper
1   red onion, diced
2   (15-ounce) cans black beans, drained and rinsed
12 large romaine lettuce leaves

FOR THE MANGO SALSA
2   whole mangoes, peeled, pitted, and chopped
½   cup chopped fresh cilantro leaves
¼   cup diced red onion
2   limes, juiced
1   jalapeño pepper, diced
1   teaspoon honey
⅛   teaspoon kosher salt

Use a 6-quart slow cooker. Place the pork into the insert. In a small bowl, combine the sugar, garlic powder, chili powder, cumin, salt, oregano, and cayenne pepper. Rub this seasoning blend all over each piece of pork. Add the onion, and pour the beans over the top. Cover, and cook on low for 8 hours, or until the pork has relaxed and can be easily shredded with a fork. Remove the pork from the pot, shred completely, and stir back into the beans. Meanwhile, in a medium bowl, combine all the salsa ingredients. Scoop the pork and beans with a slotted spoon onto large pieces of lettuce and top with the mango salsa.

THE VERDICT
YOU WILL LOVE THESE WRAPS: EVERYTHING BOUNCES WITH FLAVOR AND THE LETTUCE AND HOMEMADE SALSA PROVIDE LOTS OF FUN TEXTURE AND FRESHNESS. MIXING IN THE BLACK BEANS ALLOWS YOU TO USE A SMALLER CUT OF MEAT— GREAT FOR ENTERTAINING, FOR TRIMMING THE GROCERY BUDGET, OR FOR TRIMMING YOUR WAISTLINE.

PHILLY JOES

Serves 4

1	pound extra-lean ground beef
8	ounces fresh button mushrooms, thinly sliced
1	onion, diced
1	green or red bell pepper, seeded and thinly sliced
3	garlic cloves, diced
1	cup beef broth
¼	cup A1 Steak Sauce
4	hamburger buns or rolls (I use gluten-free)
4	slices provolone cheese

Use a 4-quart slow cooker. Crumble the beef into the insert, and add the mushrooms, onion, bell pepper, and garlic. Stir in the broth and steak sauce. Cover, and cook on low for 6 hours. Stir well, and serve with a slotted spoon onto the buns and top with a slice of the cheese. If you'd like, broil the open sandwiches in the oven until the cheese has melted and browned on top.

 THE VERDICT
THE SANDWICHES HAVE ALL
THE FUN OF EATING A SLOPPY
JOE, BUT WITH A FANTASTIC
PHILLY CHEESE STEAK FLAVOR.

POT ROAST FRENCH DIP SANDWICHES

Serves 8

I   (3-pound) pot roast, trimmed
2   tablespoons dried minced onion
I   tablespoon garlic powder
I   tablespoon Worcestershire sauce (I use gluten-free)
½   teaspoon ground black pepper
2   cups beef broth
8   hoagie rolls
8   slices mozzarella cheese (optional)

Use a 4-quart slow cooker. Place the roast into the insert, and add the onion flakes, garlic powder, Worcestershire sauce, and pepper. Pour the broth evenly over the top. Cover, and cook on low for 8 to 10 hours, or until the meat shreds easily with a fork. Shred completely, and scoop with a slotted spoon into the hoagie rolls and top with a slice of the cheese, if desired. Serve a small bowl of the collected drippings for dipping on the side.

🍲 The Verdict
Growing up, French dip sandwiches were one of my dad's favorite things to order at a diner. I'm so happy to recreate these at home using pantry staples and fully gluten-free ingredients.

RATATOUILLE SANDWICHES

Serves 8

I   eggplant, peeled, quartered, and sliced
I   red onion, sliced into thin rings
I   red bell pepper, seeded and thinly sliced
I   orange bell pepper, seeded and thinly sliced
I   medium zucchini, thinly sliced
2   small yellow summer squash, thinly sliced
3   ripe tomatoes, quartered
¼   cup prepared pasta sauce
I   tablespoon olive oil
½   teaspoon kosher salt
¼   teaspoon ground black pepper
8   soft sandwich buns, toasted (I use gluten-free)
8   ounces Swiss or provolone cheese, sliced (optional)

Use a 6-quart slow cooker. Put the eggplant, onion, bell peppers, zucchini, squash, and tomatoes into the insert. Add the pasta sauce, oil, salt, and black pepper, and stir well to combine. Cover, and cook on low for 8 hours, or until the vegetables have broken down quite a bit and the onion is translucent. Serve on the buns with a slice of the cheese on top, if desired.

🍲 The Verdict
Everything about these sandwiches screams "backyard summer party" to me. Simmering vegetables all day really brings out the individual flavors, and I love how I can get so many good-for-you vitamins into such a delicious package.

ROASTED BEEF SANDWICHES

Serves 10

1	(4-pound) beef chuck roast, trimmed
3	onions, sliced into thin rings
6	garlic cloves, smashed
4	cups beef broth
1	(12-ounce) bottle of beer (Redbridge by Anheuser-Busch is gluten-free)
2	tablespoons beef bouillon granules
1	tablespoon kosher salt
1	teaspoon ground black pepper
10	hoagie rolls or hot dog buns (I use gluten-free), toasted and buttered
	Butter for buns

Use a 6-quart slow cooker. Place the roast into the insert, and top with the onions and garlic. Add the broth, beer, and bouillon. Stir in the salt and pepper. Cover and cook on low for 10 to 12 hours, or until the meat can be completely shredded with a fork. Serve on the buttered buns with a small bowl of crock drippings for dipping on the side.

 The Verdict

Seriously. Good. Food. I served this to a houseful of kids, and they all gobbled up the "sloppy meat." Make sure you've got plenty of napkins on hand!

SAUCY STEAK WRAPS

Serves 6

2	pounds round steak, cut into thin strips
1	onion, thinly sliced
1	green bell pepper, seeded and thinly sliced
1	red bell pepper, seeded and thinly sliced
½	cup A1 Steak Sauce
2	teaspoons Tabasco sauce
12	small brown rice or flour tortillas, warmed

Use a 4-quart slow cooker. Place the steak into the insert, and add the onion and bell peppers. Stir in the steak and Tabasco sauces. Cover, and cook on low for 7 to 8 hours, or until the meat is super tender. Spoon into the tortillas to serve.

 The Verdict

This is exactly what the name describes—a super-saucy and tasty steak sandwich. If you're feeding really young children or those with sensitive palates, you can skip the Tabasco sauce.

SHREDDED CHICKEN SANDWICHES

Serves 6 to 8

3	pounds boneless, skinless chicken breast (frozen is fine)
1	red onion, thinly sliced
½	cup ketchup
½	cup packed dark brown sugar
2	tablespoons apple cider vinegar
2	tablespoons soy sauce (I use gluten-free)
1	tablespoon Worcestershire sauce (I use gluten-free)
1	teaspoon ground mustard
½	teaspoon ground black pepper
6	to 8 soft sandwich buns, toasted (I use gluten-free) Coleslaw, for serving (optional)

Use a 6-quart slow cooker. Place the chicken into the insert and add the onion. In a medium bowl, whisk together the ketchup, sugar, vinegar, soy sauce, Worcestershire sauce, mustard, and pepper. Pour this mixture on top of the chicken and onion. Cover, and cook on low for 8 to 10 hours, or until the chicken is thoroughly cooked and shreds easily with a fork. Serve the shredded chicken on the buns with a scoop of coleslaw on top, if desired.

 **THE VERDICT**
THESE SANDWICHES MAKE A PERFECT PICNIC OR TAILGATING MEAL. OUR MINIVAN HAS AN OUTLET IN THE TRUNK, AND WE CAN KEEP THE MEAT HOT UNTIL WE'RE READY TO EAT—PRETTY COOL!

SHREDDED GREEK CHICKEN POCKETS

Serves 4

2	pounds boneless, skinless chicken breast
1	onion, grated
1	lemon, juiced
1	cup chicken broth
1	tablespoon dried oregano
1	teaspoon kosher salt
½	teaspoon ground black pepper
1	cup plain yogurt or sour cream, at room temperature
4	pita pockets (or gluten-free brown rice tortillas)

Use a 4-quart slow cooker. Place the chicken into the insert, and add the onion and lemon juice. Add the broth, oregano, salt, and pepper. Cover, and cook on low for 6 hours, or until the chicken shreds easily with a fork. Shred completely, and stir in the yogurt. Serve in the pita pockets.

 **THE VERDICT**
I LOVE MAKING CHICKEN DINNERS LIKE THIS. CHICKEN CAN SOMETIMES GET A BIT DULL, BUT THIS IS A GREAT RECIPE TO MIX THINGS UP A BIT. MY KIDS LOVE ASSEMBLY-LINE DINNERS, AND LIKE MAKING THEIR OWN WRAPS WITH BROWN RICE TORTILLAS.

SLOPPY JOES FOR A CROWD

Serves 10 to 12

3	pounds extra-lean ground turkey
1	onion, grated
1	green bell pepper, seeded and diced
2	cups ketchup
1	cup yellow mustard
½	cup packed dark brown sugar
6	garlic cloves, chopped
¼	cup A1 Steak Sauce
10	to 12 sandwich rolls (I use gluten-free)

Use a 6-quart slow cooker. Put the turkey into the insert. Add the onion, bell pepper, ketchup, mustard, sugar, garlic, and steak sauce. Stir well to combine. Cover and cook on low for 8 hours, or on high for about 4 hours. Stir very well to break up the meat before serving. Scoop with a slotted spoon onto the rolls and serve.

The Verdict

Sloppy joes are fun, no matter your age. This is a not-too-sweet version that pleases both adults and kids. Plan a retro party! Invite me! I'll bring the sloppy joes.

SPICY BBQ BEEF SANDWICHES

Serves 8

1	(3- to 4-pound) beef chuck roast (frozen is fine)
1	onion, sliced into thin rings
4	garlic cloves, minced
1	(12-ounce) jar chili sauce
1	(4-ounce) can fire-roasted diced green chiles, undrained
2	tablespoons dark brown sugar
1	tablespoon Worcestershire sauce (I use gluten-free)
1	tablespoon red wine vinegar
1	tablespoon molasses
8	hoagie rolls or hamburger buns (I use gluten-free)
8	ounces Cheddar cheese, sliced

Use a 6-quart slow cooker. Place the roast into the insert. Add the onions, garlic, chili sauce, chiles, the sugar, Worcestershire sauce, vinegar, and molasses. Stir the sauce ingredients together and flip the meat over a few times to cover with sauce. Cover, and cook on low for 8 to 10 hours, or until the meat shreds easily with a fork. You can help speed along the process by cutting the meat into chunks an hour or two before it is finished cooking. Serve on the hoagie rolls with a slice of the cheese on top.

 The Verdict

This is a great game day or potluck dish. If you don't want to get your hands messy, serve the meat over a bed of rice or a baked potato (although sauce dripping down your forearms is kind of the fun part). If you or your guests would like more of a kick, offer Tabasco sauce at the table.

SWEET POTATO AND BLACK BEAN WRAPS

Serves 4

2   large sweet potatoes, peeled and cut into
    1-inch cubes
1   (15-ounce) can black beans, drained and rinsed
3   garlic cloves, minced
1   teaspoon ground cumin
½   teaspoon ground coriander
½   teaspoon kosher salt
¼   teaspoon ground black pepper
¼   cup vegetable broth
2   limes, juiced
8   large romaine lettuce leaves

Use a 4-quart slow cooker. Put the sweet potato into the insert. Add the beans and garlic. Add all the seasonings. Stir in the broth and lime juice. Cover, and cook on low for 6 hours, or until the sweet potato is super tender and the flavors have melded. Serve in large lettuce leaves and eat with your fingers!

 The Verdict

What a fun wrap! This recipe comes from Kalyn Denny, who writes at kalynskitchen.com and slowcookerfromscratch.com. She serves this filling in tortillas and makes little burritos. If you are gluten-free, use brown rice or corn tortillas.

THE WORLD'S EASIEST BUFFALO CHICKEN SANDWICHES

Serves 6

3   pounds boneless, skinless chicken breast
    (frozen is fine)
1   (1-ounce) packet ranch salad dressing mix (for
    homemade, see recipe below)
1   (12-ounce) bottle buffalo wing sauce
6   hamburger buns, toasted (I use gluten-free)
6   ounces Cheddar cheese, sliced (optional)

Use a 4-quart slow cooker. Place the chicken into the insert, and sprinkle with the salad dressing mix. Add the buffalo wing sauce. Cover, and cook on low for 6 to 7 hours. Shred the chicken completely with a fork, and serve on the buns with a slice of the cheese, if desired.

The Verdict

A reader sent me this recipe after finding it in a Weight Watchers guide. There is no added fat or oil in the pot, and the lean chicken soaks up the buffalo flavor without sacrificing your waistline. Yay!

HOMEMADE RANCH SALAD DRESSING MIX

Makes ½ cup

2½ tablespoons dried minced onion
2½ teaspoons paprika
2½ teaspoons dried parsley
2   teaspoons kosher salt
2   teaspoons dried minced garlic
2   teaspoons ground black pepper
2   teaspoons sugar

In a bowl, combine all the ingredients. Store in an airtight container for up to 3 months, and use 1 tablespoon in lieu of packaged ranch dressing.

SPICY BEEF DIP SANDWICHES

Serves 10

1 (5-pound) beef chuck roast
1 (1-ounce) packet onion soup mix (for homemade, see page 109)
2 tablespoons dried oregano
2 tablespoons dried basil
1 teaspoon cayenne pepper
½ teaspoon anise seed
1 (8-ounce) jar pepperoncini peppers, drained
1 (12-ounce) bottle beer (Redbridge by Anheuser-Busch is gluten-free)
10 hoagie rolls or hamburger buns, toasted (I use gluten-free)
8 ounces sliced cheeses, such as Swiss, Cheddar, or mozzarella

Use a 6-quart slow cooker. Place the roast into the insert, and add the onion soup mix. Add the remaining seasonings, and sprinkle in the pepperoncini peppers. Pour in the beer. Cover, and cook on low for 10 to 12 hours, or until the meat shreds easily with a fork. Serve on the buns with a slice of cheese, and a bowl of juice from the crock for dipping.

 **THE VERDICT**
MEGHAN, WHO USED TO LIVE IN CHICAGO, MAKES THIS SANDWICH REGULARLY FOR GET-TOGETHERS. IT'S A HEARTY, DELICIOUS SANDWICH AND IT CAN FEED A HOUSEFUL OF HUNGRY COMPANY. MY KIDS FOUND THE MEAT TO BE RATHER SPICY, BUT ADAM AND OUR FRIENDS COULDN'T GET ENOUGH. THANK YOU, MEGHAN!

MEATLESS

ARROZ CON QUESO

Serves 8

1½ cups long-grain white rice, rinsed
1 (10-ounce) can tomatoes and chiles, undrained
1 (15-ounce) can black beans, drained and rinsed
2 cups shredded mozzarella cheese
1 cup ricotta or cottage cheese
1 onion, diced
2 garlic cloves, minced
½ cup water

Use a 4-quart slow cooker. Coat the insert with cooking spray. Place the rice into the greased insert, and add the tomatoes and chiles and the beans. Add both cheeses, the onion, and garlic. Stir in the water. Cover, and cook on low for 6 to 7 hours, or until rice is bite-tender. Uncover, and cook for an additional 20 to 30 minutes to release moisture.

The Verdict

I love hearty casseroles like this. The cheese holds the beans and rice together, and the chiles provide just a hint of spice. Adam added taco sauce to his bowl, and the kids used tortilla chips instead of spoons.

AUNT JEANNE'S EGG DISH

Serves 4

½ tablespoon olive oil
1 tablespoon butter, melted
4 large eggs
1½ cups milk
2 tablespoons all-purpose flour (I use a gluten-free flour mixture)
¼ teaspoon kosher salt
½ teaspoon ground black pepper
2 (7-ounce) cans whole fire-roasted green chiles, drained
3 cups shredded Monterey Jack cheese

Use a 4-quart slow cooker. Rub the oil and melted butter around the sides and bottom of the insert. In a large bowl, whisk together the eggs, milk, flour, salt, and pepper until clump-free. Spread a layer of the chiles into the insert, and add a layer of cheese. Repeat with the rest of the chiles and then the remaining cheese. Pour the egg mixture evenly over the top. Cover, and cook on low for 5 hours, or on high for about 2½ hours. Uncover, and let cook on high for 20 minutes to release condensation. Your egg dish is finished when it is set in the middle, begun to brown on top, and has pulled away from the sides.

The Verdict

I found this recipe stuck to the refrigerator at my in-laws' cabin. Adam's aunt Jeanne is "famous" for this chile casserole, and I wanted to test it out in the slow cooker. It came out beautifully, and we all really enjoyed it. If you would like to add meat, I'd suggest thinly sliced hot link smoked sausage or linguiça.

BAKED POTATO BAR

Serves 10

10	**large Russet or Yukon Gold potatoes**
1	**cup sour cream**
½	**pound bacon (or a vegetarian alternative), cooked and crumbled**
3	**green onions, thinly sliced**

Use a 6-quart slow cooker. Scrub your potatoes well with a vegetable brush, and poke them a few times with a fork. Place all the potatoes into the insert, and cover. Cook on low for 8 to 10 hours, or on high for about 6 hours. Your potatoes are finished when a fork or knife inserts easily. Slice in half, fluff the pulp, and top with the sour cream, bacon, and green onions.

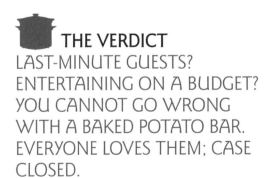 **THE VERDICT**
LAST-MINUTE GUESTS? ENTERTAINING ON A BUDGET? YOU CANNOT GO WRONG WITH A BAKED POTATO BAR. EVERYONE LOVES THEM; CASE CLOSED.

BLACK BEAN AND TOMATO QUINOA

Serves 4 as a side dish, 2 as a main course

I   **cup dried black beans, soaked overnight and drained (for quick-soak method, see page 82)**
I   **cup quinoa, rinsed**
2   **ripe tomatoes, diced**
¼   **cup chopped fresh cilantro leaves**
2   **garlic cloves, chopped**
4   **green onions, thinly sliced**
I   **lime, juiced**
2   **cups vegetable or chicken broth**
    Freshly grated Parmesan cheese, for serving (optional)

Use a 4-quart slow cooker. Put the beans into the insert. Add the quinoa, tomatoes, cilantro, garlic, green onion, and lime juice. Stir in the broth. Cover, and cook on low for 6 hours, or on high for 3 hours, until the beans have reached desired tenderness. Uncover and unplug the slow cooker. Fluff the quinoa with a fork, and let the pot sit for 10 minutes with the lid off to let condensation escape. Serve as is, or with a sprinkle of cheese, if desired.

THE VERDICT

ONLY ONE OF MY CHILDREN WANTED TO TRY THIS DISH, BUT SHE ATE EVERYTHING ON HER PLATE. THIS IS QUITE FILLING—AND THE LEFTOVERS MAKE A GREAT LUNCH. ADAM HAD HIS AS A SIDE DISH WITH LEFTOVER TRI-TIP, BUT I ATE IT AS A MAIN COURSE.

BLACK BEAN PIE

Serves 4 to 6

4	brown rice or flour tortillas
1	onion, diced
1	(15-ounce) can black beans, drained and rinsed
1	cup frozen white corn kernels
3	garlic cloves, minced
2	jalapeño peppers, seeded and diced (wear gloves!)
1	lime, juiced
1	tablespoon ground cumin
1	teaspoon kosher salt
½	teaspoon ground black pepper
3	cups shredded Mexican blend cheese
	Suggested toppings: sour cream, avocado slices

Use a 4-quart slow cooker. Coat the bottom and sides of the insert with cooking spray, and place 1 tortilla on the very bottom. In a large bowl, combine the onion, beans, corn, garlic, jalapeños, lime juice, cumin, salt, and black pepper. Scoop a third of this mixture onto the tortilla. Add a healthy handful of the cheese, and put another tortilla on top. Push down gently on the tortilla before adding more bean filling. Repeat the layers until you run out of ingredients. Cover, and cook on low for 6 hours, or on high for about 3 hours. Unplug, and let your pie sit in the cooling cooker with the lid off for about 15 minutes before slicing. Serve as is, or with a dollop of sour cream and avocado slices.

🍲 The Verdict

We used brown rice tortillas to keep our meal gluten-free, and I was pleased with how they held up in the slow cooker. This is a fun, new twist on bean burritos. I liked how the crunch from the corn and the tart hint of lime really came through in each bite.

BLACK BEAN TAMALE PIE

Serves 6

2	(15-ounce) cans black beans, drained and rinsed
1	(10-ounce) can tomatoes and chiles, undrained
1	(15-ounce) can corn, drained
1	red bell pepper, seeded and diced
1	yellow onion, diced
½	cup shredded sharp Cheddar cheese
1	teaspoon chili powder
1	teaspoon ground cumin

FOR THE CORNBREAD TOPPING

1¼	cups baking mix (I use a gluten-free baking mix)
1	cup milk
¾	cup cornmeal
¼	cup sugar
1	large egg, beaten
½	teaspoon paprika

Use a 4-quart slow cooker. Coat the insert well with cooking spray. Add the beans, tomatoes and chiles, corn, bell pepper, onion, cheese, chili powder, and cumin and stir very well to combine. To make the topping, whisk together in a large bowl the baking mix, milk, cornmeal, sugar, and egg to form a batter. Pour this batter evenly over the top of the ingredients already in the slow cooker. Sprinkle the paprika on top. Cover, and cook on low for 5 to 6 hours, or on high for about 3 hours. Your tamale pie is finished when the cornbread is fully cooked, set in the middle, and has begun to pull away from the sides. Uncover, and let it sit in a cooling slow cooker for 10 minutes before cutting into.

🍲 The Verdict

I like to scoop this pie out with a large spoon and flop it into a bowl, so the cornbread topping ends up at the bottom, and gets juicy from the bean and tomato filling.

BOMBAY BEANS AND POTATOES

Serves 6

2   (15-ounce) cans chickpeas, drained and rinsed
2   pounds white potatoes, scrubbed and cut into
    1-inch pieces
1   yellow onion, diced
4   ripe tomatoes, diced
2   tablespoons olive oil
1   teaspoon ground mustard
1   teaspoon chili powder
1   teaspoon ground cumin
1   teaspoon ground turmeric
1   teaspoon garam masala (for homemade,
    see following recipe)
1   teaspoon ground ginger
1   teaspoon kosher salt
½   teaspoon ground black pepper
    Corn tortilla or naan wedges, for serving (optional)

Use a 6-quart slow cooker. Toss together the chickpeas, potatoes, onion, and tomatoes in the insert. In a small bowl, whisk the oil and all the seasonings together. Toss again to evenly coat the beans and potatoes with the spice mixture. Cover, and cook on low for 6 to 7 hours, or until the potatoes have reached desired tenderness. Serve as is, or with tortilla or naan wedges to use as scoopers.

The Verdict
We eat a lot of Indian food in our house, and I love how this simple recipe is packed with so much flavor. These potatoes make a fantastic lunch, and I like to cook a batch on the weekend, then separate into single-serving portions for quick and easy lunches. I sometimes add a scoop of nonfat yogurt to the kid plates to soften the spices a bit.

GARAM MASALA
Garam masala is an Indian spice mixture that is readily available in most grocery stores, but you can also make it yourself.

4   tablespoons coriander seed
1   tablespoon cumin seed
1   tablespoon black peppercorns
1   teaspoon ground ginger
4   cardamom pods
¾   teaspoon ground cloves
¾   teaspoon ground cinnamon
2   bay leaves, crumbled

Combine all the ingredients by crushing them together using a mortar and pestle. Store in an airtight container for up to 4 months.

BRAZILIAN BLACK BEAN AND VEGGIE STEW

Serves 6

1	cup dried black beans, soaked overnight and drained (for quick-soak method see page 82)
3	cups vegetable broth
1	sweet potato, peeled and diced
1	red bell pepper, seeded and diced
1	orange bell pepper, seeded and diced
1	onion, diced
1	cup chopped kale leaves
2	ripe tomatoes, chopped
2	cinnamon sticks
2	bay leaves
1	tablespoon garlic powder
1	tablespoon ground cumin
2	teaspoons dried thyme
1	teaspoon kosher salt
2	limes, juiced
¼	cup chopped fresh cilantro leaves (optional)

Use a 6-quart slow cooker. There's a lot of chopping to do here—don't get annoyed. Put the beans into the insert, and add the broth. Add the sweet potato, bell peppers, and onion. Add the kale and tomatoes, and drop in the cinnamon sticks and bay leaves. Add the garlic powder, cumin, thyme, and salt, and stir in the lime juice. Cover, and cook on low for 6 to 7 hours, or until the beans are completely soft. Remove the cinnamon sticks and bay leaves and stir in the fresh cilantro before serving, if desired.

 THE VERDICT

THIS IS MY NEW FAVORITE VEGAN DISH. EVERYTHING ABOUT THIS IS PERFECT. THE SWEET POTATO BREAKS DOWN THROUGH COOKING AND STIRRING AND CREATES A MILD SWEET, CREAMY SAUCE FOR THE BEANS AND OTHER VEGETABLES. SOME PEOPLE FEEL CILANTRO TASTES LIKE SOAP. IF THIS IS TRUE FOR YOU, DON'T USE IT.

CARROT RISOTTO

Serves 2 to 4

1	tablespoon butter, melted
1½	cups **Arborio rice**
½	onion, finely diced
1	cup shredded carrots
4	garlic cloves, minced
½	teaspoon kosher salt
¼	teaspoon ground black pepper
3	cups chicken or vegetable broth
1	cup dry white wine
1	cup freshly grated Parmesan cheese

Use a 4-quart slow cooker. Add the butter to the insert, and swirl the rice in it. Add the onion, carrots, garlic, salt, and pepper. Stir in the broth and wine. Cover, and cook on high for 2 to 4 hours, or until the rice is tender. Remove the lid and stir in the cheese. Unplug the slow cooker, and let it sit with the lid off for 10 minutes before serving.

THE VERDICT

A READER WROTE IN THAT SHE ADDED SHREDDED CARROTS TO HER RISOTTO BECAUSE SHE HAD A SURPLUS OF CARROTS AFTER MAKING BATCHES OF BABY FOOD. I LOVED THE IDEA OF THE SAVORY PARMESAN MIXED WITH SWEET CARROTS AND WAS EAGER TO TEST IT OUT. THE RESULT IS A LUSCIOUS, CREAMY RISOTTO WITH A GORGEOUS SUNNY COLOR. FOR FUN, YOU CAN USE A VARIETY OF COLORED CARROTS AS WE DID IN THE PHOTOGRAPH.

CHILES RELLENOS

Serves 4

8   **canned green chiles**
3   **cups shredded Cheddar cheese**
1   **(14.5-ounce) can plum tomatoes, drained**
1   **green bell pepper, seeded and thinly sliced**
4   **large eggs**
½   **cup chicken broth**
½   **cup milk**
1   **teaspoon dried oregano**
½   **teaspoon kosher salt**
½   **teaspoon ground black pepper**

Use a 6-quart slow cooker. Coat the insert well with cooking spray. Slice 6 of the chiles lengthwise, and stuff ½ cup of the cheese into each pepper. Nestle the chiles next to each other in the insert. In a blender, combine the remaining 2 chiles with the tomatoes, bell peppers, eggs, broth, milk, oregano, salt, and black pepper. Pour the mixture evenly over the stuffed chiles. Cover, and cook on low for 6 hours, or on high for about 3 hours. Your relleno is finished when the egg has set, and the top has browned and begun to pull away from the sides of the insert.

 THE VERDICT
THIS IS A BEAUTIFUL RELLENO DISH THAT IS SURE TO LIVEN UP YOUR BRUNCH TABLE. THE CHEESE-FILLED PEPPERS ARE BAKED IN A TOMATO CREAM SAUCE WITH EGG.

CREAMY PUMPKIN PENNE PASTA

Serves 6

1	cup canned pumpkin puree (not pumpkin pie filling)
1	onion, grated
1	cup chicken or vegetable broth
¼	cup freshly grated Parmesan cheese, plus extra for serving
4	garlic cloves, minced
1	teaspoon ground sage
1	teaspoon kosher salt
½	teaspoon ground black pepper
1	pound penne pasta
½	cup heavy whipping cream

Use a 4-quart slow cooker. Add the canned pumpkin to the insert. Add the onion, broth, cheese, garlic, sage, salt, and pepper and stir well—the mixture will be like a thick soup. Cover, and cook on low for 7 hours, or until the onion is translucent and the mixture has thinned. Meanwhile, cook the penne according to package directions. Stir the cream into the sauce. Toss the sauce with the hot pasta, and sprinkle with a bit more cheese at the table.

THE VERDICT

I HAD A CREAMY PUMPKIN PASTA DISH ON VACATION IN A SEAFOOD RESTAURANT (I WAS THE ONLY ONE NOT TO ORDER FISH; I JUST WASN'T IN THE MOOD) AND I'VE BEEN TRYING TO FIND A GOOD PUMPKIN SAUCE EVER SINCE. THIS IS IT! IT'S THE SAGE— IT REALLY BRINGS OUT THE PUMPKINY FLAVOR.

DOUBLE-THE-SPINACH RAVIOLI LASAGNA

Serves 4

- 1 (25-ounce) package frozen spinach and cheese ravioli (I use gluten-free)
- 1 (26-ounce) jar prepared pasta sauce (retain jar)
- 1 (6-ounce) bag fresh baby spinach
- 2 cups shredded mozzarella cheese
- ¼ cup warm water

Use a 4-quart slow cooker. Coat the insert with cooking spray. Add the ravioli. Stir in the pasta sauce, spinach, and cheese. Add the warm water to the empty pasta sauce jar, and shake. Pour this liquid evenly over the top of the ingredients in the cooker. Cover, and cook on low for 6 hours, or on high for 3 to 4 hours.

 The Verdict

I like that I can get tons of extra vitamin A and C into the kids without them noticing. The fresh spinach shrivels down to hardly anything—it's wonderful. We scrape the crock clean every time. I can find frozen gluten-free ravioli at our local Costco, and one of the gluten-free bakeries in town makes its own variety. Read the packages carefully! Serve with garlic bread (I like the Against The Grain gluten-free baguettes for our garlic bread).

EGGPLANT STEAKS WITH BAKED GARLIC

Serves 4

- 2 tablespoons olive oil
- 1 large eggplant, cut into 8 slices (no need to peel)
- 1 teaspoon paprika
- 1 head garlic, slightly mashed (about 10 cloves)
- ¼ cup torn fresh basil leaves
- 6 ounces fresh mozzarella cheese, sliced
- 1 (14.5-ounce) can fire-roasted tomatoes, undrained

Use a 6-quart slow cooker. Brush 1 tablespoon of the oil into the insert, and place the eggplant slices on top. Brush the remaining tablespoon of oil on top of the eggplant, and sprinkle on the paprika. Add the garlic and basil. Top with the cheese, and pour in the tomatoes. Cover, and cook on low for 5 hours, or until the eggplant is tender and the cheese has melted completely and has begun to brown at the edges.

 The Verdict

Oh yum. I love fresh basil and eggplant anything, and couldn't get enough of this simple dish. My kids aren't huge eggplant fans, but ate enough to warrant dessert. Serve this with polenta if you'd like.

HONEY BEANS AND SPINACH DINNER

Serves 4 to 6

1	(15-ounce) can chickpeas, drained and rinsed
1	(15-ounce) can black beans, drained and rinsed
1	onion, finely diced
2	medium sweet potatoes, peeled and chopped
3	garlic cloves, minced
2	teaspoons ground cumin
½	teaspoon ground coriander
½	teaspoon kosher salt
½	teaspoon ground black pepper
¼	cup honey
1	lemon, juiced
1	(12-ounce) bag fresh baby spinach
2	tablespoons cream cheese (optional)
	Hot cooked white or brown basmati rice, for serving

Use a 6-quart slow cooker. Put the beans into the insert. Add the onion, sweet potatoes, and garlic. Add the cumin, coriander, salt, and pepper, and stir in the honey and lemon juice—you want the beans and veggies in the pot to be coated with them. Add the spinach. You'll need to squish it all in, but I promise it'll fit. Plop the cream cheese on top, if desired. Cover, and cook on low for 6 hours, or on high for about 3 hours. Stir well before serving over a bed of rice.

 The Verdict

The spinach leaves on top may stick to the edges of the pot and get a bit crispy. This is okay, just peel them off and stir them in. The bit of cream cheese mixes with the lemon and honey to create a fabulous sauce. I love everything about this dish, and it's been highly reviewed online. But my kids prefer to eat salami and cheese.

INDIAN BUTTER TOFU

Serves 4

12	ounces extra-firm tofu, drained
1	(14.5-ounce) can diced tomatoes, undrained
1	onion, sliced
4	garlic cloves, chopped
1	tablespoon garam masala (for homemade, see page 264)
1	tablespoon ground cumin
1	teaspoon ground turmeric
½	teaspoon cayenne pepper (optional)
½	teaspoon kosher salt
1	(1-inch) piece fresh ginger, peeled and grated
1	cinnamon stick
½	cup plain yogurt or sour cream

Use a 4-quart slow cooker. Place the tofu into the insert and add the tomatoes, onion, and garlic. Now add the garam masala, cumin, turmeric, cayenne pepper, and salt. Add the ginger, and toss in the cinnamon stick. With a large spoon, carefully mix the ingredients to evenly coat the tofu. Cover, and cook on low for 4 to 5 hours. Before serving, remove the cinnamon stick and stir in the yogurt.

The Verdict

Plain yogurt is the traditional add-in at the very end, but I've used sour cream in a pinch, and actually prefer the texture and creaminess—it's your choice. Indian food is a comfort food to me. I'll happily sit on the couch and eat bowl after bowl while watching a *Brothers and Sisters* marathon via Netflix. Serve over a bed of rice or with naan or gluten-free corn tortilla wedges, if you'd like.

KALAMATA OLIVE MARINARA

Serves 4

1	**(28-ounce) can diced tomatoes, undrained**
1	**onion, grated**
½	**cup dry red wine**
6	**garlic cloves, minced**
¼	**cup chopped pitted kalamata olives**
¼	**cup freshly grated Parmesan cheese**
1	**tablespoon dried Italian seasoning**
1	**pound pasta (I use gluten-free fusilli), cooked**
½	**cup crumbled feta cheese (optional)**

Use a 4-quart slow cooker. Dump the tomatoes into the cooker and add the onion, wine, garlic, olives, Parmesan, and Italian seasoning. Cover, and cook on low for 8 hours, or until the olives break down and the flavors have melded. Meanwhile, cook the pasta according to package directions. Serve the sauce tossed with the hot pasta and top with the feta, if desired.

 **THE VERDICT**
THIS PERFECT MEDITERRANEAN PASTA DISH USES PANTRY STAPLES AND REALLY WAKES UP THE REGULAR "WEDNESDAY NIGHT SPAGHETTI" WE'RE ALL ACCUSTOMED TO. IT'S VEGETARIAN, YET COMPLETELY SATISFYING.

LENTIL AND SWEET POTATO CURRY

Serves 6

2	large sweet potatoes, peeled and diced
I	onion, diced
I ½	cups dried brown or green lentils, rinsed
I	teaspoon ground ginger
I	teaspoon curry powder
I	teaspoon ground turmeric
½	teaspoon kosher salt
¼	teaspoon ground black pepper
4	cups chicken or vegetable broth
I	(13.6-ounce) can coconut milk

Use a 4-quart slow cooker. Place the sweet potato and onion into the insert. Rinse the lentils and add them to the pot. Add the ginger, curry powder, turmeric, salt, and pepper. In a large bowl, whisk together the broth and coconut milk until fully combined. Pour this mixture over the top of the ingredients in the pot. Stir well. Cover, and cook on low for 6 to 7 hours, or on high for about 4 hours.

THE VERDICT

WE'VE GOT TWO SUPER FOODS IN ONE POT HERE—LENTILS AND SWEET POTATOES ARE BOTH AMAZING SOURCES OF FIBER AND NUTRIENTS. THIS DISH WILL PROVIDE MORE THAN ENOUGH OF YOUR DAILY INTAKE OF VITAMINS A, C, AND A HEALTHY DOSE OF IRON. AND IT'S DELICIOUS!

LENTIL CROQUETTES

Serves 6 to 8

2	tablespoons olive oil
2	cups cooked green or brown lentils
1	cup cooked rice
1	small onion, diced
6	garlic cloves, minced
3	tablespoons tomato paste
2	tablespoons Dijon mustard
2	tablespoons flax meal
1	tablespoon ground cumin
1	teaspoon chili powder
1	teaspoon ground turmeric
1	teaspoon kosher salt
	Tzatziki Sauce (page 156), for serving

Use a 6-quart slow cooker. Swirl the oil into the insert, and set aside. In a large bowl, mash together the cooked lentils and rice. Add the onion, garlic, tomato paste, mustard, flax meal, cumin, chili powder, turmeric, and salt. Stir until all the ingredients are well combined. Using your hands, form golf ball–size mounds of the mixture, and flatten slightly with your hands. Place into the insert, dipping each side briefly in the oil. Continue until you run out of ingredients. It's okay to stagger-stack your croquettes. Cover, and cook on low for 5 to 6 hours, or on high for about 3 hours. Your croquettes are finished when they are dry to the touch, and have browned on all sides. Serve with the tzatziki sauce on the side.

 The Verdict

These will remind you of falafel. Since they are packed with rice, I served them on a plate with a bit of the tzatziki sauce and a spinach salad. The leftovers pack well for lunch, and can be eaten cold.

LOADED VEGETABLE CHILI

Serves 8

1	tablespoon oil
1	red onion, diced
4	garlic cloves
1	(28-ounce) can fire-roasted tomatoes, undrained
1	yellow bell pepper, seeded and diced
1	red bell pepper, seeded and diced
2	carrots, thickly sliced
2	cups cubed butternut squash
1	sweet potato, peeled and diced
1	(15-ounce) can black beans, drained and rinsed
2	teaspoons ground cumin
2	teaspoons chili powder
1	teaspoon kosher salt
½	teaspoon ground black pepper
1	lime, juiced
1	or 2 jalapeño peppers
2	cups vegetable broth
	Limes wedges, favorite grated cheese, for serving (optional)

Use a 6-quart slow cooker. Add the oil to the insert and swirl the onion and garlic into it to fully coat. Add all the vegetables, the beans, and all the seasonings. Pour in the lime juice. Throw in the jalapeños, and stir in the broth. Cover, and cook on low for 8 hours. Discard the jalapeños and use a handheld immersion blender to blend some of the beans and vegetables (or carefully remove a cup of beans and vegetables, blend in a traditional blender, and mix back into the mixture in the cooker). Stir well. Serve with lime wedges and a sprinkle of cheese, if desired.

The Verdict

This recipe is Karina Allrich's (glutenfreegoddess.blogspot.com) favorite chili. She makes it completely vegan, but we threw on cheese and sour cream in our house. It's hearty, delicious, and packed full of nutritional goodness.

MACARONI AND CHEESE

Serves 8

- 4 **cups milk**
- 2 **cups elbow macaroni (I use gluten-free)**
- 8 **ounces American cheese, cubed or shredded**
- ¼ **teaspoon ground black pepper**
- 2 **cups shredded Cheddar cheese**

Use a 4-quart slow cooker. Coat the insert with cooking spray. Add the milk and pasta, American cheese, and pepper. Stir well to combine. Top with the Cheddar cheese. Cover, and cook on low for 4 to 5 hours, or on high for about 2½ hours. The pasta will break down if overcooked, but still tastes amazing.

 The Verdict

Holy Batman and Robin, this is good mac and cheese. I've made dozens of different variations of this dish the past few years, but good ol' American cheese is what it takes to make a winner. My apologies to the cheese snobs!

MEDITERRANEAN EGGPLANT

Serves 4

- 1 **tablespoon olive oil**
- 1 **pound eggplant, peeled and cut into 1-inch cubes**
- 1 **red bell pepper, seeded and thinly sliced**
- 1 **onion, thinly sliced**
- 4 **ripe tomatoes, diced**
- 1 **small zucchini, thinly sliced**
- 4 **garlic cloves, chopped**
- 2 **teaspoons dried basil**
- 4 **ounces feta cheese**

Use a 6-quart slow cooker. Add the oil to the insert along with the eggplant, bell pepper, onion, tomatoes, zucchini, garlic, and basil. Toss together to evenly coat everything with the oil and basil. Cover, and cook on low for 5 to 6 hours, or on high for about 3 hours. Crumble in the cheese, and serve.

 The Verdict

Eggplant and feta belong together, I've just decided. Alanna Kellogg, from A Veggie Venture blog (kitchen-parade-veggieventure.blogspot.com), shared this recipe and it is perfect—the vegetables create their own cooking liquid to form a ratatouille. The baby ate a good amount off my plate, but her older sisters weren't feeling up to the adventure.

MUSHROOM AND BEAN RAGOUT

Serves 6

1	pound fresh cremini mushrooms, thinly sliced
2	onions, chopped
4	garlic cloves, minced
1	tablespoon chopped fresh thyme or 1½ teaspoons dried thyme
½	teaspoon kosher salt
½	teaspoon ground pepper
1	tablespoon olive oil
1	(28-ounce) can diced tomatoes, undrained
1	(15-ounce) can cannellini beans, drained and rinsed
	Hot cooked brown rice or polenta, for serving

Use a 6-quart slow cooker. Put the mushrooms into the bottom of the insert, and add the onion and garlic. Add the thyme, salt, pepper, and swirl in the oil. Add the tomatoes and beans, stir once more, and cover. Cook on low for 8 to 10 hours, or until flavors have melded and the tomatoes and mushrooms have broken down. Serve over rice or polenta.

 **THE VERDICT**
I LOVE HOW CREMINI MUSHROOMS MIMIC MEAT IN THIS SAUCE, PROVIDING A THICK AND HEARTY TEXTURE. THIS RECIPE WAS RECOMMENDED BY A READER FROM COOKINCANUCK.COM.

MUSHROOM RISOTTO

Serves 4

½ ounce dried shiitake or porcini mushrooms, finely chopped
2 cups boiling water
1 tablespoon olive oil
1½ cups Arborio or short-grain white rice
½ pound fresh cremini mushrooms, sliced
1 small onion, finely diced
4 garlic cloves, minced
1 tablespoon chopped fresh rosemary
½ teaspoon kosher salt
¼ teaspoon ground black pepper
4 cups chicken or vegetable broth
1 cup shredded Swiss cheese (optional)

Use a 4-quart slow cooker. Place the dried mushrooms into a glass measuring cup, and pour the water over them. Set aside. Add the oil to the insert, and swirl the rice into it—you want all the grains coated with the oil. Add the fresh mushrooms, onion, garlic, rosemary, salt, and pepper, and stir in the broth. Drain the soaked mushroom pieces and add to the mixture. Cover, and cook on high for 2 to 4 hours, or until the rice is tender. Remove the lid and unplug the cooker. Let the rice sit in the cooling cooker for 10 minutes before serving. Top with the cheese, if desired.

 **THE VERDICT**
RISOTTO IN THE SLOW COOKER JUST COULDN'T BE EASIER—NO NEED TO STIR, NO NEED TO WATCH FOR SCORCHING, NO NEED TO MISS OUT ON VALUABLE FAMILY TIME (OR A *GOSSIP GIRL* MARATHON). LOADED WITH MUSHROOMS, THIS IS ONE OF MY FAVORITE RICE DISHES.

NO-MEAT TACOS

Serves 6

2   cups dried green or brown lentils, rinsed
2   cups vegetable or chicken broth
I   onion, diced
I   (1-ounce) packet taco seasoning (for homemade, see page 28)
    Taco shells or corn tortillas, for serving
    Suggested toppings: shredded Cheddar cheese, salsa, avocado slices, sour cream, black olives

Use a 4-quart slow cooker. Place the lentils into the insert, and add the broth, onion, and taco seasoning. Stir well. Cover, and cook on low for 5 to 6 hours, or until the lentils are bite-tender. Spoon into taco shells or tortillas and top with the desired goodies.

 The Verdict

When I told Adam and the kids we were having meatless tacos, they were pretty skeptical, but they all did like their dinner. This is a great rotation item for your meatless Monday dinner plan, or to win over a reluctant vegetarian diner.

PEANUTTY HONEY TOFU

Serves 4

I   (16-ounce) package extra-firm tofu, drained
¼   cup peanut butter
¼   cup honey
¼   cup soy sauce (I use gluten-free)
I   (1-inch) piece fresh ginger, peeled and grated
3   garlic cloves, minced
I   lemon, juiced
I   tablespoon sesame oil
I   teaspoon chili powder
2   green onions, thinly sliced
2   tablespoons chopped peanuts

Use a 4-quart slow cooker. Drain and press the tofu to release any extra moisture, and cut into 1-inch pieces. Place the tofu into the insert. In a small bowl, combine the peanut butter, honey, soy sauce, ginger, garlic, lemon juice, oil, and chili powder. Pour this mixture over the top of the tofu, and stir gently to fully cover each piece. Cover, and cook on low for 5 to 6 hours, or on high for about 2½ hours. Before serving, toss the tofu squares with the green onion and peanuts.

 The Verdict

Tofu is a great source of protein, calcium, and iron and has less than 100 calories per ½-cup serving. The great thing about tofu is that the flavor comes from whatever you cook it in—in this case, it marinates and cooks in a lovely peanut sauce: slightly salty, slightly tangy, and delicious. Serve with brown rice and a steamed vegetable. Enjoy!

NUTTY FOR ACORN SQUASH

Serves 2

2	**acorn squashes**
½	**cup warm water**
½	**cup chopped pecans**
¼	**cup chopped walnuts**
¼	**cup dried cranberries (1-ounce snack box is perfect)**
4	**tablespoons (½ stick) butter, melted**
2	**tablespoons dark brown sugar**

Use a 6-quart slow cooker. Cut the acorn squashes in half, and scoop out the seeds. If you have a hard time cutting the squash, try microwaving each on high for 30 seconds. Pour the water into the insert. Place the squash halves, flesh-side up on top of the water. In a small bowl, combine the pecans, walnuts, cranberries, butter, and sugar. Spoon this mixture evenly into each acorn squash half. Cover, and cook on low for 6 to 7 hours, or until the squash has reached desired tenderness.

THE VERDICT
ACORN SQUASH DOESN'T NEED TO REMAIN A SIDE DISH—BRING IT FRONT AND CENTER BY STUFFING IT WITH NUTS AND DRIED CRANBERRIES. THE TOUGH SQUASH STEAMS PERFECTLY IN THE SLOW COOKER, AND BECOMES A LIGHT, HEALTHY, AND DELICIOUS MEAL.

PUMPKIN SPAGHETTI

Serves 6

1   cup canned pumpkin puree (not pumpkin pie filling)
2   (14.5-ounce) cans fire-roasted tomatoes, undrained
1   (6-ounce) can tomato paste
1   onion, diced
6   garlic cloves, minced
¼   cup freshly chopped flat-leaf parsley
1   tablespoon dried Italian seasoning
2   teaspoons kosher salt
½   teaspoon ground black pepper
1   pound spaghetti (I use gluten-free)

Use a 4-quart slow cooker. Add the pumpkin, tomatoes, and tomato paste to the insert. Add the onion, garlic, parsley, Italian seasoning, salt, and pepper, and stir well to combine. Cover and cook on low for 7 to 8 hours, or until onion is translucent and the sauce is bubbly. Use a handheld immersion blender to blend to desired consistency (or carefully remove a cup of sauce, blend in a traditional blender, and mix back into the cooker). Cook the spaghetti according to package directions. Toss the sauce with the hot pasta and serve.

THE VERDICT

I DID A BIT OF FREELANCE WORK FOR DINNERTOOL. COM, AND THEY E-MAILED ME THIS RECIPE TO TEST OUT. IT'S DELICIOUS, AND A VERY NICE CHANGE OF PACE FROM OUR NORMAL SPAGHETTI SAUCE. THE PUMPKIN PROVIDES A LOVELY BUTTERY SWEETNESS, AND CREATES A VERY RICH TEXTURE WITHOUT A DROP OF OIL OR CREAM.

QUICK CHILI AND CORNBREAD CASSEROLE

Serves 6

3   (15-ounce) cans of your favorite beans, drained and rinsed
1   onion, chopped
3   garlic cloves, minced
2   (6-ounce) cans tomato paste
2   tablespoons chopped pickled jalapeño peppers
1   tablespoon dried Italian seasoning
2   cups chicken or vegetable broth

FOR THE CORNBREAD TOPPING

1¼   cups all-purpose flour (I use a gluten-free mix)
1   cup milk
¾   cup cornmeal
¼   cup sugar
1   large egg, beaten
1   teaspoon baking powder

Use a 6-quart slow cooker. Coat the insert well with cooking spray. Add the beans to the insert along with the onion and garlic. Spoon in the tomato paste, and add the jalapeños and Italian seasoning. Stir in the broth. In a large bowl, whisk together all the ingredients for the cornbread topping, and spread it over the top of the chili. If it doesn't cover completely, that's okay—this is what gives it its homemade character! Cover, and cook on low for 6 to 7 hours, or until the cornbread has browned on top and has begun to pull away from the sides.

 **THE VERDICT**
CHILI AND CORNBREAD BELONG TOGETHER. THIS IS A GREAT CLEAN-OUT-THE-PANTRY MEAL. I ENDED UP USING A MIXTURE OF BLACK BEANS, KIDNEY BEANS, AND PINTO BEANS. THE BIG KIDS ADDED A BIT OF SHREDDED CHEESE AND SOUR CREAM TO THEIR BOWLS, AND THE BABY PICKED OFF ALL THE CORNBREAD FIRST AND ATE IT WITH HER FINGERS.

ROASTED GARLIC AND EGGPLANT MARINARA

Serves 8

2	medium eggplants, peeled and cubed
1	onion, diced
1	(14.5-ounce) can diced tomatoes, undrained
1	whole head garlic, peeled (about 10 cloves)
1	cup dry red wine
2	tablespoons tomato paste
2	teaspoons dried basil
1	tablespoon sugar
1	teaspoon dried oregano
½	teaspoon crushed red pepper flakes
1	pound pasta (I use gluten-free)

Use a 6-quart slow cooker. Add the eggplant, onion, tomatoes, and garlic to the insert. Add the wine, tomato paste, basil, sugar, oregano, and red pepper flakes, and toss the ingredients together. Cover, and cook on low for 6 to 8 hours, or on high for 4 to 5 hours. After the vegetables are fully soft, blend (carefully!) with a handheld immersion blender or in batches in a traditional blender. Cook the pasta in salted water until al dente. Toss the sauce with the hot pasta and serve.

THE VERDICT

EGGPLANT AND GARLIC ARE MEANT TO GO TOGETHER, AND THE WHOLE GARLIC CLOVES CREATE A MILD NUTTY FLAVOR THAT INFUSES THE SAUCE—IT'S EXQUISITE. I LIKE TO MAKE BATCHES OF THIS PASTA SAUCE TO FREEZE FOR LATER USE; WHEN THAWED, THIN WITH A BIT OF BROTH OR WATER IF NEEDED.

ROASTED GRAPE AND GOAT CHEESE SWEET POTATO BAKE

Serves 6

1	tablespoon olive oil
3	sweet potatoes, washed and halved lengthwise
¼	teaspoon kosher salt
¼	teaspoon ground black pepper
⅛	teaspoon ground cinnamon
⅛	teaspoon ground nutmeg
2	cups red seedless grapes
4	ounces goat cheese
2	tablespoons honey

Use a 6-quart slow cooker. Add the oil to the insert and swirl it around. Place each potato half flesh-side up into the insert. It's okay if they overlap a bit. Sprinkle on the salt, pepper, cinnamon, and nutmeg. Add the grapes, and crumble the cheese on top. Drizzle the honey evenly over the top. Cover, and cook on low for 5 to 6 hours. Serve hot or cold.

🍲 The Verdict

I looked forward to trying this recipe from the How Sweet It Is website (howsweeteats.com) in the slow cooker to see if the grapes roasted as described. They do! This is such a decadent dish—the grapes are sweet and pucker beautifully in the cooker, and the goat cheese is smooth, creamy, and delicious. My oldest daughter ate three halves!

ROASTED VEGETABLE DINNER

Serves 6

1	large butternut squash, peeled, seeded, and cut into 1-inch pieces
3	sweet potatoes, peeled and cut into 1-inch pieces
1	head cauliflower, stem removed and separated into florets
1	head broccoli, separated into florets
1	onion, cut into wedges
6	to 8 garlic cloves, peeled
¼	cup olive oil
2	teaspoons dried rosemary (optional)
1	teaspoon kosher salt
½	teaspoon ground black pepper
⅓	cup freshly grated Parmesan cheese (optional)

Use a 6-quart slow cooker. Add the squash and sweet potatoes to the insert, along with the cauliflower, broccoli, onion, and garlic. Pour the oil evenly over the top. Sprinkle with the rosemary, if using, and the salt and pepper. Toss the vegetables to coat evenly with the oil and spices. Cover, and cook on low for 5 to 6 hours, or until the garlic is soft and onion translucent. Toss with cheese, if desired, and serve.

🍲 The Verdict

This is a great way to roast a large batch of vegetables. I love curling up on the couch with a great big bowl of veggies—you can feel good about getting seconds and thirds! The rosemary is optional because my friend Georgia doesn't like it. But we do!

ROOT VEGETABLE AND SWEET POTATO SHEPHERD'S PIE

Serves 8

1	large butternut squash, peeled, seeded, and cubed
1	onion, diced
4	red potatoes, peeled and cubed
4	large carrots, cubed
2	Granny Smith apples, peeled and diced
3	garlic cloves, minced
1	tablespoon butter, melted
1	teaspoon ground sage
½	teaspoon kosher salt
¼	teaspoon ground black pepper
2	cups mashed sweet potatoes
½	teaspoon ground nutmeg

Use a 6-quart slow cooker. Add the squash, onion, potatoes, carrots, apples, and garlic into the insert. Pour the butter over the vegetables, and sprinkle in the sage, salt, and pepper. Toss the vegetables together to evenly coat with the butter and spices. Add the sweet potatoes to the top, flattening with the back of a spoon. Dust with the nutmeg. Cover and cook on low for 6 hours, or on high for 3 to 4 hours. Uncover the slow cooker and cook on high for 20 to 30 minutes to cook away any accumulated condensation.

 THE VERDICT

THIS IS A GREAT WAY TO USE UP THE FORGOTTEN VEGETABLES IN THE BACK OF YOUR PRODUCE DRAWER AND TO GET A LARGE DOSE OF VITAMINS A AND C. THE SWEET POTATOES MAKE THIS HEARTY MEATLESS DISH TASTE LIKE DESSERT. FEEL FREE TO SWAP OUT THE BUTTER WITH A DAIRY-FREE ALTERNATIVE TO MAKE THIS A VEGAN MEAL.

ROASTED VEGETABLES ENCHILADA STACK

Serves 6

1	red onion, sliced into thin rings
1	yellow bell pepper, seeded and thinly sliced
1	red bell pepper, seeded and thinly sliced
2	cups cauliflower florets, cut into ½-inch pieces
1	sweet potato, peeled and thinly sliced
2	tablespoons olive oil
2	teaspoons ground cumin
½	teaspoon kosher salt
2	cups salsa
8	corn tortillas
4	cups shredded Mexican blend cheese
	Suggested toppings: sour cream, avocado slices

Use a 4-quart slow cooker. The first thing you need to do is roast the vegetables—you can do this the night before, if you'd like. Divide the onion, bell peppers, cauliflower, and sweet potato into 2 large baking pans that can fit into your oven. Toss the vegetables with the oil, and bake in a preheated 400°F oven for 20 minutes, stirring halfway through. Set aside to cool. When the vegetables are cool enough to handle, put them into a large bowl. Add the cumin and salt, and stir in the salsa. Scoop a ladleful of the vegetable mixture into the insert, and add a layer of tortillas (you may need to tear them to get a good fit). Finish with a handful of cheese, and repeat layers until you run out of ingredients. Cover, and cook on low for 6 hours, or on high for about 3 hours. The cheese will have melted and begun to brown on top and pull away from the sides when finished cooking. Uncover, and let sit in the cooling cooker for about 10 minutes before cutting. Serve with sour cream and avocado slices, if desired.

THE VERDICT

I'M NOT A HUGE FAN OF COOKING BEFORE I COOK, BUT TAKING THE TIME TO ROAST THE VEGETABLES BEFOREHAND IS A REALLY BIG COMPONENT IN THIS ENCHILADA STACK. THIS IS A GREAT DISH— PERFECT FOR ENTERTAINING OR FOR A FAMILY POTLUCK.

SAFFRON RISOTTO

Serves 2 as a main dish

1	tablespoon butter, melted
3	tablespoons olive oil
1¼	cups Arborio rice
1	teaspoon dried minced onion
1	teaspoon saffron threads
¼	teaspoon ground black pepper
3¾	cups vegetable broth
½	cup freshly grated Parmesan cheese
¼	cup dry white wine

Use a 4-quart slow cooker. Add the butter and oil into the insert, and swirl the rice around in it. Add the dried onion, saffron, and pepper. Stir in the broth, cheese, and wine. Cover, and cook on high for 3 to 4 hours. Stir well before serving.

 The Verdict

We are lucky enough to have an Iranian saffron connection and have a good supply in the cupboard. If you can't find it for a reasonable price locally, you can use ground turmeric in its place.

SNEAKY TOFU LASAGNA

Serves 6

1	(26-ounce) jar prepared pasta sauce (retain jar)
1	(14.5-ounce) can fire-roasted tomatoes, drained
½	cup shredded zucchini
½	cup shredded carrots
10	uncooked lasagna noodles (I use gluten-free)
1	(16-ounce) package tofu, drained
1	cup cottage cheese
¼	cup freshly grated Parmesan cheese
1	tablespoon dried Italian seasoning
4	cups shredded mozzarella cheese, divided
¼	cup warm water

Use a 6-quart slow cooker. Pour the pasta sauce and the tomatoes into a large bowl. Add the zucchini and carrots to the mix. Add a ladleful of this sauce into the insert. Put a layer of noodles on top (you may have to break a few to get a good fit). In a separate large bowl, stir together the tofu, cottage cheese, Parmesan, and Italian seasoning. Spread a layer of this cheese concoction on top of the uncooked noodles, and add a handful of mozzarella. Repeat the layers until you run out of ingredients. Put the warm water into your empty pasta sauce jar, seal, and shake. Pour this liquid evenly over the top of your assembled lasagna. Cover, and cook on low for 6 to 7 hours, or on high for about 4 hours. Uncover, and let cook on high for 20 to 30 minutes, uncovered, to release condensation.

 The Verdict

I call this "sneaky" tofu lasagna because my kids have no idea it's in there—they just think the center is a beautiful creamy cheese filling. Shh . . . don't tell!

SPINACH AND FETA RISOTTO

Serves 2 as a main dish

¼ cup olive oil
1¼ cups Arborio rice
2 cups sliced fresh button mushrooms
1 teaspoon dried minced onion
1 teaspoon dried dill
¼ teaspoon ground black pepper
3¾ cups vegetable broth
¼ cup dry white wine
7 ounces feta cheese, crumbled
10 ounces fresh baby spinach

Use a 4-quart slow cooker. Add the oil to the insert, and swirl the rice in it to fully coat with the oil. Add the mushrooms, dried onion, dill, and pepper. Stir in the broth and wine. Cover, and cook on high for 3 hours. Stir well, then crumble in the cheese, and add the spinach. You may need to shove the spinach in to get it all to fit. Recover, and cook on high for 20 minutes, or until the spinach has wilted. Stir well and serve.

 The Verdict

I hardly got to eat any of this, because my seven- and ten-year-old children came home from school starving and devoured pretty much the whole pot while I was stuck on a conference call. This is creamy deliciousness in a bowl.

SPINACH FRITTATA

Serves 8

3 (10-ounce) packages frozen leaf spinach, thawed and drained
2 cups cottage cheese
2 cups cubed American cheese
3 large eggs, lightly beaten
¼ cup baking mix (I use a gluten-free baking mix)
½ teaspoon kosher salt
½ teaspoon ground black pepper

Use a 2-quart slow cooker. Coat the insert well with cooking spray. Squeeze the spinach well to get rid of any extra liquid, and place the spinach into a large bowl. Add the cottage and American cheese, the eggs, baking mix, salt, and pepper. Stir well with a spoon; the mixture will be quite lumpy. Pour it all into the prepared insert. Cover, and cook on high for 3 to 4 hours, or until the top has begun to brown and pull away from the edges. Uncover, and cook on high for an additional 20 minutes to release condensation.

The Verdict

My kids love this creamy spinach dish. It can be served hot, cold—but it will cut better when it has fully cooled. For a heartier dish, add cooked and crumbled bacon to the mix.

SPINACH-STUFFED MANICOTTI

Serves 4

1   (8-ounce) package jumbo pasta shells (I use
    gluten-free)
1   (16-ounce) package tofu, drained and pressed
1   (10-ounce) package frozen chopped spinach, thawed
    and drained
½   cup freshly grated Parmesan cheese
6   garlic cloves, minced
1   tablespoon dried Italian seasoning
1   (26-ounce) jar prepared pasta sauce
2   cups shredded mozzarella cheese

Use a 4-quart slow cooker. Rinse the pasta shells in water
and set aside. In a large bowl, combine the drained tofu,
spinach, Parmesan, garlic, and Italian seasoning. Stir until
everything is fully incorporated and creamy. Use a spoon
to stuff each shell with a scoopful of tofu-spinach filling.
Place the filled shells into the insert—it's okay if they
overlap. Pour the pasta sauce evenly over the top. Spread
the mozzarella over the top. Cover, and cook on low for
6 hours, on high for about 4 hours, or until the pasta has
reached desired tenderness.

 THE VERDICT
I WAS THRILLED TO FIND
GLUTEN-FREE PASTA SHELLS AT
ONE OF OUR NEIGHBORHOOD
GROCERY STORES; IF YOU'RE
GLUTEN-FREE AND CAN'T
FIND THE SHELLS LOCALLY,
AMAZON.COM CARRIES THEM.
THIS IS A GREAT VEGETARIAN
DINNER—LOTS OF LOVELY
CHEESY GOODNESS.

SWEET-AND-SOUR TOFU

Serves 4

12 ounces extra-firm tofu, drained
1 (20-ounce) can pineapple chunks, drained
1 head broccoli, cut into bite-size pieces
1 cup chopped baby carrots
1 onion, sliced
1 red bell pepper, seeded and thinly sliced
4 garlic cloves, chopped
2 tablespoons soy sauce (I use gluten-free)
1 (1-inch) piece fresh ginger, peeled and grated
½ cup chicken or vegetable broth
  Hot cooked rice or pad thai rice noodles, for serving

Use a 4-quart slow cooker. Cube the tofu, and place it into the insert. Add the pineapple, broccoli, carrots, onion, bell pepper, and garlic. Add in the soy sauce and ginger, and pour the broth evenly over the top. Carefully toss the ingredients to distribute the flavors. Cover, and cook on low for 5 hours, or on high for 3. Serve over a bed of rice or toss with pad thai noodles.

THE VERDICT

MY KIDS DIDN'T EAT THE TOFU, BUT ATE EVERYTHING ELSE, WHICH TO ME EQUALS A VICTORY. ALTHOUGH THE COOKING TIME IS ONLY 5 HOURS, THIS CAN HAPPILY STAY ON THE "WARM" SETTING IN THE COOKER FOR MUCH LONGER.

SUN-DRIED TOMATO AND SUMMER SQUASH BAKE

Serves 4

- ½ cup sun-dried tomatoes (not oil-packed)
- 4 cups sliced yellow summer squash (about three large)
- 1 teaspoon dried rosemary or 1 tablespoon chopped fresh rosemary
- 1 teaspoon dried parsley or 2 tablespoons chopped fresh parsley
- ½ teaspoon ground sage or 1 tablespoon chopped fresh sage leaves
- ½ teaspoon kosher salt
- ¼ teaspoon dried thyme or 2 teaspoons chopped fresh thyme
- ¼ teaspoon ground black pepper
- ¼ cup baking mix (I use a gluten-free variety)
- 1 tablespoon olive oil
- 1 cup shredded mozzarella cheese

Use a 4-quart slow cooker. Soak the sun-dried tomatoes in hot water until pliable, then drain the liquid, and coarsely chop the tomatoes. Place into the insert. Add the squash, rosemary, parsley, sage, salt, thyme, and pepper. Add the baking mix and oil and toss to distribute everything evenly. Top with the cheese. Cover, and cook on low for 6 hours, or on high for about 3 hours.

🍲 The Verdict

Although we ate this as a main dish, this would be an excellent side to a grilled steak or lamb chop if you've got meat eaters in the house to please. The squash and sun-dried tomatoes bake together in a flavorful cheesy sauce.

TOFU CHILI

Serves 4 to 6

- 1 (16-ounce) package extra-firm tofu, drained
- 1 (15-ounce) can kidney beans, drained and rinsed
- 1 (15-ounce) can corn, drained
- 1 onion, diced
- 1 red bell pepper, seeded and chopped
- 1 orange bell pepper, seeded and chopped
- 4 garlic cloves, minced
- 1 small jalapeño pepper, seeded and diced (wear gloves!)
- 1 (14.5-ounce) can diced tomatoes, undrained
- 1 (14.5-ounce) can tomato sauce
- 1 tablespoon ground cumin
- 2 tablespoons chili powder
- 1 teaspoon kosher salt
- ½ teaspoon ground black pepper
  Suggested toppings: sour cream, shredded Cheddar cheese, and sliced avocado

Use a 6-quart slow cooker. Crumble the tofu into the insert, and add the beans, corn, onion, bell peppers, garlic, and jalapeño. Stir in the tomatoes, tomato sauce, and all the seasonings. Cover, and cook on low for 8 hours, or until the vegetables have lost shape and the onion is translucent. Serve with sour cream, shredded cheese, and avocado slices, if desired.

🍲 The Verdict

This tofu chili had been on my list of "must try" reader recipes for quite a while, and I'm happy to report back that this is a wonderful vegan chili that will satisfy everyone in your household. My kids unveganized it with lots of cheese, but happily ate everything in their bowl. I was surprised at how much the tofu crumbled and really did mimic ground beef, even though I opted not to brown it on the stove before adding it into the pot.

TOFU YELLOW DAL

Serves 4

2   cups dried yellow split peas, rinsed
1   (16-ounce) package extra-firm tofu
3   cups chicken or vegetable broth
3   cups water
1   onion, diced
1   large ripe tomato, diced
4   garlic cloves, diced
1   teaspoon ground cumin
½   teaspoon ground coriander
½   teaspoon ground turmeric
¼   teaspoon cayenne pepper
½   teaspoon kosher salt
¼   cup diced fresh flat-leaf parsley
    Hot cooked white or brown basmati rice, for serving
    (optional)

Use a 4-quart slow cooker. Dump the split peas into the insert. Drain and press all liquid out of your block of tofu, and cut it into ½-inch cubes. Add the tofu cubes to the insert along with the broth, water, onion, tomato, garlic, cumin, coriander, turmeric, cayenne pepper, and salt. Stir in the parsley. Cover, and cook on low for 6 to 7 hours, or on high for about 4 hours. Stir again, and serve as is or over rice.

 THE VERDICT
THIS DISH HAS A BEAUTIFUL YELLOW COLOR AND A WONDERFUL INDIAN FLAVOR—MY WHOLE FAMILY LOVED IT, ALTHOUGH I MUST ADMIT THE KIDS ATE AROUND THE TOFU. I FOUND ¼ TEASPOON OF CAYENNE PERFECT—IF YOU LIKE THINGS SPICY, FEEL FREE TO KICK IT UP A NOTCH!

YELLOW CURRY TOFU

Serves 2 to 4

1	**(16-ounce) package extra-firm tofu**
¼	**cup cornstarch**
1	**tablespoon butter or olive oil**
1	**tablespoon curry powder**
1	**teaspoon ground cumin**
1	**teaspoon ground coriander**
½	**teaspoon kosher salt**
¼	**teaspoon ground black pepper**
1	**(15-ounce) can chickpeas, drained and rinsed**
1	**sweet potato, peeled and chopped**
1	**(14-ounce) can coconut milk**
	Hot cooked brown basmati rice, for serving

Use a 4-quart slow cooker. Drain and press the tofu to release any moisture. Cut the tofu into 1-inch squares, and shake in a zippered plastic bag with the cornstarch. Pan-fry the tofu in the butter in a skillet over medium heat until it's golden brown on all sides, then add to the insert. Add the curry powder, cumin, coriander, salt, and pepper. Gingerly stir in the chickpeas and sweet potato. Pour the coconut milk evenly over the top. Cover, and cook on low for 6 to 7 hours. Serve with basmati rice.

THE VERDICT

I'M NOT USUALLY ONE WHO LIKES TO COOK BEFORE I COOK, BUT I DEFINITELY RECOMMEND TAKING THE TIME TO BROWN THE TOFU IN A BIT OF BUTTER OR OLIVE OIL BEFORE TOSSING IT INTO THE SLOW COOKER; THIS STEP HELPS THE TOFU RETAIN ITS SHAPE AND ADDS TEXTURE. IF YOUR MORNINGS ARE RUSHED, YOU CAN DO THIS STEP THE NIGHT BEFORE.

ZUCCHINI AND CHARD COVERED DISH

Serves 4

3 cups sliced zucchini

1 bunch Swiss chard, stems removed and leaves torn

6 garlic cloves, minced

¼ cup almond flour

1 teaspoon paprika

½ teaspoon ground chipotle chile

4 tablespoons (½ stick) butter, melted

1 cup shredded Monterey Jack cheese

Use a 4-quart slow cooker. Add the zucchini, chard, and garlic to the insert, and toss to distribute. In a small bowl, combine the almond flour, paprika, and chipotle. Sprinkle this evenly over the top of the vegetables. Pour the butter on top. Add the cheese, and cover. Cook on low for 4 hours, or on high for about 2 hours. Uncover, and let the casserole sit in the cooling slow cooker for 10 minutes before serving.

 The Verdict

Swiss chard has a rather strong taste, and can be off-putting to even the most die-hard vegetable fans. But guess what? Smothering it in cheese and butter works. You'll like this. Your kids will like this. And your guinea pigs will really like the discarded chard stems.

ZUCCHINI FRITTATA WITH SWEET POTATO

Serves 4 to 6

1 tablespoon olive oil

3 yams or sweet potatoes, peeled and sliced into ¼-inch rounds

3 medium zucchini, peeled and grated

1 onion, grated

2 cups shredded Cheddar cheese

1½ cups 1% milk

4 large eggs

1 teaspoon ground mustard

½ teaspoon kosher salt

½ teaspoon ground black pepper

Use a 4-quart slow cooker. Grease the bottom and sides of the insert with the oil. Separate the sweet potato rounds with your fingers, and place them into the insert. In a large bowl, combine the grated zucchini and onion with the cheese, milk, eggs, mustard, salt, and pepper. Stir well. Pour this mixture evenly over the top of the sweet potatoes. Cover, and cook on low for 5 to 6 hours, or on high for 3 to 4 hours. The frittata is finished when it is fully set, has browned on the top, and has begun to pull away from the sides.

The Verdict

Adam, my grandma, and I love everything about this dish. The bit of mustard and black pepper provides a bit of contrast to the sweet potatoes, although you could certainly add Tabasco at the table if you'd like (I did on the leftovers). The baby ate two bowls, but the older girls thought it sounded weird. While filling enough for dinner, this is an elegant dish for breakfast or brunch.

FISH & SEAFOOD

BASS WITH FENNEL, LIME, AND GARLIC

Serves 4

4	**bass fillets**
I	**fennel bulb, thinly sliced**
I	**lime, juiced**
8	**garlic cloves, minced**
2	**tablespoons olive oil**
I	**teaspoon kosher salt**
½	**teaspoon ground black pepper**
	Steamed spinach, lime wedges, for serving

Use a 4- or 6-quart slow cooker. Spread 4 long sheets of aluminum foil out on the countertop. Place a fish fillet into the center of each piece of foil. Separate the fennel into 4 equal parts, and add the slices to the top of each fish fillet. In a small bowl, whisk together the lime juice, the garlic, oil, salt, and pepper. Spoon this sauce evenly over the top of the fennel. Fold the foil over and crimp the sides to create a fully enclosed packet. Place these packets into the insert. Cover, and cook on high for 2 hours, or until the fish flakes easily with a fork. Serve over a bed of steamed spinach with lime wedges.

 **THE VERDICT**
FENNEL HAS A MILD LICORICE FLAVOR AND IS HIGH IN ANTIOXIDANTS, AND HELPS TO LOWER BAD CHOLESTEROL. WHILE SOMEWHAT BORING ON ITS OWN, IT WORKS WELL COOKED THIS WAY AND IS A GREAT VEGETABLE TO ADD TO YOUR FAMILY'S DIET.

BACK TO THE BAYOU SOUP

Serves 6

1	pound white fish fillets, such as cod, cut into 1-inch pieces
2	(14.5-ounce) cans fire-roasted tomatoes, undrained
1	(15-ounce) can tomato sauce
1	onion, grated
6	garlic cloves, minced
¼	teaspoon cayenne pepper
1	teaspoon celery seed
1	teaspoon dried thyme
3	bay leaves
1	(16-ounce) package frozen mixed vegetables

Use a 6-quart slow cooker. Put the fish into the insert. Add the tomatoes and tomato sauce to the insert. Now add the onion, garlic, cayenne pepper, celery seeds, thyme, and bay leaves. Fold in the vegetables until all the ingredients are evenly dispersed. Cover and cook on low for 7 hours, or until the fish flakes easily with a fork and the onion and garlic are translucent. Discard the bay leaves before serving.

 The Verdict

There's a slight kick to this fish soup—it's enough to wake up the back of your tongue and warm you on a chilly evening, but not overpowering. If you'd like more of a spicy bite, add hot sauce at the table.

BLACKENED TILAPIA

Serves 4

4	tilapia fillets
3	tablespoons butter, melted
1	lemon, ½ juiced, ½ thinly sliced, for garnish
1	teaspoon dried oregano
½	teaspoon ground chipotle chile
½	teaspoon onion powder
½	teaspoon garlic powder
¼	teaspoon kosher salt
¼	teaspoon ground black pepper
	Hot cooked rice pilaf, for serving

Use a 4- or 6-quart slow cooker. Place the tilapia fillets side by side onto a large sheet of aluminum foil. In a small bowl, combine the butter, the lemon juice, oregano, chipotle, onion powder, garlic powder, salt, and pepper. Spoon this mixture evenly over the top of each piece of fish. Fold the foil over to fully enclose the fillets, and crimp the edges to form a packet. Place this packet into the insert. Cover, and cook on high for 2 hours. Serve with rice pilaf and garnish with sliced lemon.

 The Verdict

I made this recipe after falling in love with a restaurant's version of blackened catfish while on a beach vacation. Our local grocery store didn't have catfish, but they always have tilapia in the freezer. This brought me back to my August vacation, although I was sitting at our kitchen table in the middle of winter.

CRAB AND TOMATO CHOWDER

Serves 4

2	(14-ounce) cans crushed tomatoes, undrained
4	red potatoes, washed and diced
1	cup chopped celery
½	cup chopped baby carrots
1	(6.5-ounce) can clams, undrained
1	cup chicken broth
¼	teaspoon cayenne pepper
½	pound lump crabmeat, picked through, or
	1 (6-ounce) can crabmeat, drained
½	cup half-and-half or heavy whipping cream

Use a 4-quart slow cooker. Add the tomatoes to the insert, then add the potatoes, celery, and carrots. Pour in the clams, and add the broth and cayenne pepper. Cover, and cook on low for 6 to 8 hours, or until the potatoes are quite tender. Stir in the crabmeat and half-and-half. Recover and cook on high for about 20 minutes, or until fully hot.

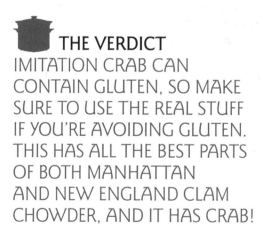 THE VERDICT
IMITATION CRAB CAN CONTAIN GLUTEN, SO MAKE SURE TO USE THE REAL STUFF IF YOU'RE AVOIDING GLUTEN. THIS HAS ALL THE BEST PARTS OF BOTH MANHATTAN AND NEW ENGLAND CLAM CHOWDER, AND IT HAS CRAB!

CAJUN SHRIMP CHOWDER

Serves 4

1	(16-ounce) package frozen white corn
3	cups chicken broth
1	onion, diced
1	tablespoon butter
1	tablespoon Cajun seasoning
½	teaspoon kosher salt
1	cup peeled cooked mini bay shrimp
½	cup heavy whipping cream or half-and-half
	Sliced green onions, for garnish (optional)

Use a 4-quart slow cooker. Add the corn, broth, onion, butter, Cajun seasoning, and salt to the insert. Cover, and cook on low for 6 to 7 hours. Use a handheld immersion blender to puree—it will be thick. (If you want the soup to be chunkier, puree only part of it.) Stir in the shrimp and cream. Cover, and cook on high for 30 minutes or until soup is fully hot. Garnish with green onions, if desired.

 THE VERDICT
CAJUN SEASONING IS A GREAT SPICE MIX TO HAVE IN YOUR PANTRY, BUT YOU CAN EASILY MAKE YOUR OWN BY COMBINING EQUAL PARTS OF WHITE PEPPER, GARLIC POWDER, ONION POWDER, RED PEPPER, BLACK PEPPER, AND PAPRIKA.

CREAMY LEMON TILAPIA

Serves 4

4	tilapia fillets
2	ounces cream cheese, softened
¼	cup freshly grated Parmesan cheese
3	garlic cloves, minced
1	lemon, juiced
¼	teaspoon kosher salt
¼	teaspoon ground black pepper

Use a 4- or 6-quart slow cooker. Place the tilapia fillets side by side onto a large sheet of aluminum foil. In a small bowl, whisk together the cream cheese, Parmesan, garlic, lemon juice, salt, and pepper. Spread this cheese sauce evenly over the top of each fillet. Fold the foil over to fully enclose the fish, and crimp the edges to form a packet. Place this packet into the insert. Cover, and cook on high for 2 hours.

THE VERDICT

I LOVE TO SERVE THIS FISH TO A FINICKY GUEST WHO SWEARS UP AND DOWN THAT HE HATES FISH, AND THEN SLOWLY NODS AND QUIETLY SMILES AS HE PRETTY MUCH LICKS THE PLATE CLEAN. THIS IS SUCH A FANTASTIC FISH DISH, YOU SHOULD REALLY GIVE IT A TRY.

DILL-ICIOUS FISH FILLETS

Serves 4

4	fish fillets, such as salmon or tilapia
1	cup plain yogurt
½	cup chopped fresh dill or 1 tablespoon dried dill
4	garlic cloves, minced
1	teaspoon dried Italian seasoning
½	teaspoon kosher salt
½	teaspoon ground black pepper
1	lemon, cut into 4 wedges

Use a 4- or 6-quart slow cooker. Spread a length of aluminum foil on the countertop, and place the fish fillets into the center of the strip (or you can make individual packets). In a small bowl, whisk together the yogurt, dill, garlic, Italian seasoning, salt, and pepper. Smear this sauce evenly over the top of each fish fillet. Fold the edges of the foil together and crimp to make a fully enclosed packet. Place this packet into the insert—do not add water. Cover, and cook on high for 2 hours, or until the fish flakes easily with a fork. Serve with the lemon wedges.

The Verdict

I recently began growing dill in the garden, and love the slightly tart flavor it brings to dishes. This sauce reminds me of a light tartar sauce—always a good pairing with fish! We had our fish with asparagus, and the kids dipped their spears into the dill sauce.

FISH PARMESAN

Serves 4

4	tilapia fillets
1	(14.5-ounce) can whole tomatoes, undrained
¼	cup freshly grated Parmesan cheese
1	tablespoon dried Italian seasoning
4	slices mozzarella cheese

Use a 4-quart slow cooker. Place the fish into the insert, and pour in the tomatoes. Sprinkle the Parmesan and Italian seasoning over the top. Add the mozzarella slices on top. Cover, and cook on high for 3 hours, or until fish flakes easily with a fork.

The Verdict

I threw this together on a super-busy day, when I knew we'd be in and out of the house from 4 to 7 p.m. My fish fillets were still pretty frozen, and I didn't have time to make individual packets, so I threw everything in together and held my breath. I shouldn't have worried—the fish cooked perfectly and was beautifully seasoned. The kids ate early, and Adam snarfed down the leftovers later in the evening.

HONEY AND MISO GLAZED SALMON

Serves 4

4   **salmon fillets**
1   **packet dried miso soup mix, large chunks of tofu removed**
3   **tablespoons creamed or spun honey**
1   **lemon, juiced**

Use a 4- or 6-quart slow cooker. Place the salmon fillets side by side on a large sheet of aluminum foil. In a small bowl, combine the miso soup mix, honey, and lemon juice. Smear this paste all over the top of the salmon pieces. Fold the foil over to fully enclose the fish, and crimp the edges to form a packet. Place this packet into the insert. Cover, and cook on high for 2 hours. The salmon will flake easily with a fork when finished.

THE VERDICT

OH GOSH, I LOVE THIS SIMPLE FISH RECIPE. I ADAPTED A RECIPE I FOUND ONLINE BECAUSE I WASN'T ABLE TO FIND PLAIN MISO IN MY LOCAL GROCERY STORE, BUT LIKE THIS COMBINATION EVEN BETTER BECAUSE OF THE BOUILLON GRANULES AND THE BITS OF GREEN ONION IN THE SOUP MIX. I SHARED THIS FISH WITH OUR NEIGHBORS, JEN AND EJ, WHO ALSO REALLY LIKED IT. SERVE THIS WITH RICE AND A GREEN SALAD.

FISHERMAN'S CHOWDER

Serves 8 to 10

1	**pound white fish fillets, such as sole, tilapia, or swordfish, cut into ½-inch cubes**
6	**slices bacon, diced**
1	**onion, diced**
3	**baking potatoes, such as Yukon Gold or Russet, peeled and cut into bite-size pieces**
1	**(15-ounce) can corn, undrained**
1	**(6.5-ounce) can clams, undrained**
1	**teaspoon kosher salt**
¾	**teaspoon ground black pepper**
3	**(12-ounce) cans evaporated milk**

Use a 6-quart slow cooker. Place the fish into the insert. In a skillet over medium heat, add the bacon and onion and cook, stirring occasionally, until the bacon is fully cooked and the onions are translucent. Drain off the accumulated grease and scrape the pan contents into the insert. Place the potatoes into the insert, and add the corn and clams. Add the salt and pepper, and stir in the evaporated milk. Cover, and cook on low for 7 to 8 hours, or until the potatoes are tender. If you'd like a thicker chowder, pulse a few times with a handheld immersion blender or blend in batches in a traditional blender.

 The Verdict

This creamy and filling chowder feeds a crowd—serve with homemade drop biscuits (I make mine with a gluten-free baking mix) for an added treat.

LEMONY BALSAMIC HONEY SALMON

Serves 4

4	**salmon fillets**
2	**tablespoons balsamic vinegar**
2	**tablespoons honey**
1	**lemon, juiced**
1	**teaspoon dried dill**
½	**teaspoon kosher salt**
¼	**teaspoon ground black pepper**

Use a 4- or 6-quart slow cooker. Spread a long sheet of aluminum foil on the kitchen countertop. Place the fish fillets into the center of the foil (or you can make separate packets). In a small bowl, make a paste out of the vinegar, honey, lemon juice, dill, salt, and pepper. Spoon this paste evenly over the top of each fish fillet. Fold the foil over and crimp the edges to create a fully enclosed packet. Place the packet into the insert. Cover, and cook on high for 2 hours, or until fish flakes easily with a fork.

The Verdict

Honey and balsamic vinegar pair with dill and lemon to make a fabulous sauce for this deliciously simple summer fish dinner.

LIMEONY SALMON

Serves 4

4	**salmon fillets**
1	**lemon, juiced**
2	**limes, juiced**
2	**teaspoons Dijon mustard**
1	**teaspoon soy sauce (I use gluten-free)**
½	**teaspoon ground ginger**
½	**teaspoon garlic powder**

Use a 4- or 6-quart slow cooker. Place the salmon fillets into a zippered plastic bag and add the lemon juice, lime juice, mustard, soy sauce, ginger, and garlic powder. Seal the bag well, and squish it around to ensure the salmon is coated in marinade. Refrigerate for 2 to 12 hours. After marinating, remove the salmon from the bag and discard the leftover marinade. Put the salmon fillets onto a large length of foil and fold it over and crimp the edges to make one large fully enclosed packet. Cover, and cook on high for 2 hours, or until the salmon flakes easily with a fork.

 THE VERDICT
TWO OF MY THREE CHILDREN HAPPILY ATE THIS FISH WITH A BIG SCOOP OF WHITE BASMATI RICE. ADAM AND I REALLY LIKED IT—THE DIJON MUSTARD AND LIME FLAVOR CAME THROUGH WITHOUT DROWNING OUT THE NATURAL SALMON FLAVOR.

MAHI MAHI WITH CILANTRO CREAM SAUCE

Serves 4

4	**mahi mahi fillets**
I	**cup chopped fresh cilantro leaves**
4	**garlic cloves, minced**
4	**tablespoons cream cheese, softened**
I	**lemon, juiced**
½	**teaspoon kosher salt**
¼	**teaspoon ground black pepper**

Use a 4- or 6-quart slow cooker. Spread a large sheet of aluminum foil on the countertop. Place the fish fillets into the middle of the foil. In a small bowl, combine the cilantro, garlic, cream cheese, lemon juice, salt, and pepper into a paste. Spoon this mixture evenly over the top of each fish fillet. Fold the edges of the foil together and crimp to make a fully enclosed packet. Place this packet into the insert. Cover, and cook on high for 2 hours. The fish is done when it flakes easily with a fork.

 **THE VERDICT**
THIS PERFECTLY STEAMED FISH PAIRS WELL WITH QUINOA AND VEGETABLES. YOU CAN MAKE ANOTHER FOIL PACKET WITH FRESH VEGETABLES AND A LITTLE BUTTER OR OLIVE OIL TO COOK ALONG WITH THE FISH FOR A COMPLETE MEAL.

MEDITERRANEAN ISLE FISH PACKETS

Serves 6

6   white fish fillets, such as haddock or sole
2   small zucchini, thinly sliced
2   small yellow crookneck squash, thinly sliced
1   red onion, sliced into thin rings
1   (14.5-ounce) can diced tomatoes, drained
½   cup freshly grated Parmesan cheese
¼   cup sliced pitted black olives
2   garlic cloves, chopped
½   teaspoon ground black pepper
¼   teaspoon kosher salt

Use a 6-quart slow cooker. Spread 6 long sheets of aluminum foil on the countertop. Place a fish fillet into the center of each piece of foil. Top with a handful of the zucchini, squash, and onion. In a small bowl combine the tomatoes, cheese, olives, garlic, pepper, and salt. Spoon this tomato relish evenly on top of the fish and vegetables. Fold the foil over and crimp the edges to create a fully enclosed packet. Place all of the packets into the insert. If you need to add more foil to the top, do so. Cover, and cook on high for 2 hours, or until the fish flakes easily with a fork.

 The Verdict

Many of my friends have been speaking quite highly about living the "Paleo" life, which is simply a low-carb, back-to-basics approach to eating. These fish packet meals are perfect for this type of eating lifestyle, and taste wonderful.

MUSTARD-LEMON HADDOCK

Serves 6

6   haddock fillets
1   tablespoon Dijon mustard
1   lemon, juiced
1   teaspoon paprika
½   cup shredded mozzarella cheese

Use a 6-quart slow cooker. Spread 6 long sheets of aluminum foil out on the countertop. Place a fish fillet into the center of each piece of foil. In a small bowl whisk together the mustard, lemon juice, and paprika. Spoon this sauce evenly over the top of each piece of fish. Sprinkle a tablespoon or so of cheese on top of each piece of fish. Fold the foil over and crimp the sides to fully enclose the fish. Place the packets into the insert. Cover, and cook on high for 2 hours, or until the fish flakes easily with a fork.

The Verdict

Haddock is a hearty white fish that holds up beautifully in the slow cooker. Pair the fish with a side of roasted asparagus and a serving of quinoa for a light, yet still filling dinner.

NANTUCKET SCALLOP CHOWDER

Serves 4

6   slices thick-cut bacon, cooked and crumbled
1   onion, diced
1   cup diced white potatoes
6   garlic cloves, minced
1   teaspoon dried thyme
2   cups bottled clam juice
1   cup dry white wine
1   (16-ounce) bag frozen scallops
½   cup heavy whipping cream

Use a 4-quart slow cooker. Put the bacon into the insert. Add the onion, potato, garlic, and thyme. Stir in the clam juice and wine. Cover, and cook on low for 5 to 6 hours, on high for 3 hours, or until the onion is translucent and the potato has reached desired tenderness. Stir in the scallops. Recover, and cook on high for 30 minutes, or until the scallops are fully cooked. Stir in the cream. If you'd like a thicker texture, pulse a few times with a handheld immersion blender to smash up some potatoes (or puree a cup in a traditional blender and return to the soup) before serving.

The Verdict

Delicious and creamy—just like you'd get on the pier, but without the seagulls. I made bread bowls by using boxed gluten-free bread mix. I followed package instructions, but formed rounds with my hands before baking.

RANCH FISH FLORENTINE

Serves 4

1   (16-ounce) bag fresh baby spinach
4   white fish fillets, such as tilapia, haddock, or sole
¼   cup ranch salad dressing
1   tablespoon mustard
1   lemon, juiced
¼   teaspoon kosher salt
¼   teaspoon ground black pepper
½   cup freshly grated Parmesan cheese

Use a 4-quart slow cooker. Add the spinach to the insert (you may need to press to fit it in). Put the fish fillets on top. In a small bowl, whisk together the salad dressing, mustard, lemon juice, salt, and pepper. Pour this sauce evenly over the top of the fish fillets. Sprinkle with the cheese. Cover, and cook on high for 3 hours, or until the fish flakes easily with a fork.

The Verdict

I couldn't think of a name for this fish recipe—everyone in the house absolutely loved it, but Ranch Mustard Fish sounded weird. I asked Twitter for name suggestions, and Sue @slml32 came up with Ranch Fish Florentine. This is a delicious, tangy fish. The spinach wilts quite a bit; it's rather startling!

SALMON LOAF

Serves 4 to 6

1	**pound skinless salmon fillets, coarsely chopped**
1	**large egg**
2	**tablespoons breadcrumbs (I use gluten-free)**
1	**tablespoon dried dill**
1	**lemon, juiced**
1	**tablespoon prepared horseradish**
1	**teaspoon kosher salt**
½	**teaspoon ground black pepper**

Use a 6-quart slow cooker with an inserted 9 x 5 x 3-inch glass or metal loaf pan. In a large bowl, combine the salmon, egg, breadcrumbs, dill, lemon juice, horseradish, salt, and pepper. Combine the ingredients until everything is wet and goopy. Don't overmix; you want the salmon to still be recognizable. Coat the loaf pan well with cooking spray, and press the fish mixture into the loaf pan. Put this pan into the insert—do not add water. Cover, and cook on low for 6 to 7 hours, or until the loaf is cooked through and begun to brown on top and pull away from the sides.

 **THE VERDICT**

WHO SAYS YOU HAVE TO EAT SALMON THE SAME WAY EVERY WEEK? I LIKE THAT THIS TASTES LIKE A GREAT BIG HUGE CRAB (SALMON) CAKE BUT IS STILL LIGHT, HEALTHY, AND PACKED WITH ALL THE GOOD OMEGAS AND OTHER THINGS THE EXPERTS TELL YOU YOU'RE SUPPOSED TO EAT (UNTIL THEY CHANGE THEIR MINDS).

PALEO JAMBALAYA

Serves 4

½   **pound boneless, skinless chicken breast, cubed**
1   **pound andouille turkey sausage, thickly sliced**
1   **onion, diced**
6   **garlic cloves, minced**
1   **(28-ounce) can diced tomatoes, undrained**
3   **tablespoons Cajun seasoning (for homemade, see page 305)**
5   **cups chicken broth**
2   **to 4 tablespoons hot sauce**
½   **head cauliflower**
1   **pound large shrimp, cooked, peeled, and cleaned**

Use a 6-quart slow cooker. Place the chicken into the insert and add the sausage, onion, and garlic. Pour in the tomatoes, and add the Cajun seasoning. Stir in the broth and 2 tablespoons of the hot sauce. Cover and cook on low for 6 hours. Place the cauliflower into the bowl of a food processor, and pulse until the cauliflower resembles grains of rice. Stir this "rice" into the insert, and add the shrimp. Cover, and cook on high for 20 to 30 minutes, or until the shrimp is fully hot. Add more hot sauce, to taste, at the table if you'd like.

 THE VERDICT
THIS PALEO-STYLE JAMBALAYA COMES FROM ANDREANNA OF LIFEASAPLATE.COM. SHE HAD THE BRILLIANT IDEA TO SWAP OUT THE TRADITIONAL RICE WITH BLENDED CAULIFLOWER TO KEEP THE DISH LOW CARB AND TO ADD NUTRITION. THIS IS A FANTASTIC JAMBALAYA, FIT FOR ANY MARDI GRAS FEAST. THANK YOU, ANDREANNA!

SALMON WITH CANDIED PECANS

Serves 4

4	salmon fillets
1	cup pecans, chopped
¼	cup packed dark brown sugar
2	tablespoons butter, melted
1	lemon, juiced
½	teaspoon kosher salt

Use a 4- or 6-quart slow cooker. Place the salmon fillets side by side on a large sheet of aluminum foil. In a small bowl, combine the pecans, sugar, butter, lemon juice, and salt. Smear this mixture over the top of the fish pieces. Fold the foil over to fully enclose the fish, and crimp the edges to form a packet. Place this packet into the insert. Cover, and cook on high for 2 hours. The fish will flake easily with a fork when finished.

THE VERDICT

THE BROWN SUGAR, BUTTER, AND PECANS MIX WITH THE LEMON JUICE TO CREATE A BEAUTIFUL SWEET-AND-SOUR CANDIED FLAVOR THAT COMPLEMENTS THE FISH PERFECTLY. MY CHILDREN ATE SO MUCH, MY HUSBAND BARELY GOT A TASTE WHEN HE ARRIVED HOME FOR THE DAY. THIS IS A NEW STAPLE IN OUR MEAL ROTATION.

SHRIMP ARRABBIATA

Serves 4

2	(14.5-ounce) cans fire-roasted tomatoes, undrained
1	onion, diced
½	cup dry red wine
½	cup chopped fresh flat-leaf parsley
4	garlic cloves, diced
1	tablespoon dried Italian seasoning
½	teaspoon kosher salt
½	teaspoon crushed red pepper flakes
1	pound cooked jumbo shrimp, peeled and cleaned (frozen is fine)
½	cup heavy whipping cream
1	pound spaghetti or linguini pasta (I use gluten-free)

Use a 4-quart slow cooker. Pour the tomatoes into the insert. Add the onion, wine, parsley, garlic, Italian seasoning, salt, and red pepper flakes, and stir well. Cover, and cook on low for 5 to 6 hours. Add the shrimp and cream. Cover, and cook on high for 20 to 30 minutes, or until the shrimp is pink and the sauce is fully hot. Cook the pasta according to the package instructions. Toss the hot pasta with the sauce and serve.

 The Verdict

My friend Kim adapted this recipe from one she found in an old *Cooking Light* magazine. *Arrabbiata* means "angry" in Italian, but you will not be angry after eating this!

SPINACH AND FETA FISH DINNER

Serves 4

1	tablespoon olive oil
3	cups fresh baby spinach
4	white fish fillets, such as tilapia, catfish, or sole
1	(14.5-ounce) can diced tomatoes, drained
¼	cup Italian salad dressing
½	cup crumbled feta cheese

Use a 6-quart slow cooker. Rub the oil on the bottom and sides of the insert, and load the spinach in. Place the fish fillets directly on top of the bed of spinach, and pour in the tomatoes and salad dressing. Add the cheese. Cover, and cook on high for 2 to 3 hours, or until the fish flakes easily with a fork.

 **The Verdict**

I love everything-in-one-pot meals, and this spinach and fish dinner is perfect. The salad dressing and feta provide great flavor with very little fuss, and the spinach steams nicely and creates a flavorful side dish.

SHRIMP IN A FOIL PACKET WITH PASTA

Serves 6

2	**pounds cooked jumbo shrimp, peeled and cleaned (frozen is fine)**
6	**ripe tomatoes, diced**
2	**tablespoons olive oil**
4	**garlic cloves, minced**
2	**tablespoons chopped fresh basil**
¼	**teaspoon kosher salt**
¼	**teaspoon ground black pepper**
I	**pound linguini pasta (I use gluten-free)**
	Freshly grated Parmesan cheese, for serving

Use a 4-quart slow cooker. In a large bowl, combine the shrimp and tomatoes. Add the oil, garlic, basil, salt, and pepper. Stir gingerly or toss with your hands to combine the ingredients. Pour the shrimp and tomato mixture onto a large sheet of aluminum foil, then fold the foil over and crimp the edges to form a very large fully enclosed packet. Place this packet into the insert. Cover, and cook on high for 2 hours, or until the shrimp is pink and bite-tender. Cook the pasta according to the package instructions. Toss the shrimp mixture with the hot pasta and sprinkle with cheese before serving.

THE VERDICT

SHRIMP STEAMS PERFECTLY IN THIS SLOW COOKER FOIL PACKET AND THE FLAVORS OF THE BASIL AND GARLIC SEASON EVERY BITE. I LIKE HOW THE SHRIMP STAYS MOIST AND JUICY WITHOUT DRYING OUT OR TURNING RUBBERY—THIS IS A GREAT PASTA DISH. IF YOU'D LIKE A BIT OF SPICE, YOU CAN ADD CRUSHED RED PEPPER FLAKES TO THE PACKET.

SUN-DRIED TOMATO AND GARLIC TILAPIA

Serves 4

4   **tilapia fillets**
2   **tablespoons coarsely chopped sun-dried tomatoes packed in oil**
¼   **cup chopped fresh flat-leaf parsley**
4   **garlic cloves, minced**
¼   **teaspoon kosher salt**
¼   **teaspoon ground black pepper**

Use a 4- or 6-quart slow cooker. Place the tilapia fillets side by side on a large sheet of aluminum foil. Add the tomatoes to a small bowl, and whisk together with the parsley, garlic, salt, and pepper. Spoon this mixture evenly over the top of the fish pieces. Fold the foil over to fully enclose the fish, and crimp the edges to form a packet. Place this packet into the insert. Cover, and cook on high for 2 hours. The fish will flake easily with a fork when finished.

 The Verdict

This recipe comes from a reader, Ann, who cans her own oil-packed tomatoes. This is such a great way to eat fish; my entire family really enjoyed it.

SWEET-AND-SOUR SHRIMP PACKETS

Serves 4

1   **pound uncooked jumbo shrimp, peeled and cleaned (frozen is fine)**
1   **cup pineapple chunks**
1   **red bell pepper, seeded and thinly sliced**
1   **orange bell pepper, seeded and thinly sliced**
3   **green onions, thinly sliced**
⅓   **cup orange marmalade**
2   **tablespoons dark brown sugar**
1   **tablespoon soy sauce (I use gluten-free)**
¼   **teaspoon kosher salt**
¼   **teaspoon crushed red pepper flakes (optional)**
     Hot cooked white or brown rice, for serving

Use a 4-quart slow cooker. In a large bowl, toss together the shrimp, pineapple, bell peppers, and green onions until everything is evenly distributed. In a smaller bowl, whisk together the marmalade, sugar, soy sauce, salt, and red pepper flakes, if desired. Pour this sauce over the top of the shrimp and vegetables, and toss to coat. Spoon into a large length of aluminum foil. Fold the foil over and crimp the edges to create one very large packet. Place this packet into the insert. Cover, and cook on high for 3 hours, or until the shrimp is pink and the vegetables have reached desired tenderness. Serve over rice.

 The Verdict

You'll love this! I couldn't get enough of this sauce—I ended up making another batch to drizzle on the leftover rice because it was just so good. I love cooking shrimp in foil—it comes out non-rubbery and packed with flavor every time!

TANDOORI FISH

Serves 6

6	tilapia fillets or other white fish
1	tablespoon ground cumin
1	teaspoon ground ginger
1	teaspoon ground coriander
1	teaspoon kosher salt
¼	teaspoon ground cloves
¼	teaspoon ground cardamom
¼	teaspoon cayenne pepper
	Lime wedges, for serving

Use a 6-quart slow cooker. Spread 2 large sheets of foil onto the kitchen countertop, and place 3 of the fish fillets onto each piece. In a small bowl, combine the cumin, ginger, coriander, salt, cloves, cardamom, and cayenne pepper. Rub this mixture into each fish fillet, and fold over the edges of the foil and then crimp to form a fully enclosed packet. Place the packets into the insert—no need to add water. Cover, and cook on high for 2 hours, or until the fish flakes easily with a fork. Squeeze lime on each piece of fish before serving.

 **THE VERDICT**
THIS EXOTIC SPICE BLEND WILL MAKE YOUR WHITE FISH COME ALIVE. IT'S TASTY, WITH A WARM (BUT NOT HOT) AFTERTASTE. THE LIME IS A NICE TOUCH, AND I LIKED HOW I COULD TASTE THE INDIVIDUAL SPICES—WHICH IS SOMETIMES LOST WHEN PAIRING SAVORY WITH SWEET. MY KIDS DUNKED THEIR FISH INTO TARTAR SAUCE, BUT STILL ATE EVERY BITE.

TERIYAKI TILAPIA

Serves 4

4	tilapia fillets
¼	cup packed dark brown sugar
3	tablespoons soy sauce (I use gluten-free)
1	(1-inch) piece fresh ginger, peeled and grated
4	garlic cloves, smashed

Use a 4- or 6-quart slow cooker. Place the tilapia fillets side by side on a large sheet of aluminum foil. In a small bowl, combine the sugar, soy sauce, ginger, and garlic. Spread this paste evenly over the top of each piece of fish. Fold the foil over to fully enclose the fillets, and crimp the edges to form a packet. Place this packet into the insert. Cover, and cook on high for 2 hours.

THE VERDICT

THERE'S NO NEED TO SAVE TERIYAKI FLAVOR FOR CHICKEN OR BEEF—ENJOY THIS FISH OVER A BED OF SPINACH LEAVES, OR WITH A SCOOP OF RICE. I LIKE TO PAIR IT WITH STEAMED BROCCOLI, WHICH CAN COOK AT THE SAME TIME AS THE FISH: PUT CHOPPED BROCCOLI IN ANOTHER FOIL PACKET SQUEEZED WITH THE JUICE OF 1 LEMON.

TOMATO AND CAPER TILAPIA

Serves 4

4	tilapia fillets
1	(14.5-ounce) can diced tomatoes, drained
4	garlic cloves, chopped
1	tablespoon capers, drained
1	tablespoon dried Italian seasoning
¼	teaspoon ground black pepper

Use a 4- or 6-quart slow cooker. Place the tilapia fillets side by side on a large sheet of aluminum foil. In a large bowl, combine the tomatoes, garlic, capers, Italian seasoning, and pepper. Spoon this mixture evenly over the top of each piece of fish. Fold the foil over to fully enclose the fillets, and crimp the edges to form a packet. Place this packet into the insert. Cover, and cook on high for 2 hours, or until the fish flakes easily with a fork.

The Verdict

The moisture from the capers and tomatoes helps steam the fish in the foil and infuses it with a beautiful, robust Mediterranean flavor. Serve with polenta or rice pilaf.

TUNA AND NOODLE CASSEROLE

Serves 6

2	cups frozen peas, thawed
8	ounces fresh button mushrooms, thinly sliced
1	(6.5-ounce) can tuna packed in water, drained
2	tablespoons butter
¼	cup all-purpose flour (I use rice flour)
1	cup milk
1	cup chicken broth
½	cup freshly grated Parmesan cheese
½	teaspoon kosher salt
½	teaspoon ground black pepper
	Hot cooked pasta (I use gluten-free corn fusilli)

Use a 4-quart slow cooker. Add the peas, mushrooms, and tuna to the bottom of the insert. In a small saucepan over low heat, melt the butter. Stir in the flour to make a roux, and whisk in the milk, broth, cheese, salt, and pepper until fully combined. Pour this evenly over the top of the ingredients in the slow cooker. Cover, and cook on low for 5 hours, or on high for about 2½ hours. Ladle over hot, cooked pasta, or stir the pasta directly into the sauce.

The Verdict

My kids love this casserole. If you'd prefer not to use canned tuna, it tastes just as good when I substitute canned chicken. I have also swapped out the Parmesan cheese with a half-block of cream cheese for an even creamier version.

INDEX

Note: Page references in *italics* indicate photographs.